Military Psychology

Chetwodean Value

The Honour, Safety and Welfare of the Country come first always and every time. The Honour, Safety and Welfare of the Men you command come next. Your own Safety and Welfare comes last, always and every time.

Military Psychology

International Perspectives

Edited by

Lt. Col. Dr Samir Rawat

RAWAT PUBLICATIONS

Jaipur • New Delhi • Bangalore • Guwahati • Kolkata

ISBN 978-81-316-0842-5

Disclaimer:
The opinions and assertions expressed in the papers are those of the authors and need not be construed as those as official or as reflecting views in consonance with the Indian Armed Forces or the Ministry of Defence in India or the countries from where the authors hail.

Published by
Prem Rawat for **Rawat Publications**
Satyam Apts, Sector 3, Jawahar Nagar, Jaipur 302 004 (India)
Phone: 0141 265 1748 / 7006 Fax: 0141 265 1748
E-mail: info@rawatbooks.com
Website: www.rawatbooks.com

New Delhi Office
4858/24, Ansari Road, Daryaganj, New Delhi 110 002
Phone: 011 2326 3290

Also at *Bangalore, Guwahati* and *Kolkata*

Typeset by Logiciels Info Solutions Pvt. Ltd, Chennai

Printed and bound in India

Contents

Foreword

If one is looking for a book which explores the entire gamut of 'Military Psychology' he would home in on to *Military Psychology: International Perspectives* edited by Soldier Scholar, Lt. Col. Dr Samir Rawat. The book starts with 'Polemology: an imperative field in military psychology' by Lt. Col. Dr Jacques J. Gouws. He asserts that those with abnormal human minds take their countries to war. War, like a feast, unifies people. Human nature drives a nation to war to prove civilisational supremacy. Nations perceive even acts of deterrence by neighbours as increased threat of war. Wars are real and one cannot wish them away!

The second chapter by Dr Rawat himself goes into the aspect of 'Stress in the armed forces'. When demands of the mission exceeds the human capacity, which is most likely in most cases, it creates imbalance and generates stress. If one perceives it as stress, it manifests in soldier's behaviour, which obviously would not be in sync with the mission, accomplishment. The chapter explores different types of stresses and explains the causes and their remedies. The modern battlefield transparency and night vision devices have driven troops to sleeplessness, thus accentuating stress and alienating them from their mission. Attitudinal orientation is required to perceive 'stress' as a 'challenge'.

In the third chapter 'Coping resources in the armed forces: a psychological perspective', Ms Basu articulates how in a combat situation responses could be either 'fight' or 'flight'; aggression or avoidance, and how religion, peer support, humour, leadership, and altruism enable forces to cope with demands of combat. In the fourth chapter, 'Resilience among military spouses during soldiers deployment in operational areas', Ms Patil argues that the military spouses adapt themselves to a life without their spouses and can deftly handle the demands of children, parents, schooling, and household matters. With years of experience they get better at it. She has taken an adequate sample for her research and comes to the conclusion that the military spouses become far more independent than spouses from civilian walk of life. Such adaptations are good for a soldier, which enables him to concentrate on his operational tasks.

The fifth chapter is on 'Competency-based human resource management: selecting future leaders in the Indonesian Army.' In this chapter, Colonel Dr Hidayat argues that the concept of minimum essential forces levels mandated by Indonesia demanded 'world class soldiers'. In the competency-based selection system one evaluates the characteristics of superior-performing individuals as it would predict better performance than relying on traditional psychometric tests. In the 'competency-based model' one can determine the surface competencies such as skill and knowledge and also behavioural competencies such as traits, attitudes, values, and motivation. During training one can identify underperformers and train and develop in them both institutional competencies such as values and patriotism and above-the-surface competencies like technical skills. Officers need to develop 'creativity and risk-taking abilities' in addition to those required of soldiers.

In the sixth chapter, Dr Ole Boe covers 'Character strengths and their relevance for military officers' and asserts their indispensability to a successful military officer. The combat environment is characterised by Volatility, Uncertainty, Complexity, and Ambiguity (VUCA). They get further exacerbated when terrorism and guerrilla warfare become part of the same conflict. It requires officers with strong character, courage, tenacity, integrity, and fair play to be successful in such combat situations. Many countries have different qualities they see in their officers. Psychometric tests also exist to assess character qualities. A consolidated list of 24 qualities have been listed; however, the author feels all may not be relevant and only about half of them would be sufficient to make a successful officer. A unique quality has also come up for discussion is the 'Capacity for Love'. This is essential, as an officer needs to love the troops under his command to build bonds for success in war.

In Chapter 7, Col Dr Cristian Dobre explores 'Cyber-psychology and the soldier of the future'. War has transcended from ground, air, and sea dimensions to social, economics, diplomacy, and cybernetics. It is easy to transport a combatant in to a virtual world of future wars. How does 'human psychology' adjust to the virtual environment? What is the cyber psychology of a human in a virtual battle field environment? It explores multidimensional manifestation in his personality. The need to study human behaviour in cyber space and real life and ability to function rationally in times of conflict would be a challenge for a future soldier. The virtual environment enables training of combatants in war environment.

In Chapter 8, Col Dr Hubert Annen dwells on 'Research and teaching of military psychology at the Swiss Military Academy'. It covers the selection, training and motivation, and leadership aspects covered in the academy. Stress is caused by excessive demands, and motivated people are less stressed, and, simultaneously, bad leaders impart stress to their troops. Hence, the training in the academy is aimed towards motivation and development of leadership. Self-awareness in individuals is a continuous process and helps in development of a good leader. Cultivating in students the right mind-set and instilling appropriate attitude and empowering them with knowledge develop leadership elements in the students. Character and personality are keys to leadership development. Military psychology is an important part of the curriculum as it makes one understand its requirement in the profession of arms.

In Chapter 9, 'Health beyond symptoms: multidimensional approach to functional fitness in military organisations', Dr Merle Parmak perceives in military organisations that the pride to remain fit restrains them from seeking timely medical treatment, which only aggravates their ailments. The physical tests during training also do not encompass the entire range of performance components that may need to be demonstrated while fighting a battle. Hence, individuals with a predisposition towards soldiering obviously tend to fair better as they take the stress as a challenge and involve themselves in problem-solving rather than passively cope up stress. Review of a soldier's fitness is at a bare minimum multidimensional, which includes assessing soldier's fitness in the following areas – physical, psychological, behavioural, medical, occupational, environmental, spiritual, social, and family – to ascertain whether he is ready to be a total combatant. Medical and non-medical interventions are required to keep a soldier fit in all dimensions. In the situation of poor leadership there is 'sick building syndrome' with troop reporting illness with 'medically unexplained symptoms'. Preparation of troops mentally enhances motivation and pain tolerance in them.

Dr Yvonne R. Masakowski in the last chapter explores 'Cultural competence and leadership in multinational military operations'. To command troops from different nationalities, language, religion, and cultures, a commander needs to develop 'Cross-cultural Competence'. He should have knowledge, skill, abilities, motivation, and cross-cultural sensitivity. He should be able to communicate his intent to all his troops effectively. He should develop intellectual, social, and emotional intelligence keeping in mind the cultural diversity among his own troops and also that of the enemy. This would enable him to take informed decisions. He needs to develop leadership styles encompassing both transactional leadership and the more important transformational leadership. He should encourage transparency, practice integrity, and develop moral perspectives, which would influence and motivate followers to aspire towards becoming leaders of tomorrow. He should imbibe the environment and understand the 'human terrain' of the combat area and comprehend how his actions would impact on local population. He should be adept in mediation and conflict resolution by respecting cultural sensitivity of all stakeholders.

An array of authors from different parts of the globe give the book an international perspective. Their mastery in their respective chapters stands out prominently. The reference section at the end of each chapter gives a wealth of study resources based on which the authors' have offered ideas, data, and arguments. Thus, this book is a rich source for students of 'Military Psychology' to enable them to carry out further research on the subject. The book is a prized souvenir for students, .teachers, academicians, researchers, and, most importantly, to those who have joined the 'profession of arms'.

Lt. Gen PG Kamath, PVSM, AVSM, YSM, SM.
Formerly Commandant, Army War College, Mhow, India.

Preface

As I edit this book in 2016, the global war on terrorism becomes more pronounced in the wake of unfortunate innocent lives lost across the globe; be it in Syria, France, US, UK, Germany, or closer home in India. Not many books in the field of military psychology appear to have been written, especially books that delve into areas that are now receiving considerable attention and are of great relevance in such challenging times that we live in. These topics have been overlooked or touched upon very briefly in other psychology books; here, these are discussed in various chapters to emphasise their significance.

For many of you, as young leaders in military and students of psychology in various colleges and institutions across the country, this may well be your first educational foray in the field of military psychology. It is my proud privilege to introduce you to this work. If the learning acquired from reading this book gives you a better understanding of the military environment and personnel who serve in them, it will have made my efforts more than worthwhile.

This book is the creation of many minds that put their heart and soul in writing chapters relevant to the times we live in. I hope it provides you with a scientifically sound, practical, and an eye-opening journey in the lives of military personnel. I hope that readers from the non-military background will recognise that military culture is an important diverse group that society can no longer afford to ignore. I am sanguine that universities and academic institutions will soon consider inclusion of military psychology and counselling as an area of study in their course curriculum.

I wish to express my gratitude to all my professional colleagues and my 'military role model' father – Lt. Col. S.C. Rawat and his course mates from the first course at the National Defence Academy (NDA) for their evaluations and constructive criticisms of this book. I would like to also thank my colleagues and researchers at Military MIND Academy, Pune, my wife of 25 years Neelima, and son Suryang who meticulously read the manuscript for this edition and provided many invaluable suggestions, most of which have been incorporated.

All the royalties from the sale of this book are being utilised for educational and learning-development initiatives benefiting military personnel and their families.

Lt. Col. Dr Samir Rawat

Acknowledgements

It would be very difficult for me to attempt acknowledging my gratitude to people who have enabled me in this endeavor to edit a book on Military Psychology.

I am grateful to the men and women in the Armed Forces in India and across the globe that I have had the privilege of knowing as I journeyed through the wonderful surroundings that is the military environment.

I am privileged to have known eminent military psychologists like Hubert Annen, Ole Boe, Chris Dobre, Jacques Gouws, Eri Hidayat, Yvonne Masakowski, and Merle Parmak; they have contributed towards writing interesting chapters for this book. I shall remain indebted to them forever.

The timely help and motivation from my research colleagues at Military MIND Academy, Pune, deserve a special mention – Tintisha helped me in tackling the typing errors and editing the book while Vrashali sifted through voluminous references in the book. The onerous task of timely publishing of this book would not have been possible without the timelines adhered to by not only the contributors but also Pranit Rawat and his dedicated team. I am personally thankful to each one of them; their enthusiasm and patience was a learning for me as they provided outstanding assistance on behalf of Rawat Publications.

I would especially like to thank Ms Tintisha Basu for the tremendous resilience shown in diligently helping me with reference entries and chapter-proofing work.

Closer home, I owe a lot to my parents, relatives, and friends. The tremendous social support I have received from them has sustained me during editing this book. My son Suryang and wife Neelima deserve special mention as they relentlessly endeared my unsocial behavior and unpredictable circadian rhythm so that I could battle the book editing on a war footing with complete abandon.

Any questions, suggestions, or comments will be highly appreciated and should be directed to Lt. Col. Dr Samir Rawat, PhD (Retd) at the Military MIND Academy, Pune; or by e-mail to samtanktrooper@yahoo.com.

Pune, India **Lt. Col. Dr Samir Rawat**

Abbreviations

BSC	Bachelor's Study Course
CBHRM	Competency-Based Human Resource Management System
CBT	Competency Based Training
CCC	Cross-cultural Competencies
CONOPS	Continuous Operations
DSC	Diploma Study Course
ETHZ	Eidgenössische Technische Hochschule; or ETH Zurich
FAOs	Foreign Area Officers
HR System	Human Resource System
HTT	Human Terrain Teams
ISIS	Islamic State of Iraq and Syria
ISTIP	Italian Institute of Polemology
MEF	Minimum Essential Force
MILAK	Military Psychology of the Swiss Military Academy at the Swiss Federal Institute of Technology in Zurich
MUS	Medically Unexplained Syndrome
NATO	North Atlantic Treaty Organisation
NCO	Non-commissioned Officer
NMA	Norwegian Military Academy
OBSCIF	OBServation of Character in Field
PCAP	Position Competencies Assessment Program
PDs	Psychological Disabilities
PMF	Para Military Forces
PTSD	Post-traumatic Stress Disorder

SUSOPS	Sustained Operations
TNI AD	Indonesian Army (*Tentara Nasional Indonesia Angkatan Darat*)
USAFM	United States Army Field Manual
VIA	Values in Action
VIAIS	Values in Action Inventory of Strengths

Introduction

These are indeed challenging times for all countries and its soldiers as unconventional warfare gets a new dimension in the wake of terrorism reaching our very backyards; the enemies no longer lie across borders. While the stressors of combating terrorism make it a daunting task in itself for soldiers to manage; they need to shoulder additional responsibilities towards own families, friends, and the society itself which is at an increased risk of life and limb. A very unique and hugely pertinent subject, which has not yet been explored in the way advanced countries use it as a force multiplier, but is now taking centre stage is Military Psychology and Counselling and its application in real-life contexts for uniformed personnel. It is now fast becoming an interdisciplinary field of international relevance all over the globe as world armies prepare to ensure security not just on their own borders and within but across continents as well.

In the wake of terror attacks all over the world, military psychology is gaining currency and assuming greater significance to encompass not just the military, but Police, Para Military Forces (PMF), and Central Armed Police Forces (CAPF) as well in an effort to understand the psychology of terror and develop tactics and strategies to deal with this growing menace.

As uniformed personnel the world over grope to deal with an assortment of responsibilities ranging from border management and handling internal security to dealing with the fog of war and terror attacks, this book comes at an appropriate time to create an awareness of military psychology as a field of study which introduces information as relevant to the Armed Forces, and in light of increasing threats and terror attacks, it is also relevant for Police, PMF, as well as CAPF. The theme of the book is diverse with chapters from experienced military psychologists from eight countries; on one hand, it infuses fresh blood into the subject matter by introducing and discussing initiatives to deal with psychology of terror, and on the other it provides strategies for reducing burnout of uniformed personnel. Furthermore, it comes at a time when the need of the hour is for collective synergy to dismantle the old, archaic constitutional structure and use best practices in military psychology to act as a force multiplier in the collective war against terror. India, which is now high on growth trajectory, needs to battle with an overwhelmingly stretched army fighting on more than one front, and this causes immense unwanted stress on the battle-returned soldiers; it is exactly here that Military Psychology comes into play! Military Psychology refers to the science and application of human behaviour to military contexts.

Who should read this book?

Whether you are a student of psychology, a specialist military officer or military spouse, police or PMF personnel, a policymaker in Ministry of Defence or Home or External Affairs, or a practicing psychologist/counsellor/psychiatrist – this book provides you with a better understanding of the military environment and all those who put their lives at stake while working in it.

Subsequent to my invitation in an International Military Conference in Germany in 2014 and having participated in similar conferences in Austria, Croatia, Indonesia, Portugal, South Korea, Switzerland, and in Sweden where I met military psychologists from across the globe, I felt the need to create an awareness of military psychology as a field of study among students in India as well.

The rationale of this book was to create awareness among students of psychology, counsellors, practising psychologists, military and other uniformed personnel about military psychology and counselling as a field of study. This book introduces psychology students, consultants and counsellors to psychological information as relevant to the Armed Forces and in the light of increasing threats and terror attacks. While this book is designed to expand the outlook of young psychology students, it also has great relevance to practitioners, counsellors, and all uniformed personnel, including Military, Police, PMF and CAPF and their spouses at large since there are eminent international military psychologists with rich experiences keen on sharing their perspectives on unique topics.

The book is a conglomeration of diverse chapters written by experienced and eminent military psychologists from eight different countries; their writings give a new flavour to the application of psychology in military contexts of challenging circumstances under which uniformed personnel must now operate.

Chapter 1 makes a case for military psychology, as an applied science in the military context, to include polemology as a primary tool to limit and reduce short-sighted engagement in war and regional conflicts. It is quite possible that the application of polemology principles may serve to curb humankind's self-destruction, thus preventing planetary suicide.

Chapter 2 examines how stress may adversely affect performance, commitment, retention, cohesion, morale and physical health of military personnel. Military leaders can contribute to prevent or reduce unwanted stress in the military environment.

Chapter 3 considers various dimensions of coping resources available to military personnel, be it in the realm of problem-focused coping or emotion-focused coping.

Chapter 4 discusses a very important aspect of resilience among military spouses during soldier deployment in operational areas and makes a case for addressing resilience building for this neglected population which makes as much a sacrifice for the nation as the soldier.

Chapter 5 discusses the concept of Competency-Based Human Resource Management (CBHRM) and Assessment Centre and their application in military organisation and subsequently elaborate on its implementation in the Indonesian Army.

Chapter 6 discusses character strengths, their relevance for military officers, and some subjective and objective measures of character strengths and makes a case for 12 character strengths considered most important for military officers.

Chapter 7 identifies aspects related to influence which cyber-warfare will play against emotions and behaviour of the world's future soldiers and attempts to explain this new dimension of security with the help of cyber-psychology.

Chapter 8 discusses research on psychological aspects of selection, training, motivation, and leadership of military personnel with a clear focus on application and use of methods, which foster critical thinking and individual processing by leaders of men.

In Chapter 9, a multidimensional approach to functional fitness in military organisations is proposed to highlight the importance of understanding performance restrictions by considering both physical and psychological factors.

Chapter 10 examines challenges to military leaders by a decentralised adversary; one which is geographically distributed in power and organisation, culturally diverse, ideologically driven, and is able to act as non-state actors who function within a coordinated social network which affords the adversary an asymmetric advantage. The chapter highlights the importance of understanding cultural and sociopolitical underpinnings of such ideologies that challenge global security and suggests that each nation must deem cross-cultural competence as a vital prerequisite for all future military leaders.

I wish you an interesting developmental journey as you page through this book, hoping that young students of psychology as well as uniformed personnel find this book appealing enough to factor in the learning of their professions.

5 November 2016 **Lt. Col. Dr Samir Rawat**
Pune, India

1

Polemology: an imperative field in military psychology

Jacques J. Gouws

Introduction

Many authors have claimed that humankind is the only living species on earth capable of intelligent reasoning and experiencing emotional feelings through which an understanding of their world eventually leads to innovative technological development. In doing so, humankind has accomplished much: conquering land, sea, and air, and even the moon. Now humans have set their sights on the stars and planets.

The underlying belief system to these achievements is that these many accomplishments make it possible to conquer disease and poverty, and at the more altruistic level, slavery and subjugation, including class and social differences. The ultimate goal is that once these inequities are conquered human suffering on earth will be replaced by healthy, affluent societies, where each individual will be free to express their views and opinions in an environment free from prejudice and intimidation. This proffered ideal towards which humankind is striving, once achieved, will supposedly ensure lasting peace and security, free from all the restrictions that have bound humankind from time immemorial to the quirks of other humans who are beholden to a belief system that at its core only promotes inequality.

Historians may well one day look back upon the twentieth century as having equal importance as the Italian Renaissance era. The past century brought about a paradigm shift in how the human race perceived the world and its place therein. The Renaissance was a reawakening to the science, art, and culture of the time, resulting in a cultural movement that challenged every aspect of society as it existed at the time, be it politics or religion, philosophy or science; in fact no area of life was devoid of intellectual inquiry. If nothing else, the Renaissance laid the foundation of what became the Industrial Revolution of the 1700s and 1800s. The significant advances this brought to technology in the nineteenth century changed economic paradigms, thus creating a new world order. These developing technologies also served to enhance military armaments, the application of which in turn brought about another paradigm shift. The doctrine and strategy of warfare changed rapidly as the wars of the late 1800s and early 1900s benefited from the application of these new technologies to create ever more destructive weapons of war. At the start of the twentieth-century, technology advanced even more rapidly in the development of more destructive weapon systems, making possible the mass slaughter witnessed during the First World War; the war that formally gave birth to what became the field of military psychology.

A century of rapid paradigm shifts

As technological advances exploded after the First World War, paradigm shifts continued to occur at increasing rates. The world changed forever during a defining moment of the Second World War – the creation of the ultimate weapon of self-destruction, the nuclear bomb, and its subsequent use. This resulted in decades of a Cold War, defined by constant fear of total mutual destruction. When this era finally ended, humankind breathed a sigh of relief, only to be rudely awakened to a completely new type of warfare. Not even two decades into the twenty-first century the world appears on the verge of what may well become the final battle for the survival of humankind – waging war against fanatic forces with apparently only one objective – to bring about a new world order that harks back to some of the darkest ages in human history. While it would be the ultimate insanity to resort to the use of tactical nuclear weapons, it would not be a surprising action from a psychological perspective, given the rhetoric espoused by various world leaders.

One can only wonder how it is possible that humankind, at this point in the twenty-first century, still finds itself captive in the remorseless chains of 'primitive' forces, apparently coming out of nowhere, yet capable of binding 'progressive' communities helplessly to the pillars of their Temple of War. It seems that humankind, even after the euphoria of the end of the Cold War, remains completely unable to break free from the ever-present violence and destruction imposed by the powerful on the weak, the rich on the poor, the aggressive on the passive, the devious on the ignorant, and the fanatic on the non-believer. Humankind during the twentieth century created a cult of war, with its temples of worship being the theatres of conflict in various parts of the world. In order to break free from this cult-like bondage, humankind will have to bring down this Temple of War. This brings to mind the story of Samson, the ancient Jewish strongman who, betrayed by his Philistine lover, blinded and enslaved, was brought to the Temple in Gaza by his captors to be displayed for the amusement of the Philistine worshipers. However, in a final burst of strength, Samson, bound to the two pillars supporting the temple roof, brings down the temple upon himself and all those inside. The chilling conclusion in the Book of Judges is that Samson, at his death, killed more people than he had killed during his life.

One can be forgiven for thinking that ancient history is repeating itself today in especially the Middle East. Despite best efforts, all the peace talks, negotiations, sanctions, military action, and other actions taken by international leaders, world organisations, and individual groups failed to bring about curtailment of the perpetual engagement in war operations. Even a cursory study of all these failed efforts reveals the stark absence of a scientifically based, thorough understanding of human motives, beliefs, and drives in the waging of these war operations. It is ironic that for centuries warring factions employed military principles to 'better wage war' based on what is now part of psychological application but not its prevention or curtailment!

In the formalised military context, military psychology at its inception during the First World War was tasked with selection and placement based on cognitive tests. In time, this new science matured, and now its primary applied focus is to create soldiers whose skill sets surpass those of their predecessors in dealing with the ever-increasing complex demands of the modern battlefield. A study of the Cold War certainly provides ample examples of the psychological games involved in the posturing of East and West against each other. The resulting arms race ravaged whole economies, while arms manufacturers and dealers walked away with lucrative contracts. Meanwhile these weapon systems were field-tested by opposing forces locked in civil wars, with East and West respectively supporting their 'side' of the conflict. Throughout this time military psychology in all of its sub-disciplines worked hand-in-hand with national military forces to enhance the capabilities of the modern fighting soldier, whether psychologically, physically, or technologically.

However, in less than three decades since the fall of the Berlin Wall on 9 November 1989, (considered by many the pivotal event that signalled the end of the Cold War), twentieth-century conventional warfare had been replaced by twenty-first-century unconventional warfare. Indeed, the face of war has changed dramatically, and the traditional approaches to war that served the military well for many centuries no longer apply. Insurgency war operations are at the core of the *Jihad* (Holy War) fought by fanatic forces who may well have a reasonable rationalisation as to why, in an 'eye-for-an-eye' belief system, they want to destroy the aberrant modern civilisation in Europe, and in particular the United States as the main enemy. These operations involve non-statutory forces, drawn from various populations, acting either as 'lone wolves' or organised militia groups.

At the statutory level, new technology applied in military operations may well replace 'boots on the ground.' This is already the case with the use of unmanned aerial vehicles (UAV) or remotely piloted aircraft (RPA) used by the US Air Force. If anything, soldiering as we know it may become obsolete. That said, while these weapon systems are designed to reduce casualties among land forces while neutralising enemy forces, long-distance warfare by operating drones will not be sufficient to attack an enemy consisting of primarily civilian-based, non-statutory militia.

Psychological motives play a major role in every conflict; hence, there is a requirement for a thorough analysis of these motives on all sides in order to prevent a catastrophe arising from ill-informed international intervention decisions against largely invisible opponents. This is where the inclusion of polemology, based on sound scientific principles, may serve traditional military psychology in advising military leadership and government decision-makers on conflict resolution and prevention of catastrophic, drawn-out wars.

What is polemology?

Early days

The foundation for the structured and systemised study of the war phenomenon has been in existence for close to eight decades, still it remains a great unknown to most military psychologists. *Polemology*, a term coined by Gaston Bouthoul after the end of the Second World War, is the study of war and its precursors and consequences, given the ability that humankind had developed to wipe out itself and the earth with nuclear weapons. *Polemology* is a word derived from the contraction of the Greek words *polemos* (πόλεμος) and *logos* (λόγος). Hence, polemology is the study of the war phenomenon, with a more literary meaning being the logic or science of war.

Following the Second World War, Bouthoul, a sociologist, became the first social scientist to openly and actively initiate the scientific, systematised study of the phenomena of aggression and wars as they manifest in strategy, tactics, economics, politics, ideology, and cultural contexts. Bouthoul postulated that by a better understanding of conflicts and wars one can find positive ways to prevent them. Sadly, these very worthy aspirations died with Bouthoul in 1980. Lately, there has been a revival in the interest in Bouthoul's work with a fairly recent, landmark publication, *The Ashgate Research Companion to War*. In the Introduction to this work, Gardner and Kobtzeff offered some insights as to why the work of Bouthoul was ignored:

> By the time postmodernism became very influential in France as well as in the world, around the 1980s and 1990s, marking the decline of the Annales school (which had itself reached the peak of its influence in the French intelligentsia and public in the 1970s), war was still not a subject that the New Historians had been able to interpret. The original prejudice against

war studies in particular and political science in general still prevailed after three generations.

This probably explains the isolation of French sociologist Gaston Bouthoul (1896–1980) who devoted his career to fusing the knowledge and methodologies of all social sciences into a new interdisciplinary field of research and reflection for which he invented a new word: polemology. Originally published in 1951 as Les guerres (Wars), and renamed Traité de Polémologie (Treatise on Polemology) in 1970 (published in Paris by Payot), Bouthoul's landmark monograph and his other writings are known to only a few specialists. The word 'polemology' remains either almost unheard of or is mistakenly associated with the kind of practical academic programs delivered by military institutions. In the aftermath of First World War, and later, again, following Second World War, it had been too difficult to explain to a battle-fatigued public the need for a large-scale effort to create a science of wars. The tens of millions of casualties made it difficult to accept that war can be quietly studied as an object of science, an 'ordinary' social phenomenon. Bouthoul had to defend his project and explain that it was not just a laboratory for the amusement of cold-blooded scientists oblivious to the sufferings of the victims. Also, when Bouthoul and his team of researchers founded, in 1945, a modest research centre named the French Institute of Polemology (Institut Français de Polémologie) they were met with suspicion which was typical of the late forties to mid-to-late 1960s. On one hand, the now dominating Annales school suspected too much political comment over war; on the other, an increasingly radical leftwing intelligentsia rejected any activity in the arts or social sciences that could not justify itself as politically and socially useful for the Revolution (peace studies, like hippies, risked demobilising the working masses). The fact that Bouthoul's institute cooperated with the French military academic system made him even more suspicious. Nevertheless, Bouthoul, a socialist who loathed war, strongly argued that his scientific activities were pacifist in nature. Although he conceived polemology as a discipline based on scientific methods, academic objectivity

> was not meant to abolish the scientist' ability to function as a thinking and responsible citizen striving for peace. Fortunately, other scholars initiated comparable efforts in other parts of the world. At a time when nuclear holocaust appeared to be a real possibility, it became evident that conflict prevention or resolution was hampered by the dramatic lack of research structures that could offer the necessary broad array of conflict analysis tools. The urgency of the need for more research on war and peace became evident after such dramatic moments as the Cuban missile crisis, or under the growing pressure from peace movements in the 1960s. The emerging disciplines or sub-disciplines of sociology or political science became better known as 'Peace Studies' with the creation of such groups and institutions as PRIO, the Peace Research Institute Oslo (associated with Johan Galtung); or the Malmö group that established the Peace Research Society (which initially included Walter Isard, Kenneth Boulding and Anatol Rapoport, and which became in 1973 the Peace Science Society), or many teaching and research institutions in a variety of departments housed by prestigious universities in Anglo-Saxon academia in Scandinavia, Italy and the Netherlands.

The above reasoning adequately explains why nations have a general reluctance to study war scientifically and to use the knowledge gained from research to effect peaceful change in a conflict-ravaged world. Ironically, traditional military psychology remains largely unaware of this important field of study. The reality is that military psychologists are in an exquisitely well-placed position to study and analyse aberrant behaviours and develop counter-strategies to the new global, ideological-based threat fuelled by religious fervour. It is only through the scientific study of war that an understanding can be gained of the psychological factors that perpetuate war at a time when the world can ill-afford the risk of fanatics using dirty bombs (or worse) to achieve their aims.

Bouthoul on polemology

The work of Bouthoul is monumental in its scope and application, making it almost impossible to summarise in brief. There is no question that even touching the surface of his work opens up new insights into the phenomenon of war.

Probably the most significant early commentary on the work of Bouthoul was offered by Franco Fornari (1921–1985), an Italian psychiatrist and psychoanalyst who became interested in polemology in the 1960s. He subsequently found the first 'anti-H group' as well as established the Italian Institute of Polemology (ISTIP). Fornari was a very productive author and wrote several landmark works in psychoanalysis related to a variety of topics. One of his most provocative books was published in 1966 under the title *Psicoanalisi della Guerra*. It was later made available in translation in 1974, titled *The Psychoanalysis of War*.

Military psychologists need to gain an insight into the motives behind decisions to go to war (or not) and especially carefully study the intentions and consequences of what is taking place in conflict regions. In this, the work of Bouthoul, as quoted by Fornari, plays an important role. Fornari, quoting from the work of both Bouthoul and Durkheim, provides an insight into the origins of much of the military action and subsequent ritual that still take place today. World leader's reactions to the Twin Towers Attack of 9/11, the current conflict in Ukraine and Crimea, as well as the conflicts in the Middle East pertaining to Syria, ISIS/ISL/DAESH, Libya, and others, serve to illustrate the following arguments:

> The splitting of the world into friend and enemy represents an extreme simplification whereby the good and the bad are no longer integrated in the same instinctual situation and in the same object relationship, but the same situation assumes different characters according as it is consummated upon the self, or upon the other, in the paranoid aphorism of 'mors tua vita mea.' The enormous weight of human ambivalence is suddenly lifted when love and hate find two separate objects of attention.

Clearly then war is a method to bring about a radical transformation of values, to make people think, feel, and act differently from before, and to make them distinguish between 'good and bad'. However, to bring about this transformation, the powerbase of the initiator must first be coaxed into action and then become unified in its aggression against the opposition. This is achieved through mass behaviour taking place in a specific context, which, as explained by Fornari, is analogous to a feast:

> In Bouthoul's opinion war has all the characteristics of a feast, whose principal function, according to Durkheim, is to unify the group. The most typical psychological aspects of a feast, in the sociological sense of the word, are the following: 1) It brings about a meeting of the members of a group; 2) it is a rite of expenditure and dissipation; 3) it is accompanied by a modification of certain moral laws; 4) it is a rite of collective exaltation; 5) it brings about a state of physical insensibility; 6) it is accompanied by sacrificial rites. As every one of these characteristics is found in war, war might be regarded as the *supreme feast*.

Little elaboration, if any, is needed on the characteristics of a feast, as described above, and how this relates to many public ritualistic activities that still take place in both the waging and commemoration of war. Fornari noted that in primitive peoples one finds that war preparations include dances, something that appears to be preserved in modern day military parades.

Furthermore, the manner in which the rules of war transcend civilian law is similar to the modification of morals at a feast – the tunnel-vision, lack of feeling, and sensation often found in battle – is likewise a state of physical insensibility at a feast. In the aftermath of war, however, the ritual ceremonies recall the sacrifices made by combatants:

> Among primitive peoples, in fact, war is intimately joined to the idea of a human sacrifice that is pleasing to the gods, i.e. to the cult of death. . . . Bouthoul notes that in Western civilisation, concurrently with the decline of religions, the cult of the fallen in war has been revived in the form of monuments and parks. He interprets this situation as the return of the archaic customs in our civilisation. The cult of the fallen in war therefore tends to replace the cult of the saints.

Phenomenon of war

Many theories have been postulated to attempt to explain the almost instinctive manner in which humans settle their disputes by violent, destructive means. Though the various religions proclaim war as an unacceptable act, even they make provision for waging war under certain conditions, these being mostly defined as 'the most threatening of situations'. In all theologies certain stringent rules are thus applied before engagement in any form of war can be authorised on religious grounds. Humans in both the spiritual and secular settings of life strive towards peace and prosperity, only to have these noble strivings thwarted by someone else who feels dispossessed, unfairly treated, or 'left with a raw deal'. Even pacifists, for all their well-meant intentions, eventually find themselves in a position where they have to take a stand, very often violently opposing the very violence of which they wanted no part of, in either a physical or psychological manner. The greatest contradiction is humankind's willingness to save the lives of the elderly, the weak, and the infirm in society, while at the same time sending the younger, fitter, and stronger members of society off to war to be killed, injured, maimed, and crippled for life.

The first of the explanations for the war phenomenon blames the soldier. Arguments abound that those who are commanding the forces, that is, the generals, are the warmongers, the ones who really give an essence, a right to existence, for armies, and thus war. The solution is to terminate the defence budget and dissolve the military. Then war and violence would disappear, because soldiers, so explains the believer, actually foster and enhance the spirit of conflict. Likewise, if societies were to disarm, violence will disappear.

This argument is countered by Boatner who stated that soldiering is not only the third oldest profession, but the soldier himself is the only element that has varied least through the ages, since the dawn of humankind. He quotes Ardent duPicq:

> Centuries have not changed human nature. Passions, instincts – particularly the most powerful instinct of self-preservation – these things are expressed differently in accordance with the times, the circumstances, the character and temperament of races. . . . But, beneath it all, the same man is to be found.

A clue to the rhetorical question about the reasons for war and the war phenomenon is found in the reference to human nature as discussed above. Humankind appears to have something within (let us call it the 'psyche' for convenience sake) that will always drive them towards some form or another of conflict or war. Conflict seems to be an inherent part of human nature, and war is the 'legalised' method by which this conflict is made both manifest and resolved. Humans in their societies appear to be in perpetual conflict with each other, even while both sides are actively striving towards conflict resolution. It is the perception of others as a threat to their continued existence that drives war preparations to 'deter' the perceived enemy. To deter, is to pre-empt, but the defensive measures taken by one will always be interpreted by the other side as an increased threat to self. Thus, subjective perceptions become the rationale for war, regardless of the region where it is waged.

Rationale for war

Walsh very bluntly identified the rationale for war:

> It is now quite universally recognised that the superficial and naive statement that war maintains the balance of nature in humans in the same way that predators do in the animal world is a myth, since the present studies show that the expression of naked aggression, manifested through the destruction of other human beings, is largely led and initiated by psychologically abnormal individuals.
>
> One can say with certainty that the time-honoured human habit, unfortunately not rare, of placing nations under the control of psychologically abnormal, aggressively perverted persons, together with the modern factor of the ever-increasing new invention of massive weapons of destruction, is certain to be suicidal for the human race unless interrupted. This tendency of societies to select psychiatrically and pathologically charismatic abnormal individuals, of the nature of aggressive perverts, to control nations and to lead them into war indicates that intra-specific aggression in the human race has gotten out of hand and has become a serious threat to the survival of the species. This can only mean that natural selection in the human is being interfered with, and that unconscious forces, basically responsible for the existence of aggressive perversions as well

as for the uncanny ability of such pathologically charismatic individuals to seduce normal human beings into selecting them as leaders and following them to death, can effectively upset the balance of human nature and can brutalise and destroy human beings en masse with enormous damage to the painfully attained process of civilisation.

These statements have important implications in the interpretation of rationalisations offered by political and military leaders to engage in war operations. If the characterisation of elected leaders going to war because of being psychologically abnormal is correct, it follows logically that the rationalisations to go to war would reflect an imperative to intervene to rectify the *abnormal imbalance* that had developed in the targeted party, which also poses *a threat* to the initiating party's goals. A commonly used rationalisation is a saying of Xenophon:

The art of war is, in the last result, the art of keeping one's freedom of action.

This *freedom of action* is a highly controversial and subjective issue, defined by the whims of those entering into war operations, as illustrated in the following quote:

'War' must be regarded as a finite, extraordinary and unnatural state of affairs. . . . War permits one man – if he is a 'privileged belligerent', consistent with the laws of war – to kill another. War violates the natural order of things, in which children bury their parents; in war parents bury their children. In its twelfth year, we must not accept the current conflict, and all that it entails, as the 'new normal'. Peace must be regarded as the norm toward which the human race continually strives.

This statement, with particular chilling aspects to it, was made in a speech delivered at Oxford University by Jeh Charles Johnson in late 2012. At the time he was the Pentagon's general counsel. The contradiction is clear: acknowledgement of the abnormal psychological nature of war while at the same time giving it a sense of legality. The late Senator William Fulbright articulated it very forcefully:

> The more I puzzle over the great wars of history, the more I am inclined to the view that the causes attributed to them – territory, markets, resources, the defense or perpetuation of great principles – were not the root causes at all but rather explanations or excuses for certain unfathomable drives of human nature. For lack of a clear and precise understanding of exactly what these motives are, I refer to them as the 'arrogance of power' – as a psychological need that nations seem to have in order to prove that they are bigger, better, or stronger than other nations. Implicit in this drive is the assumption, even on the part of normally peaceful nations, that force is the ultimate proof of superiority – that when a nation shows that it has the stronger army, it is also proving that it has better people, better institutions, better principles, and, in general, a better civilisation.

Fulbright is not alone in this position, as the many historic examples of why war was declared show that the rationalisation from ancient to modern times remains unchanged:

> 'War for the sake of war' towards a more 'civilised' rationale: superiority in values, power and status. During the period in which the Crusades took place the Church and Church Fathers invoked racial, religious and economic prejudices in order to militarily save Christianity from the Muslim infidel. This 'Christian' approach brought about an awareness in Western thought that even today still prevents rational negotiation from taking place, rather than war, viz., that of a subjective superiority that favours the subjugation of a subjectively perceived inferior in order to safeguard all aspects of the perceived superior system. One also finds this in certain other quarters of society, especially with regard to the Third World, where the perception still persists that 'the chosen people are the guardians of the lesser human beings'.

There is little doubt that most of the conflicts currently taking place is based on a perception of inferior and superior forces 'battling it out for the good of all'. Whatever the rationale offered to engage in war, history shows that when peace reigned it was shattered by war, when war was waged, it was overcome by peace. William James, quoted by Montross offers the following insight:

> Every up-to-date dictionary should say that 'peace' and 'war' mean the same thing. . . . It may even reasonably be said that the intensely sharp competitive preparation for war by nations is the real war, permanent, unceasing; and that the battles are only a sort of public verification of the mastery gained during the 'peace' interval.

Regardless of the degree to which any war may be more justifiable than others, war is a mechanical process whereby humans create a war machine, and once created, the functioning of these machines must be demonstrated, often by their application in actual war operations. In the end, regardless of the rationale, war is caused by human behaviour.

Causes of war

Regardless of the myriad of books, papers, and articles on war and its causes, in the end war is caused by people, regardless of malice or good intentions. Ordinary everyday citizens, considered good people, are drawn into the political rhetoric and the perceptions put forward by political leadership and even bureaucrats, who may claim to be taking action for all the right reasons, but in the end, on final assessment, had been pursuing their own political agendas. If anything, just as was the case a 100 years ago when the First World War started, nations today continue to act in a manner similar to what Hegel had stated almost 170 years ago:

> The first glance at History convinces us that the actions of men proceed from their needs, their passions, their characters and talents; and impresses us with the belief that such needs, passions and interests are the sole spring of actions.

This statement by Hegel is not news to anyone with even a basic knowledge of psychology. However, as an applied science that is performing its role within the military organisation, military psychology has to be cognisant of the needs and passions that drive national leaders and their allies' actions, including the choice of going to war or not. No one would argue that without the complacency and complicity of the German military, Hitler would not have been able to start the Second World War. Often however, military psychology lacks a thorough understanding of the underlying ideological belief systems and specific leader personality traits and even the psychopathology that drive the political decision-making processes, and with that, the choice towards military deployment rather than addressing the core issues underlying conflict situations. After all:

> War is something that people do, not something that happens: activity with a military dimension is activity, not mere blind process and event.

Analysis of the armed conflicts since the fall of the Berlin Wall, and particularly after 9/11, chillingly suggests that the deployment of military forces had simply been based on political decision-making for short-term political expediency rather than long-term exigency. Conflict analysis also suggests that in these deployments there were no well-thought-through exit strategy before allied governments committed their forces to military operations in various parts of the world. Indeed, the American political scientist and historian, Michael Parenti, noted that:

> Through much of history the abnormal has been the norm. This is a paradox to which we should attend. Aberrations, so plentiful as to form a terrible normality of their own, descend upon us with frightful consistency.

This statement is an echo of Stoessinger's questioning of the archaic arguments on the causes of war:

> I read that wars were caused by nationalism, militarism, alliance systems, economic factors, and by some other bloodless abstraction that I could not understand.
>
> Often I was told that war was an ineradicable part of human nature. . . . I wondered if this could be true. . . . The conventional wisdom . . . somehow always missed the human

> essence of the problem. After all, wars were begun by people. Yet this personality dimension was seldom given its due weight in traditional books on war. Instead, forces over which men had no control often were enthroned as 'fundamental' causes.

Even a cursory review of daily news statements indicates that established and legitimate political and military entities appear to engage in actions that are designed to perpetuate regional war operations simply because it is politically convenient to do so. There is an almost surreal quality to media statements that seem to suggest a video-game-like, virtual reality that reduces real-life events to just another set of electronic images on a screen:

> 'Deter', 'degrade' and 'defeat' flow from our leaders' tongues with the ease of salesman selling a new mouthwash; 'precision' bombing is discussed as if this was equivalent to tossing curling stones in downtown Moose Jaw; training by foreign troops of local forces is accepted as if this was a woodworking class in the local trades school; recovery of downed pilots from ISIS-controlled territory is glossed over with the suggestion that the Americans will handle this nasty possibility; and the legality of extending the war to Syria is justified by parsing sections of the United Nations Charter by the chief lawyer for the Canadian military, hardly an unbiased observer.
>
> Unfortunately there is one aspect of the war that is being ignored, and as with most modern wars it is the most important. No one, especially the militaries involved, has offered any assessment of success in understandable terms of what this war will achieve. Most will only say that a conclusion is years away, which in today's world is no answer whatsoever.
>
> We have dressed for a ball that we do not understand, and invited ourselves, knowing we have no capability of influencing the outcome. Instead, leaders who should know better see the war as a means of scratching a small itch in the national body politic – fear of an imprecise national security threat. In response, they send our soldiers into harm's way, and this even

> before they have satisfactorily dealt with the wounded from the last war.
>
> We do not have to go back to Vietnam for a detailed understanding of the futility of fighting forces on their own land. Eleven years of fighting the Afghans with overwhelming force and money, the creation of comprehensive new security and military forces, the fostering of civilian political measures of electoral politics and the holding of elections and the creation of a hothouse corrupt economy based on foreign money have done absolutely nothing to change anything of any significance in that ancient land.

Based on his in-depth studies of six major international wars that were fought in the twentieth century (First and Second World Wars, Korea, Vietnam, India and Pakistan, the Arab States and Israel, and Iran and Iraq, and the Gulf War in Kuwait), Stoessinger's causal analysis of why nations go to war is that:

1. War is a sickness.
2. No nation that began a major war in the twentieth century emerged a winner.
3. The advent of the nuclear age changed the nature of war into an indecisive, suicidal venture.
4. Where a war has been fought, the victor will seldom have a lasting peace, unless the vanquished is completely destroyed.

Stoessinger's findings on the leaders of the countries involved in the wars he studied confirm that humans are the actual causes of war, in that

1. The personalities of the leaders are of crucial importance with regard to the outbreak of war. When the actions, reactions, and general rationality of the leaders involved in the waging of war is considered, it appears that these attributes are decisive in the decision of going to war or not.
2. The single most important precipitating factor in the outbreak of war is misperception, manifesting itself in four different ways:

    a. The leader's image of him or herself.
    b. *The leader's view of the adversary's character.*

c. *The leader's view of the adversary's intentions toward him or herself.* This is an important factor: should a leader, when on the brink of war, believe that attack by the adversary is imminent, the chances of war are fairly high. Should both leaders share this perception about each other's intent, war becomes a virtual certainty. The mechanisms of the self-fulfilling prophecy then come into motion, totally overwhelming all reason and rationality. When leaders attribute evil designs to their adversaries and nurture these beliefs for long enough, they will eventually be proved right.
d. *The leader's view of his or her adversary's capabilities and power.* Perception, and not the actual situation, is the quintessential cause of war. A war will start when nations disagree over their perceived strength. The war itself then becomes a dispute over the measurement of this power.

These theses as discussed above all suggest that the world has become far too dangerous to accommodate the uncontrolled decision-making on going to war by popular leaders in positions of power over nations and minority or majority ethnic groups alike. Military psychology, as one of the most significant applications of the field of psychology, may well hold the key to both the survival and the demise of humankind for the foreseeable future. This is because military psychology, more than any other scientific field, is intimately involved with the military conduct of conflict in all its forms in the modern world.

Conclusion

In a rapidly changing world, it is imperative to recognise that the changes of the past almost three decades brought a major shift in how people see the world. The most important tool in any government's hands is its military. However, the government and military are as much subject to the identified human frailties as any other societal structure.

The phenomenon of war is a fact of life across human history. It is almost as if it is one of few certainties in life: there will always be conflict giving rise to war for as long as human nature remains unchanged. As for the rationale for war, it seems as though there are only three categories of war rationale: war for the sake of war, war for freedom of action, and war for superiority. However, war is caused by humans, regardless of the many reasons offered for engaging in war. In the final analysis it is humans who decide to take up arms and fight. Therefore, it is imperative to gain a thorough understanding of the human drives and needs that lead to the preparation for and declaration of war. The groundwork for this understanding has already been laid in the field of polemology, and ample research indicates the degree to which aberrant behaviours and even psychopathology play a role in the decision to go to war. As the science of human behaviour it would therefore be incumbent upon military psychology to provide guidance to pursue normal rather than aberrant behaviour when leaders are facing challenging political and international situations. This guidance comes from the study of war and its aberrations.

Failure by military psychology to understand the psychological factors and drives that result in decisions on military and quasi-military operations will simply enhance the incredible violence resulting from the application of modern weapon systems. What the world had witnessed during more than a century of modern weapon systems in global war operations will pale in the face of the ever faster growing technological advances and their application in the annihilation of opposing forces in what has become regional conflicts rather than theatres of war.

Now, more than ever before, the role of military psychology in the study of war is paramount, as aptly articulated by Senator Fulbright, as quoted by Watson:

> in this field of the psychological aspects of war and peace, psychology's role is to provide a 'new dimension of self-understanding: We have got to understand, as we have never understood before, why it is, psychologically and biologically, that men and nations fight; and why it is, regardless of time or place or circumstances, that they always find something to fight about; why it is that we are capable of love and loyalty to our own nation or ideology and of venomous hatred toward someone else's. We have got to understand whether and how such emotions satisfy certain needs of human nature and whether and how these needs could be satisfied in a world without war.

> Only on the basis of an understanding of our behaviour can we hope to control it in such a way as to ensure the survival of the human race.

Time is running out for the prevention of conflicts that lead to the proliferation of weapons into the hands of those who would not hesitate to destroy the world. Therefore, military psychology must expand its focus beyond military recruitment, training, deployment, and treatment of post-battle casualties to include a clear understanding of the psychological forces at play in society and the world, and how these are affecting the economic, political, ideological, social, military, and moral/religious factors that lead to conflict and war. If not, the world will destroy itself while military psychology's contribution enhances armed conflict but not conflict resolution.

References

Boatner III, M. M. (1956). *Military customs and traditions*. New York: David Mckay Company.

Fornari, F. (1974). *The psychoanalysis of war* (trans. Doubleday). Markham, ON, Canada: Fitzhenry & Whiteside.

Fullbright, J. W. (1966). *The arrogance of power*. New York: Random House.

Gardner, H., & Kobtzeff, O. (2012). *The Ashgate research companion to war*. Farnham, UK: Ashgate.

Hegel, G. (1837). *The philosophy of history*. http://www.age-of-the-sage.org/history/quotations/lessons_of_history.html (Accessed 11 May 2015)

KingJamesBibleOnline.JudgesChapters 13–16. http://www.kingjamesbibleonline.org/Judges-Chapter-16/ (Accessed 1 February 2016)

Montross, L. (1946). *War through the ages*. New York: Harper and Brothers.

Pardy, G. (2015). The convenience of perpetual war. *Embassy News*. http://www.embassynews.ca/print_out_story/36897 (Accessed 21 April 2015)

Parenti, M. (2014). A terrible normality: The massacres and aberrations of history. *Global Research*. http://www.globalresearch.ca/a-terrible-normality-the-massacres-and-aberrations-of-history/5320619 (Accessed 4 April 2015)

Paskins, B., & Dockrill, M. (1979). *The ethics of war*. London: Duckworth.

Risen, J. (2014). *Pay any price. Greed, power, and endless war*. Boston: Houghton Mifflin Harcourt.

Stoessinger, J. G. (1992). *Why nations go to war* (6th ed.). New York: St. Martin's Press.

Walsh, M. N. (1971). *War and the human race*. New York: Elsevier.

Watson, P. (1978). *War on the mind: The military uses and abuses of psychology*. London: Hutchinson.

2

Stress in the armed forces: a psychological perspective

Samir Rawat

Introduction

It has been seen that at times, even highly resilient, tough, and once very efficient soldiers after prolonged, continuous exposure to combat and counterterrorism become reluctant to display the same level of enthusiasm and responsibility towards tasks, begin to show difficulty in making decisions, and prefer routine, simple tasks over more challenging ones as a result of accumulated unwanted stress. This chapter examines aspects of stress in the armed forces. The indicators of stress are physical, emotional, cognitive, behavioural, and somatic. Unwanted stress may impair combat readiness and decrease resistance to combat stress. It adversely affects teamwork and group cohesion, morale, and motivation, job performance, and physical and psychological health and well-being of a soldier. Soldiers trained for fighting terrorists and enemies from across the border are more likely to be stressed if made to operate with 'hands tied behind their backs' as skewed social engineering policies (e.g. use of pellet guns when training directives emphasise 'fire for effect') are thrust on them by policymakers who never have worn uniform for a day, leave alone face enemy bullets. This is further compounded by a perceived feeling of bereavement at weak military leadership who are unable to uphold standard operating procedures in a combat zone where 'unwarranted sensitivity training' increases loss of lives to own troops. Although enduring in a military environment can be very demanding and stressful, most armed forces personnel adapt and adjust well to rigors of combat soldiering (Bartone, 2006; Rawat, 2013). Research studies have reported that just living in a military environment can be overwhelming as it impinges on an individual's overall functioning and tests human limits (Cotton, 2001; Moore, 2006). Yet, military research is replete with studies of combat soldiers and their strong spirit in overcoming all odds to survive in battle (Edwards, 1993; Newman, 1992). Researchers have found that preparing for combat is known to lessen stress and increase survivability during war; it is one of the most important activities in armed forces (Driskell & Olmstead, 1989; Jaiswal, 1997).

It is evident that several psychological factors are associated with combat. Since the First World War, studies have focused attention on combat veterans (Cronin, 1998; Gal & Mangelsdorff, 1991; McGuire, 1990; Rawat, 2008; Taylor & Alluisi, 1994; Yerkes, 1919). Physical harm involved in fighting a war manifests itself in death, disability, and destruction. It has been found that these may have psychological fallouts in the form of war psychosis, fear, apprehensions, uncertainty, and personality disorders during and after combat (Khan, 2000; Srivastava, 2006).

Despite rigorous military life which prepares for combat and culminates in soldiers' skills, psychological factors affect cognitive and behavioural aspects of soldiers in an actual battlefield environment (Brooks, Byrne, & Hodson, 2001). Negatively, it may create fear of death, boredom and isolation, shock, confusion, bewilderment, war neurosis, and weariness. On the positive side, combat may bring loyalty, courage, patriotism, nationalism, morale, and leadership (Gruber, 2004; Labuc, 1991; Manning, 1991; Rawat & Wadkar, 2009; Snow, 1984).

A glance at research in military psychology indicates that most of the studies have explored stress and combat stress reactions (Belenky, 1987; Dekaris et al., 1993; Holmes, Tariot, & Cox, 1998; Southwick et al., 1993). Many studies have been carried out on posttraumatic stress disorder (Blake et al., 1990; Figley, 1985; Kulka et al., 1990; Weisenberg, Schwarzwald, & Solomon, 1991) and other problems occurring due to combat (Cronin, 1998; Gal & Mangelsdorff, 1991; Solomon, Openheimer, & Noy, 1986). Few studies have also recorded positive outcomes due to experiencing combat (Bartone, 2005; Fontana & Rosenheck, 1998; Gal, 1987; Kishon-Barash, Midlarsky, & Johnson, 1996; Rawat, 2008; Taylor, 1989).

India has fought many wars since independence and continues to experience low-intensity conflict with anti-national elements in Jammu and Kashmir as well as in Manipur. However, only few studies have been done on armed forces personnel in relation to negative or positive outcome due to combat (Khan, 2000; Rawat, 2008). Most studies have pertained to selection and recruitment processes. Training, task and work analysis, performance, and job satisfaction have been explored to an extent. Most of the research work is unpublished (Mitra, 1972; Narian, 1979; Parmar, 1999; Sinha, 1972; Rawat, 2008).

Deployment of armed forces is increasing and duties of military personnel are becoming multifarious. This leads to increase in levels of stress and hence the underpinnings in the chapter are crucial not just to the armed forces but police, Para Military Forces (PMF), and policymakers in government. Incidents of stress overload resulting in increased cases of suicide, homicide, fragging, and other maladaptive behaviour among soldiers have been reported in many studies (Mehrotra, 2006; Misra, 2006; Singh, 2006c). Under the given circumstances, this chapter makes an endeavour to undertake a scientific investigation to understand stress among military personnel.

Concept of stress

Most researchers agree that an acceptable definition of stress is likely to be satisfactory only to its author (Abbott, 2001; Cox, 1980; Hinkle, 1987; Kahn & Byosiere, 1992). Researchers have expressed that stress is a part of human life from which no human being can escape (Cooper & Dewe, 2004; Jones & Bright, 2001; Steptoe, 2000; Wong, 2006). Experience of stress varies among individuals and is inevitable at some time or the other in one's life (Lazarus & Cohen, 1977; Taylor, 2006).

Cox (1987) defined stress as a perceived phenomenon arising from a comparison between demands on an individual and one's ability to cope. An imbalance in this mechanism gives rise to experience of stress and to stress response. Stress may be defined as a real or interpreted threat to physiological or psychological integrity of an individual that results in physiological or behavioural responses (McEwen, 2000).

Selye (1976) emphasised nonspecificity of response to stress and considered a wide variety of environmental stressors, all producing a common specific pattern of bodily reactions. After Selye's pioneering work, several researchers have studied stress since the past few decades (Aldwin, 1999; Costa & McCrae, 1993; Hockey, 1997; Lazarus & Folkman, 1991; Monat & Lazarus, 1991; Pestonjee, 1987). The perspectives of these studies can be classified in broad terms as physiological (Cannon, 1929, 1939; Cassidy, 1999; Cohen & Herbert, 1996; Evans, Clow, & Hucklebridge, 1997; Martin, 1984; Selye, 1976, 1983), psychological (Lazarus, 1991; Wolff, 1953), and social (House, Landis, & Umberson, 1988; Levine & Scotch, 1970; Major, Zubek, Cooper, Cozzarelli, & Richards, 1997; McLean, 1974; Pearlin, 1985; Smelser, 1963).

Although the concept of stress has been a source of immense interest since the past six decades (Doublet, 2000), it has steadily evolved over a period of time (Cassidy, 1999). Six types of models or theories of stress have been studied (Brooks et al., 2001; MacDonough, 1991): stimulus-oriented, response-oriented, interactional, transactional, psychosocial, and catastrophic. Stimulus-oriented theories regard stress as a potential residing within stimulus properties of an organism's environment (Cox, 1987; Godwin, 1986; Hobfoll, 1989; Holmes & Masuda, 1974). According to response-oriented theory, it is an individual's response to environmental events that defines presence of stress. Stress is defined entirely in terms of responses resulting from stress, such as physical mobilisation (Kagan & Levi, 1975; Levi, 1984, 2002; Selye, 1980), cognitive disruption (Horowitz, 1990; Horowitz & Solomon, 1975), or behavioural disorganisation (Greenberg, 1996). The interactional model emphasises reciprocal interactions between an individual's cognitive, perceptual, and emotional functions and characteristics of external environment (Derogates, 1982; French, Caplan, & van Harrison, 1982; Godwin, 1986; House, 1974; Lazarus & Launier, 1978; McGrath, 1970, 1976). Transactional model of stress emphasises cognitive processes of appraisal and is based on five major variables: stress, appraisal, coping, person and environment antecedents of stress, and coping and short-term and long-term adaptational outcomes (Dewe, Leiter, & Cox, 2000;

Jex & Beehr, 1991; Larsen, 2000; Lazarus, 1999; Lazarus, Delongis, Folkman, & Gruen, 1985; Lazarus & Folkman, 1984). According to Levi (1984, 1990) psychosocial stimuli combined with adaptation patterns are basic determinants of psychological and physiological stress reactions. This stress can lead to disease, depending on interacting variables such as habits, adaptive behaviour, learning, coping, genetic, and acquired interaction techniques. Catastrophic model of stress lay emphasis on individual functioning and psychological effects of disasters and traumatic stress (Figley, 1985; Frederick, 1985; Hobfoll, Briggs, & Wells, 1994; Laube & Murphy, 1985; Raphael, 1986; Solomon, Laror, & McFarlane, 1996).

According to Steptoe (1998), effects of stress manifest in four distinct domains: physiological effects, behavioural effects, subjective experience, and cognitive function. Physiological effects of stress include alterations in neuroendocrine autonomic nervous system and immune function. Behavioural manifestations of stress include aggressive responses, freezing, and displacement activities in health-related behaviour and deficits in performance of complex tasks. Subjective experiences during stress include distress, feelings of dissatisfaction and anger, together with anxiety and depressive responses. Cognitive manifestations of stress include alterations in information processing and attentional and memory functions, which may influence performance and decision-making capacity.

In conclusion, an individual's functioning in an environment is determined by one's psychological needs and demands as well as physical, social, and cultural environment. When environmental demands exceed resources and capacities of person, individual experiences a state of imbalance. If this is not satisfactorily resolved, it results in stress.

Understanding military stressors

'The stress of war tries humanity as no other test that has been encountered in civilised life. Like a crucial experiment, it exposes underlying physiological and psychological mechanisms of human beings' (Grinker & Spiegel, cited in Cronin, 1998, p. 113). War is becoming more stressful, and of all stressors in a military environment the threat of biological and chemical weapons is perceived as most stressful (Coker, 2001).

Since the First World War, research on stress among combat veterans in battle has been done mostly by military psychiatrists. They have focused mainly on effective treatment of psychological casualties and their returning back to duty (Jones, 1995). Individual differences in response to extreme combat stress are regarded as a result of pre-existing neuroses or psychopathology (Grinker & Spiegel, 1945; Noy, 1987). In understanding what causes extreme stress reactions to combat, military research studies have put greatest importance on situational factors such as combat intensity and duration. At the extreme high end of stress spectrum, as in very intense combat, individual differences in response to stress are minimal. It has been demonstrated that under stress of extreme combat conditions, everyone has a breaking point, though not precisely at the same moment. From this perspective, individual combat experiences result in mental breakdown in combat (Belenky, Noy, & Solomon, 1987; Goyne, 2001; Marlowe, 1979). Few research studies have emphasised social situational factors (Labuc, 1991; Manning, 1991; Manning & Ingraham, 1987; Rawat, 2008; Taylor, 1991).

Literature on military psychology suggests that psychologists have attempted to identify major stress factors besides war situations among military personnel (Bartone, 1998; Cotton, 2001; Cronin, 1998; Gal & Mangelsdorff, 1991; Kearney, Creamer, Marshall, & Goyne, 2001; Rawat, 2011a). Besides psychopathological tendencies such as neuroticism and repression (Grossman & Siddle, 2000; Noy, 1987), even domains of normal personality of soldiers have been explored (Gal, 1983).

Most research studies have grouped stressors in military operations as stressors just prior to deployment (time pressure, not having enough time to prepare family for deployment), stressors in early deployment period (isolation, fatigue, lack of sleep, uncertainty about mission), stressors in mid-deployment period (feeling confined, lack of information, worry about family), and psychological stress in military operations (isolation, ambiguity, powerlessness, boredom, and danger; Bartone, 1996; Bartone & Adler, 1994; Doutheau et al., 1994; Gifford, Jackson, & DeShazo, 1993; Kearney et al., 2001; Miller & Moskos, 1995; Rawat, 2008; Raphel, 1995; Segal & Segal, 1983; Siebold, 1996; Stokes & Jones, 1995). Stress has been defined as physical and psychological demands and constraints that impinge on an individual as a result of operating in military environment (Staal, 2004). In the present chapter, an attempt is made to understand dimensions of stress in routine military life to include cognitive, occupational, physical, emotional, social, and personal stress. These have been operationally defined as follows:

Cognitive stress: Cognitive stress is defined as information processing load placed on the human operator while performing a particular task in a military environment. It is assumed that cognitive stress increases with task difficulty (Lively, Pisoni, van Summers, & Bernacki, 1993).

Occupational stress: Stress due to demands and constraints of operating in military environment (Staal, 2004).

Physical stress: Stress accruing due to physical pressure acting on an individual as a result of performing military duties.

Emotional stress: Emotional stress is psychological and physiological arousal due to emotions triggered before or during a task while operating in military environment (Lively et al., 1993).

Social stress: Stress in an individual due to inability to meet social demands and expectations of family, friends, and significant others due to exigencies of military service. Social stress results from interruption of the feedback loop that maintains identity processes (Burke, 1991).

Personal stress: Stress in relation to subjective, internal responses in appraisal of military environment.

Cognitive stress

In military environment, ability to perform physical and mental tasks quickly and accurately is essential. Besides, capacity to sustain and survive over an extended period of time under adverse conditions is also important. Performance in the military context includes both individual and group tasks and functions.

Most researchers have reported battle fatigue as a broad group of physical, cognitive, and emotional signs that result from heavy cognitive and emotional task of facing danger under difficult conditions in battle. Stress depends on soldier's appraisal of stressor and its content; major stressors include fear of death, disability or failure, emotions like grief and guilt, uncertainty, boredom, worries about home, and many physical and cognitive demands of combat duties (Bartone, 1998; Cronin, 1998; Gal & Mangelsdorff, 1991; Krueger, 1998; Morgan, 1993; Rawat, 2013; Salas, Jains, Cannon-Bowers, Payne, & Smith-Jentsch, 1998; US Army Field Manual, 2003).

Research studies have reported stressors due to downsizing and structural changes in armed forces despite workload continuing to increase. Soldiers have to grapple with stressors of role conflict, role ambiguity, and role overload and rely on cutting-edge technology which can itself be stressful (Kozlowski, Chao, Smith, Hedlund, & Walz, 1991; Payne, 1997; Plumridge & Brown, 2001; Rawat, 2014; Rizzo, House, & Lirtzman, 1970; Stewart-Watt, 1996).

Several studies have noted role ambiguity as a key stressor for combat-trained soldiers engaged in peacekeeping operations (Britt, 1998; Britt & Adler, 1998; Gifford et al., 1993; Litz, 1996; Miller & Moskos, 1995; Segal & Segal, 1983). Ambiguity of an unclear command structure, enforced passivity, or powerlessness to act to make things better in multinational and UN operations is stressful for most soldiers (Doutheau et al., 1994; Farley, 1995; Litz, 1996; Raphel, 1995; Weisaeth & Sund, 1982).

Results of studies on cognitive task of military personnel showed that sustained cognitive tasks can lead to general feelings of fatigue or weariness, decreased output over time, and mistakes. It has been demonstrated that sleep deprivation combined with sustained workload is more due to psychological or cognitive rather than physical tasks (Englund & Krueger, 1985; Haslam & Abhraham, 1987; Haslam, 1982; Krueger, 1991; Martin, Bender, & Chen, 1986)

It has been suggested that vigilance tasks demand considerable effort, produce significant cognitive stress, and even elicit physiological stress responses. Stress of sustained vigilance comes from maintaining a high level of alertness during a monotonous situation where there is no control over events that may occur (Davies & Parasuraman, 1982; Hancock & Warm, 1989; Thackray, 1981; Warm, 1984).

Various studies have indicated stressors due to boredom, lack of challenge, and meaningless work that act as deterrents for reenlisting (Blyth, 1985; Lundin & Otto, 1989; Motowidlo, Lawton, & Dunnette, 1980; Segal & Harris, 1993; Weisaeth, Mehlum, & Mortensen, 1996).

Research evidence has found that spreading of disinformation (e.g. realistic threat of biological and chemical weapon) to demoralise enemy troops through a willing media is a major cognitive stressor among troops from both warring sides (Bloom, 1991; Freund, 1991; Rana, 2005; Unwin et al., 1999).

In the Indian context, Khan (2006b) reported an intellectual reluctance to study military personnel. Research studies have reported that armed forces personnel get alienated, frustrated, and stressed because of public apathy, politician's distrust, and intelligentsia's lack of interest, academician's negligence, and downgrading image of armed forces by its own society (Mukherjee, 2002; Parmar, 1999; Rawat, 2008; Singh, 1985). Other research studies have reported cognitive stressors of information overload as well as under load, unpredictability of events, and difficult judgments as major stressors (Kumar & Mishra, 2006; Misra, 2006; Nazareth, 1991).

Daniel and Bhargava (2005) studied harnessing tacit knowledge in military environment and reported that lack of transfer of tacit knowledge during turnover and rotation of military personnel from posts is a source of stress when such knowledge is not shared by other battalions and paramilitary forces.

Occupational stress and physical stress

Occupational stress is the stress due to demands and constraints of operating in military environment (Staal, 2004).

Previous literature on effects of occupational stressors on soldiers' well-being demonstrated that soldiers face a climate of increasing work demands coupled with declining resources. Major stressors include work characteristics (e.g. work quantity, diversity and complexity, time availability, and deadlines), physical work environment (e.g. noise, working hours), and nature of work and human environment (e.g. leadership styles, usefulness of work; Brooks et al., 2001; Chapman, 2000; Cotton, 2001; Tucker, Sinclair, & Thomas, 2005).

Numerous studies have been conducted on stressors due to effects of hot and cold environment on military personnel. Research has demonstrated that extreme temperatures affect military personnel with respect to tasks such as vigilance, mechanical, and manipulative capabilities, cognitive tasks, as well as mood and behaviour. It has been found that crews of armoured vehicles reported thermal stress, behavioural impairment, and mood changes at extreme temperatures. This gets further intensified when personnel are required to wear protective clothing (Breckenridge & Levell, 1970; Fine & Kobrick, 1987; Kobrick & Johnson, 1991; Kobrick, Johnson, & McMenemy, 1988; Rauch et al., 1986; Tharion et al., 1986; Toner, White, & Goldman, 1981).

Research studies have reported stressful effects of high altitude on military personnel and found that altitudes greater than 3000 metres adversely affect physiological and psychological well-being, mental processes, senses, sleep, and physical work capacity (Banderet & Burse, 1991; Hackett, Rennie, Grover, & Reeves, 1986; Houston, 1987; Meehan & Zavala, 1982; Mountain, 1987; Schoene, 1987). However, perceived stress depends on prior exposure to similar environment, training, protective equipment, and clothing, and rehearsing emergency procedures in high-altitude environment (Bachrach, 1982).

It has been demonstrated that military personnel often operate in stressful, intense, and noisy environment. This includes long-duration exposure to continuous noise, armoured vehicles, as well as repetitive impulsive noise exposure from weapons and artillery fire (Ahuja & Rawat, 2015; Broadbent, 1979; Hockey, 1986; Moore & von Gierke, 1991).

Researchers have reported stressors of military personnel operating in environment of toxic fumes and indicated that military training and combat frequently expose weapon system crewmen to mixtures of potentially toxic fumes (Ase, Eisenberg, Gordon, Taylor, & Snelson, 1985; Benignus, 1991; Dalton, 1988; Snelson, Ase, Bock, & Butler, 1983).

Several research studies have stated stressful effects of sustained acceleration and vibration of military equipment on vision, memory, and central processing functions and manual control (Campise, Geller, & Campise, 2006; Von Gierke, McCloskey, & Albery, 1991).

Research literature is replete with studies on motion sickness among military personnel at sea (Keinan, Friedland, Witzhaky, & Moran, 1981; Pethybrigade, 1982; Rolnick, 1985; Rosenbaum & Rolnick, 1983), and in air (Fox & Arnon, 1988; Hixon, Guedry, Lentz, & Holtzman, 1983). An interesting study by Lerman (1987) in Israel is perhaps one of the very few reported research works on motion sickness in tanks. Besides, studies on stressful motion sickness during simulator training have also been reported among military personnel (Crowley, 1987; Gower, Lilienthal, Kennedy, Fowlkes, & Baltzley, 1987; Gower & Fowlkes, 1989a, 1989b; Gower, Fowlkes, & Baltzley, 1989; Kennedy & Frank, 1984). All these research studies have demonstrated that as an uncontrolled, stressful, and aversive event, motion sickness can give rise to a helplessness reaction which is manifested through cognitive, emotional, and motivational deficits.

Majority of studies on military personnel who engage in sustained and continuous military operations (SUSOPS) indicate that sophisticated night vision technology and other innovations bring about tactical doctrine of continuous operations (CONOPS). The research studies have found that such operations for long periods without rest produce stress, sleep loss and fatigue, thereby impairing performance, causing psychological battle stress casualties and reducing mission effectiveness (Angus & Heslgrave, 1985; Belenky, 1987; Heslgrave & Angus, 1985; Hughes, 2006; Krueger, 1991; Rawat, 2008; Tharion, Rauch, Strowman, & Shukitt, 1987; Westcott, 2005).

Various studies have been conducted in Indian context to find major organisational stressors. It has been demonstrated that stressors include prolonged deployment in operation. This leads to inadequate opportunity to rest and recoup, intense and uncertain combat conditions with threat of death or injury to self and own troops (Mehrotra, 2006; Misra, 2006; Rajan, 2004; Rawat, 2014).

As suggested by research studies, main stressors in operational area include fear of death and injury, ambiguity and uncertainty of operation and its outcome, and pressure of human rights violation. Stressors in peace location include interference by higher military formations, over commitment and workload (Kala, 2003; Rawat, 2008; Singh, 1998; Singh, 2006a)

Emotional stress

Research studies on stress in dangerous military environment have found that a soldier put in risk prone environment cannot simply be assumed to be stressed since the situation may not induce stress in the soldier if individual does not perceive situation as dangerous (Eid, Johnson, & Saus, 2005; Idzikowski & Baddeley, cited in Hockey, 1986; Thompson,

Vasterling, Benotsch, & Brailey, 2004). This is in consonance with Lazarus's (1991) view of person-environment fit.

Several researchers have discussed positive aspects of female soldiers in the armed forces (Bakshi, 2005; Coker, 2001; Elderton, 2006; George, 2007; Mitra-Sinha, 1993; Randhawa, 2004, 2005; Rawat, 2013; Sharma, 2005). However, other research studies have reported 'feminisation of military' as stressors for few male military personnel who view entry of females in armed forces as a threat to traditional military culture and enfeeblement of combat effectiveness and national defense which creates frustration, anger and stress amongst male military personnel (Dansby, 1998; Mitchell, 1993; Thomas & Barry, 1997; Thomas & Vistica, 1997).

Substantial number of research has studied effects of combat on military personnel from different theater of war belonging to different countries. It has been demonstrated that degree of stress, including vulnerability to PTSD is culture bound (Dean, 1997; Green, Grace, Lindy, & Leonard, 1989; Jones, Vermaas, McCartney, & Beech et al., 2003; Rawat & Wadkar, 2012; Solomon, Mikulincer, & Benbenishty, 1989).

One stream of study confirms that exercising military restraint in application of destruction potential on enemy is a major stressor. The research studies reported a trend of centralisation of command in military operations and found that senior officers were preventing junior officers from exercising initiative, which can be very stressful (Bartone, 1998; Dansby, 1998; Kroesen, 2001; Kumar & Mishra, 2006; Mehrotra, 2006; Misra, 2006; Nazareth, 1991).

Few research studies have found institutional discrimination issues in assignment, promotion, selection and retention and reported lack of equal opportunities to be perceived as emotional stressors amongst military personnel from minority groups (Chermol, 1985; Dansby, 1998; Moskos, 1973; Smither & Houston, 1991; St. Pierre, 1991; Thomas, 1988)

Rumour and propaganda (e.g. water contamination) as well as information warfare (also termed psychological warfare) in military environment has been reported to be a major source of emotional stress amongst military personnel (Bloom, 1991; Dyer, 1996; Freund, 1991; Marshall, cited in Idzikowski & Baddeley, 1983).

Wakin (1985) reported stressors due to false reporting, pressure to increase enemy body count and cover-up of battlefield atrocities as major emotional stressors for military personnel.

Several studies have been conducted in India to explore specific emotional stressors amongst military personnel. It has been demonstrated that anxiety producing threats due to injury, failure, loss, personal or mission failure, bereavement, boredom due to inactivity, conflicting motives like worries about home and divided loyalties, spiritual confrontation causing loss of faith are major emotional stressors (Goel, 2005; Krishnan, 2004; Misra, 2006; Rajan, 2004; Rawat, 2009, 2011, 2011a).

It has been reported that inability to control circumstances is a major cause of emotional stress in soldiers. Research studies indicate that Indian soldiers are very religious by nature and killing or injuring enemy soldiers is considered against ethos of non-violent religion, society and nation. This creates a moral conflict amongst soldiers and becomes a source of stress due to occupational and professional demands (Nazareth, 1991; Srivastava, 2006).

A substantial number of studies focused on breakaway from 'Chetwodean values' by few military officers and lowering of standards of intake in officer rank. These are major stressors amongst military personnel at all levels (Chibber, 1986; Grant, 2005; Khan, 2006b; Parmar, 1999; Singh, 1985). Other research studies have reported a transition in armed forces from being an institutional force to being an occupational force as a major stressor for military personnel amongst other countries as well, especially in officer rank (Cotton, 1981; Jans, 2001; Levitan & Alderman, 1977; Moskos, 1977; Moskos & Wood, 1988; Segal, Blair, Lengermann, & Thompson, 1983; Rawat, 2011b, 2014 Segal & Segal, 1983).

Social stress

An important focus of investigation has shown that combat stress reaction amongst military personnel is directly related to unit leadership and cohesion (Bartone & Kirkland, 1991; Noy, 1991). It has been demonstrated that breaking enemies will to fight till enemy soldiers cannot endure stress any longer results in their combat stress reaction. Research indicates that when morale has been shattered and battle seems lost, when leadership is not perceived any longer to lead to victory and survival, then number of combat stress reactions are expected to be very high (Manning, 1991; Manning & Ingraham, 1987). While most soldiers go through combat without ever succumbing to stress, few are evacuated from battlefield due to combat stress reaction, while still others go through battle seemingly unaffected, only to develop post-traumatic stress disorder (PTSD) reactions later on (Hughes, Cameron, Eldridge, & Devon, et al., 2005; Noy, 1991; Reimer, 1998; US Army Field Manual, 2003).

However, Turner, Kiernan, McKechanie, and Finch (2005) who studied military casualties from war in Iraq reported that most military personnel evacuated from war zones were suffering from combat stress reactions, or were otherwise traumatised by horrors of war.

Tillet (1996) studied stress amongst Australian Defence Forces personnel from family perspective as pre departure (e.g. lack of time/ pressure to prepare prior to departure), during mission (e.g. lack of communication with family) and post-return (e.g. residue of conflicts unresolved before departure). The researcher also reported stressors of isolation (e.g. lack of usual support systems), confinement (e.g. lack of privacy or own space) and group dynamics (e.g. personal differences within group).

Researchers have reported stressors of geographical mobility, separation from family, frequent transfers between jobs, overwork, sleep deprivation, irregular working hours and family disruption as few of the major psychosocial stressors in military environment (Gilbert, 1996; MacDonough, 1991; Goyne, 1999).

Various studies conducted in India demonstrate that military life places additional stressors on its personnel. These include: (a) sudden and prolonged isolation from families and established support systems (b) restriction of choice and freedom (c) imposed discipline (d) numerous interstate moves due to postings and frequent transfers (e) coping with situational stress e.g. dealing with terrorists and (f) performance anxiety related to high expectations (Husain, 2006; Khan, 2000; Parmar, 1999; Singh, 1985, 1998).

Most research studies on military personnel in India have reported major stressors due to break-up of joint family system, lack of value orientation, conditional loyalty, irresponsible and prejudiced media, intense media glare, criticism and sensationalism of indiscipline cases by media, perceived high handedness by civil authorities, poor image of army, lack of avenues for promotion and lack of infrastructure like accommodation, medical and education facilities for military families (Ghosh, 2003; Rajan, 2004; Singh, 2006b).

Personal stress

Majority of studies that consider combat stress amongst military personnel report that combat stress, fatigue, and psychological disabilities (PDs) are common battlefield conditions, but are largely preventable (Reimer, 1998; Takla, Koffman, & Bailey, 1994; US Army Field Manual, 2003).

Mission stress during peacekeeping operations has been extensively studied. It has been reported that while most peacekeepers emerge with positive experience, enhanced capabilities and greater self-confidence, few soldiers have difficulty in returning to their pre-mission lives due to stress experienced by them. These research studies found that challenges of stressful experience can be met by briefing and debriefing carried out before, during, and after deployment (Deahl & Martin, 2000; Downie, 2002; Solomon, Neria, & Witztum, 2000; Zeev, Iancu, & Bodner, 2001).

According to Kodama, Nomura, and Ogasawara (2000), military personnel who were not deployed had significantly higher measures of stress than deployed personnel. The selection process and training for deployment is distressful for all personnel, whether deployed or not.

Research studies of Gulf War report two kinds of stressors during war, combat stress and operational stress. Combat stress includes death of a colleague and sleep deprivation during operations, bombing, mortar, rocket and missile attacks, mines and threat of improvised explosive devices. Operational or deployment stress includes working in harsh conditions including extreme temperature, loss of privacy, lack of family support in identification with cause (Caldwell & Redeker, 2005; Pivar & Field, 2004; Platoni, cited in Munsey, 2006).

An interesting study by Kipling (2005) reported combat stressors amongst US military personnel returning from war in Iraq. Major stressors included lack of sleep, long deployment and sustained operations, inaccuracy of media, adjustment problems at home and fear of being stigmatised for being unable to deal with their problems on their own. It is found that soldiers returning from combat are troubled in dealing with loud noise. The researcher reported that during deployment, a soldier's spouse takes on additional responsibilities at home and is not eager to relinquish it when the deployed soldier returns home and this shift in family dynamics is found to be stressful.

Tillet (1996) studied personal stressors amongst military personnel and found that they include competing demands (e.g. setting priorities, allocating time, inability to have personal time or space) and expectations (e.g. of self and colleagues).

US Army Field Manual (2003) reports seven major categories of stressors for military personnel. These include: (a) stressors of offensive and defensive military operations (e.g. enemy fire including shelling and landmines, perceived threat of becoming prisoner of war, wounded or killed in action), (b) stress during operations other than war (e.g. rules of engagement may prohibit firing until fired upon, lack of confidence in fighting on enemy soil), (c) stress in insurgency operations (e.g. austere and primitive living conditions, enforced inactivity with high tension), (d) stress in counterinsurgency operations (e.g. unfamiliar terrain, difficulty in identifying enemy), (e) stress due to terrorist attacks (e.g. sudden violation of familiar setting, loss of control), (f) stress in peacetime contingency (e.g. small unit activity has great political and media interest, lack of freedom of movement), and (g) stress in peacekeeping operations (e.g. isolation, boredom, cultural alienation, repetitious or routine duties).

In the Indian scenario, it has been observed that personal stressors include separation from family, mismatch between own aspirations and expectations and that of military, and individualistic needs and growth relegated to collective needs of military organisation (Khan, 2000; Mehrotra, 2006; Rawat & Wadkar, 2009; Singh, 2006b).

To sum up, research studies have shown that when soldiers fail to merge combat experience into rest of their life experience, difficulties in facing thoughts and feelings regarding stressful event occur (Horowitz, 1976; Pennebaker & Beall, 1986; Rawat, 2011; Rawat & Wadkar, 2009; Ursano & Fullerton, 1990).

Review of above stress related literature gives an insight in understanding behaviour amongst military personnel and forces that influence such behaviour. Deciphering why military personnel respond differently under similar circumstances of combat is a critical part of this endeavour.

Conclusion

By its very nature, the military environment places heavy demands on the soldier and may lead to stress. Symptoms of stress include unwanted cognitive, emotional, behavioural and physical outcomes. Stress may adversely affect performance, commitment, retention, cohesion, morale, and physical health of military personnel. Military leaders can contribute to minimising unwanted stress among soldiers by fostering development of horizontal and vertical cohesion, by providing realistic training that prepares military personnel for the type of stressors they are likely to encounter in peacetime military service, by making sure that the sacrifices expected of subordinates are necessary and meaningful, and by increasing awareness of organisational goals and giving soldiers as much autonomy as practicable in achieving them.

References

Abbott, A. (2001). *Chaos of disciplines*. Chicago: The University of Chicago Press.

Ahuja. G., & Rawat. S. (2015, May). *Noise-induced hearing loss*. Paper Presented at the International Applied Military Psychology Symposium (IAMPS) in Lisbon, Portugal.

Aldwin, C.M. (1999). *Stress, coping, and development: An integrated perspective*. New York: Guilford.

Angus, R.G., & Heslegrave, R.J. (1985). Effects of sleep loss on sustained cognitive performance during a command and control simulation. *Behavior Research Methods, Instruments, and Computers*, 17, 55–67.

Ase, P., Eisenberg, W., Gordon, S., Taylor, K., & Snelson, A. (1985). Propellant combustion product analysis on an M16 rifle and a 105 mm caliber gun. *Journal of Environmental Science and Health*, A20, 337–368.

Bachrach, A. (1982). *The human in extreme environments* (Tech. Rep. No. 82–88). Bethesda, MD: US Naval Medical Research Institute (DTIC No. ADA 133204).

Bakshi, D. (2005). Training of women cadets in the army – Some issues and challenges. *USI Journal*.

Banderet, L.E., & Burse, R.L. (1991). Effects of high terrestrial altitude on military performance. In R. Gal & A.D. Mangelsdorff (eds), *Handbook of military psychology* (pp. 233–254). New York: Wiley.

Bartone, P.T. (1996). *Hardiness and resiliency in US peacekeeping soldiers*. Annual Convention of the American Psychological Association, Toronto, Canada.

Bartone, P.T. (1998). Stress in the military setting. In C. Cronin, *Military psychology: An introduction* (pp. 113–146). New York: Simon & Schuster.

Bartone, P.T. (2005). The need for positive meaning in military operations: Reflections on Abu Ghraib. *Military Psychology*, 17, 315–324.

Bartone, P.T. (2006). Resilience under military operational stress: Can leaders influence hardiness? *Military Psychology*, 18, S131–S148.

Bartone, P.T., & Adler, A.B. (1994). *A model for soldier psychological adaptation in peacekeeping operations*. Proceedings of the 36th Annual Conference of the International Military Testing Association (pp. 33–40), Rotterdam, Netherlands.

Bartone, P.T., & Kirkland, F.R. (1991). Optimal leadership in small Army units. In R. Gal & A.D. Mangelsdorff (eds), *Handbook of military psychology* (pp. 393–409). New York: Wiley.

Belenky, G. (1987). Psychiatric casualties: The Israeli experience. *Psychiatric Annals*, 17, 528–531.

Belenky, G.L., Noy, S., & Solomon, Z. (1987). Battle stress, morale, cohesion, combat effectiveness, heroism, and psychiatric casualties: The Israeli experience. In G.L. Belenky (Ed.), *Contemporary studies in combat psychiatry* (pp. 11–20). Westport, CT: Greenwood.

Benignus, V.A. (1991). Effects of atmospheric mix and toxic fumes on military performance. In R. Gal & A.D. Mangelsdorff (eds), *Handbook of military psychology* (pp. 313–333). New York: Wiley.

Blake, D.D., Keane, T.M., Wine, P.R., Mora, C., Taylor, K.L., & Lyons, J.A. (1990). Prevalence of PTSD symptoms in combat veterans seeking medical treatment. *Journal of Traumatic Stress*, 3, 15–27.

Bloom, R.W. (1991). Propaganda and active measures. In R. Gal & A.D. Mangelsdorff (eds), *Handbook of military psychology* (pp. 693–710). New York: Wiley.

Blyth, D.N. (1985). Study of wastage from the Territorial Army (UK Army Reserves). In *Proceedings of the 27th Annual Conference of the Military Testing Association* (pp. 741–746). San Diego, CA: Navy Personnel Research and Development Center.

Breckenridge, J.R., & Levell, C.A. (1970). Heat stress in the cockpit of the AH-1G Huey Cobra helicopter. *Aerospace Medicine*, 41, 621–626.

Britt, T.W. (1998). Psychological ambiguities in peacekeeping. In H.J. Langholtz (ed.), *The psychology of peacekeeping* ((pp. 111-128). Westport, CT: Praeger.

Britt, T.W., & Adler, A.B. (1998). *Stress, work, and health during a humanitarian assistance mission to Kazakhstan*.

Broadbent, D.E. (1979). Human performance in noise. In C.M. Harris (Ed.), *Handbook of noise control* (2nd ed., pp. 17.1 17.20). New York: McGraw Hill

Brooks, S.K., Byrne, D.G., & Hodson, S.E. (2001). Non-combat occupational stress: A review of factors and measurement issues for the Australian Defence Force. In G. Kearney, M. Creamer, R. Marshall, & A. Goyne, *The management of stress in the Australian Defence Forces* (pp. 7–19). Canberra, Australia: Defence Publishing.

Burke, P.J. (1991). Identity processes and social stress. *American Sociological Review*, 56, 836–849.

Caldwell, B.A., & Redeker, N. (2005). Sleep and trauma: An overview. *Issues in Mental Health Nursing*, 26, 721–738.

Campise, R.L., Geller, S.K., & Campise, M.E. (2006). Combat stress. In C.H. Kennedy & E.A. Zillmer, *Military psychology: Clinical and operational applications* (pp. 215–240). New York: Guilford.

Cannon, W.B. (1929). *Bodily changes in pain, hunger, fear, and rage*. New York: D. Appleton & Company.

Cannon, W.B. (1939). *The wisdom of the body*. New York: W.W. Norton.

Cassidy, T. (1999). *Stress, cognition and health*. London: Routledge.

Chapman, S.E. (2000). The measurement of stress in Australian Defence personnel: A discussion. *Australian Defence Force Journal*, 141, 19–27.

Chermol, B.H. (1985). Wounds without scars: Treatment of battle fatigue in the US Armed Forces in the Second World War. *Military Affairs*, 49, 9–12.

Chibber, M.L. (1986). *Soldiers' role in national integration*. New Delhi: Lancer International.

Cohen, S., & Herbert, T.B. (1996). Health psychology: Psychological factors and physical disease from the perspective of human psychoneuroimmunology. *Annual Review of Psychology*, 47, 113–42.

Coker, C. (2001). *Humane warfare*. New York: Routledge.

Cooper, C.L., & Dewe, P. (2004). *Stress: A brief history*. Oxford: Blackwell.

Costa, P.J., & McCrae, R.R. (1993). Psychological stress and coping in old age. In L. Goldberger & S. Breznitz (eds), *Handbook of stress: Theoretical and clinical aspects* (2nd ed., pp. 403–412). New York: Free Press.

Cotton, A. (2001). Non-operational military stress management in the ADF: Where have we been, and where are we going? In G. Kearney, M. Creamer, R. Marshall, & A. Goyne, *The management of stress in the Australian Defence Forces* (pp. 1–5). Canberra, Australia: Defence Publishing.

Cox, T. (1980). *Stress*. Baltimore, MD: University Park Press.

Cox, T. (1987). Stress, coping and problem solving. *Work & Stress*, 1, 5–14.

Cronin, C. (1998). *Military psychology: An introduction*. New York: Simon & Schuster.

Crowley, J.S. (1987). Simulator sickness: A problem for army aviation. *Aviation, Space, and Environmental Medicine*, 58, 355–357.

Dalton, B.A. (1988). Carbon monoxide in US Army tactical vehicles. *Medical Bulletin of the US Army Medical Department*, PB8-88-2, 11–13.

Daniel, A., & Bhargava, H. (2005). Harnessing tacit knowledge in military environment. *Defence Management*, Vol. 4, Issue 1.

Dansby, M. (1998). Cultural diversity and gender issues. In C. Cronin, *Military psychology: An introduction* (pp. 175–199). New York: Simon & Schuster.

Davies, D.R., & Parasuraman, R. (1982). *The psychology of vigilance*. London: Academic Press.

Dean, E.T., Jr. (1997). *Shook over hell: Post-traumatic stress, Vietnam, and the Civil War*. Cambridge, MA: Harvard University Press.

Dekaris, D., Sabioncello, A., Mazuram, R., Rabatic, S., Svoboda-Beusan, I., Racunica, N.L., & Tomasic, J. (1993). Multiple changes of immunologic parameters in prisoners of war: Assessments after release from a camp in Manjaca, Bosnia. *JAMA*, 270, 595–599.

Derogates, L.R. (1982). Self-report measures of stress. In L. Goldberger & S. Breznitz (eds), *Handbook of stress: Theoretical and clinical aspects* (pp. 270–294). New York: Free Press.

Dewe, P., Leiter, M., & Cox, T. (2000). *Coping, health and organizations* [Issues in Occupational Health]. London: Taylor & Francis.

Doublet, S. (2000). *The stress myth*. Freemans Reach, NSW, Australia: IPSILON Publishing.

Doutheau, C., Lebigot, F., Moraud, C., Crocq, L., Fabre, L.M., & Favre, J.D. (1994). Stress factors and psychopathological reactions of UN missions in the French Army. *International Review of the Armed Forces Medical Services*, 1/2/3, 36–38.

Driskell, J.E., & Olmstead, B. (1989). Psychology and the military: Research applications and trends. *American Psychologist*, 44, 43–54.

Dyer, G. (1996). Waiting foe 1989 in East Tinor. *Chicago Trlbune*, p. 31.

Edwards, J.E. (1993). *Combat service support guide*. Mechanicsburg, PA: Stackpole Books.

Eid, J., Johnson, B.H., & Saus, E.R. (2005). Trauma narratives and emotional processing. *Scandinavian Journal of Psychology*, 46, 503–510.

Elderton, C.R. (2006). *The wider employment of women in the Indian Army* (NDC Papers). New Delhi: National Defence College.

Englund, C.E., & Krueger, G.P. (1985). Methodological approaches to the study of sustained work/sustained operations: Introduction to a special section. *Behavior Research Methods, Instruments and Computers*, 17, 3–5.

Evans, P., Clow, A., & Hucklebridge, F. (1997). Stress and the immune system. *The Psychologist*, 10, 303–7.

Faris, J.H. (1976). The impact of basic combat training: The role of the drill sergeant. In N.L. Goldman & D.R. Segal (eds), *The social psychology of military service* (pp. 11–24). Beverly Hills, CA: Sage.

Farley, K.M. (1995). *Stress in military operations* (Working Paper, 95–2). Willowdale, Ontario, Canada: Canadian Forces Personnel Applied Research Unit.

Figley, C.R. (ed.). (1985). *Trauma and its wake. The study and treatment of posttraumatic stress disorder: Psychological stress series*. New York: Brunner/Mazel.

Fine, B.J., & Kobrick, J.L. (1987). Effect of heat and chemical protective clothing on cognitive performance. *Aviation, Space, and Environmental Medicine*, 58, 149–154.

Fontana, A., & Rosenheck, R. (1998). Psychological benefits and liabilities of traumatic exposure in the war zone. *Journal of Traumatic Stress*, 11, 485–505.

Fox, S., & Arnon, I. (1988). Motion sickness and anxiety. *Aviation, Space, and Environmental Medicine*, 59, 728–733.

Frederick, C.J. (1985). Selected foci in the spectrum of post-traumatic stress disorders. In J. Laube & S.A. Murphy (eds), *Perspectives on disaster recovery* (pp. 110–13). Norwalk, CT: Appleton-Century-Crofts.

French, J.R.P., Caplan, R.D., & van Harrison, R.V. (1982). *The mechanisms of job stress and strain*. Chichester, UK: John Wiley.

Freund, C.P. (1991). The war on your mind: Psychological warfare from Genghis Khan to POWs to CNN. *Washington Post*, p. C3.

Gal, R. (1983). Courage under stress. In S. Breznitz (ed.), *Stress in Israel* (pp. 65–91). New York: Van Nostrand Reinhold.

Gal, R. (1987). Combat stress as an opportunity: The case of heroism. In G.L. Belenky (Ed.), *Contemporary studies in combat psychiatry* (pp. 31–45). Westport, CT: Greenwood Press.

Gal, R., & Mangelsdorff, A.D. (1991). *A handbook of military psychology*. New York: John Wiley.

George, D.K. (2007). Mentoring women officers in the Indian Army. *Defence Management*, 6, 1.

Gifford, R.K., Jackson, J.M., & DeShazo, K.B. (1993). *Field research in Somalia during Operations Restore Hope and Continue Hope*. Paper presented at the 35th Annual Conference of the Military Testing Association, Williamsburg, Virginia.

Gilbert, J. (1996). *Failures in reporting and accountability in stress management in Department of Defence*. Canberra, Australia: Department of Defence, Defence Management Diploma Program.

Godwin, J.R. (1986). *A preliminary investigation into stress in Australian Antarctic expeditioners* (Research Report 1/85). Canberra, Australia: Directorate of Psychology, Australian Army: 1st Psychological Research Unit.

Goel, D.S. (2005). The psychopathology of military corruption. *War College Journal, Army War College*, 78–83.

Gower, D.W. Jr., & Fowlkes, J. (1989a). *Simulator sickness in the AH-1S (Cobra) flight simulator* (USAARL Tech. Rep. No. 89–20). Fort Rucker, AL: US Army Aeromedical Research Laboratory.

Gower, D.W. Jr., & Fowlkes, J. (1989b). *Simulator sickness in the UH-60 (Black Hawk) flight simulator* (USAARL Tech. Rep. No. 89–25). Fort Rucker, AL: US Army Aeromedical Research Laboratory.

Gower, D.W. Jr., Fowlkes, J., & Baltzley, D.R. (1989). *Simulator sickness in the CH-47 (Chinook) flight simulator* (USAARL Tech. Rep. No. 89–28). Fort Rucker, AL: US Army Aeromedical Research Laboratory.

Gower, D.W. Jr., Lilienthal, M.G., Kennedy, R.S., Fowlkes, J.E., & Baltzley, D.R. (1987). *Simulator sickness in the AH-64 Apache combat mission simulator* (USAARL Tech. Rep. No. 88–1). Fort Rucker, AL: US Army Aeromedical Research Laboratory.

Goyne, A. (2001). The measurement of organisational stress in the Australian Regular Army. In G. Kearney, M. Creamer, R. Marshall, & A. Goyne, *The management of stress in the Australian Defence Forces* (pp. 21–33). Canberra, Australia: Defence Publishing.

Goyne, A.N. (1999). *Report of the "Your View of AHQ" survey, DSPPR RN 10/99.* Canberra, Australia: Department of Defence.

Grant, N.B. (2005). The soldier's image – A return to traditional values. *War College Journal, Army War College*, 96–97.

Green, B.L., Grace, M.C., Lindy, J.D., & Gleser, G.C. (1990). War stressors and symptom persistence in post-traumatic stress disorder. *Journal of Anxiety Disorders*, 4, 31–39.

Green, B.L., Grace, M.C., Lindy, J.D., & Leonard, A.C. (1989). *Race differences in response to combat stress.* Cincinnati, OH: University of Cincinnati, Traumatic Stress Study Center.

Greenberg, J.S. (1996). *Comprehensive stress management.* London: McGraw-Hill.

Grinker, A.A., & Spiegel, J.P. (1945). *Men under stress.* Philadelphia, PA: Blakiston's Son & Company.

Grossman, D., & Siddle, B.K. (2000). *Psychological effects of combat.* New York: Academic Press.

Gruber, K.A. (2004). *The relationship between psychological resources, stress, and task competition in elite military training.* Baltimore, MD: University of Maryland.

Hackett, P.H., Rennie, D., Grover, R.F., & Reeves, J.T. (1986). Acute mountain sickness and the edemas of high altitude: A common pathogenesis? *Respiratory Physiology*, 46, 383–390.

Hancock, P.A., & Warm, J.S. (1989). A dynamic model of stress and sustained attention. *Human Factors*, 31, 519–537.

Haslam, D.R. (1982). Sleep loss, recovery sleep, and military performance. *Ergonomics*, 25, 163–178.

Haslam, D.R., & Abraham, P. (1987). Sleep loss and military performance. In G.L. Belenky (ed.), *Contemporary studies in combat psychiatry* (pp. 167–184). New York: Greenwood Press.

Heslgrave, R.J., & Angus, R.G. (1985). The effects of task duration and work-session location on performance degradation induced by sleep loss and sustained cognitive work. *Behavior Research Methods, Instruments and Computers*, 17, 592–603.

Hinkle, L.E. (1987). Stress and disease: The concept after 50 years. *Social Science and Medicine*, 25, 561–566.

Hixon, W.C., Guedry, F.E., Lentz, M., & Holtzman, G.L. (1983). *Airsickness during naval flight officer training: Fleet readiness squadron* (NAMRL Tech. Rep. No. 1305). Pensacola, FL: Naval Aerospace Medical Research Laboratory.

Hobfoll, S.E. (1989). Conversation of resources: A new attempt at conceptualizing stress. *American Psychologists*, 44, 513–524.

Hobfoll, S.E., Briggs, S., & Wells, J. (1994). Community stress and resources: Actions and reactions. In S.E. Hobfoll & M.W. deVries (eds), *Extreme stress and communities: Impact and intervention* (pp. 137–158). Dordrecht, The Netherlands: NATO ASI Series.

Hockey, G.R.J. (1986). Changes in operator efficiency as a function of environmental stress, fatigue and circadian rhythms. In K.R. Boff, L. Kaufmann, & J.P. Thomas (eds), *Handbook of perception and human performance* (Vol. 2, pp. 44.1–44.49). New York: Wiley.

Hockey, G.R.J. (1997). Compensatory control in the regulation of human performance under stress and high workload: A cognitive energetical framework. *Biological Psychology*, 45, 73–93.

Holmes, D.T., Tariot, P.N., & Cox, C. (1998). Preliminary evidence of psychological distress among reservists in the Persian Gulf War. *Journal of Nervous and Mental Disease*, 186, 166–173

Holmes, T.H., & Masuda, M. (1974). Life change and illness susceptibility. In B.S. Dohrenwend & B.P. Dohrenwend (eds), *Stressful life events: Their nature and effects* (pp. 45–72). New York: Wiley.

Horowitz, M. (1976). *Stress response syndromes*. New York: Aronson.

Horowitz, M., & Solomon, S.F. (1975). A prediction of delayed stress response syndromes in Vietnam veterans. *Journal of Social Issues*, 31, 67–80.

Horowitz, M.J. (1990). Stress, states, and person schemas. *Psychological Inquiry*, 1, 25–6.

House, J.S. (1974). The effects of occupational stress on physical health. In J. O' Toole (ed.), *Work and the quality of life: Resource papers for work in America* (pp. 145–170). Cambridge, MA: MIT Press.

House, J.S., Landis, K.R., & Umberson, D. (1988). Social relationships and health. *Science*, 241, 540–545.

Houston, B.K. (1987). Stress and coping. In C.R. Snyder & C.E. Ford, *Coping with negative life events: Clinical and social psychological perspectives* (pp. 373–499). New York: Plenum. http://www.military.com

Hughes, J.H., Cameron, F., Eldridge, R., & Devon, M., et al. (2005). Going to war does not have to hurt: Preliminary findings from the British deployment to Iraq. *British Journal of Psychiatry*, 186, 536–537.

Idzikowski, C., & Baddeley, A.D. (1983). Fear and dangerous environments. In G.R.J. Hockey, *Stress and fatigue in human performance* (pp. 123–144). New York: John Wiley.

Ingraham, L.H., & Manning, F.J. (1981). *Cohesion: Who needs it, what is it, and how do we get it to them? Military Review*, 6, 2–12.

Jaiswal, N.K. (1997). *Military operations research: Quantitative decision making.* Stanford, CA: Stanford University Stanford.

Jans, N. (2001). Organisational change and human resource management in the ADF. In G. Kearney, M. Creamer, R. Marshall, & A. Goyne, *The management of stress in the Australian Defence Forces* (pp. 47–57). Canberra, Australia: Defence Publishing.

Jex, S.M., & Beehr, T.A. (1991). Emerging theoretical and methodological issues in the study of work-related stress. *Research in Personnel and Human Resources Management*, 9, 311–65.

Jones, E., Vermaas, R.H., McCartney, H., & Beech, C., et al. (2003). Flashbacks and posttraumatic stress disorder: The genesis of a 20th century diagnosis. *British Journal of Psychiatry*, 182, 158–163.

Jones, F., & Bright, J. (2001). *Stress: Myth, theory, and research*. Harlow, UK: Prentice-Hall.

Jones, F.D. (1995). Psychiatric lessons of war. In J.D. Jones, L.R. Sparacino, V.L. Wilcox, J.M. Rothberg, & J.W. Stokes (eds), *War psychiatry* (*Textbook of military medicine. Part I. Warfare, weaponry and the casualty*, pp. 63–83). Washington, DC: Office of the Surgeon General, US Army.

Kagan, A.R., & Levi, L. (1975). Health and environment-psychological stimuli: A review. In L. Levi (ed.), *Society, stress, and disease* (Vol. 2, pp. 241–260). New York: Oxford University Press.

Kahn, R.L., & Byosiere, P. (1992). Stress in organizations. In M.D. Dunnette & L.M. Hough (eds), *Handbook of industrial and organizational psychology* (2nd ed., Vol. 3, pp. 571–649). Palo Alto, CA: Consulting Psychologists Press, Inc.

Kala, H.B. (2003). Demystifying military leadership. New Delhi: Manas Publications.

Kearney, G., Creamer, M., Marshall, R., & Goyne, A. (2001). *The management of stress in the Australian Defence Force: Human factors, families, and the welfare of military personnel away from the combat zone*. Canberra, Australia: Department of Defence.

Keinan, G., Friedland, N., Witzhaky, J., & Moran, A. (1981). Biographical, physiological, and personality variables as predictors of performance under sickness inducing motion. *Journal of Applied Psychology*, 66, 233–241.

Kennedy, R.S., & Frank, L.H. (1984). *A review of motion sickness with special reference to simulator sickness* (NAVTRAQUIPCEN Tech. Rep. No. 81-Cognitive-0105-16). Orlando, FL: Naval Training Equipment Center.

Khan, J.A. (2000). *Choice of military career*. Jaipur, India: Rawat Publications.

Khan, J.A. (2006b). *Indian armed forces and society* (Vol. 2). New Delhi: Anmol.

Kipling, L. (2005). *Fighting combat stress*. http://www.military.com

Kishon-Barash, R., Midlarsky, E., & Johnson, D.R. (1996). *Altruism in Vietnam PTSD*. Paper presented at the Second World Conference of the International Society for Traumatic Stress Studies, Jerusalem, Israel.

Kobrick, J.L., & Johnson, R.F. (1991). Effects of hot and cold environments on military performance. In R. Gal & A.D. Mangelsdorff (eds), *Handbook of military psychology* (pp. 215–232). New York: Wiley.

Kobrick, J.L., Johnson, R.F., & McMenemy, D.J. (1988). *Nerve agent antiodes and heat exposure: Summary of effects on task performance of soldiers wearing BDU and*

MOPP-IV clothing systems (Tech. Rep. No. T1-89). Natick, MA: US Army Research Institute of Environmental Medicine.

Kodama, Y., Nomura, S., & Ogasawara, T. (2000). Psychological changes of Japan self-defense forces personnel during selection and training for the peacekeeping mission in the Golan Heights. *Military Medicine*, 165, 653–655.

Kozlowski, S., Chao, G., Smith, E., Hedlund, J., & Walz, P. (1991). *Organisational downsizing: Individual and organisational implications and recommendation for action* (Technical Report 929). Alexandria, VA: US Army Research Institute for the Behavioral and Social Sciences.

Krishnan, K. (2004). Preparing armed forces for future. *Pinnacle: The ARTRAC Journal. Army Training Command*, 3, 24–32.

Kroesen, F.J. (2001). Korean war lessons. *USI (United Service Institution of India, New Delhi) Digest*, 3, 142–147.

Krueger, G.P. (1991). Sustained military performance in continuous operations: Combatant fatigue, rest, and sleep needs. In R. Gal & A.D. Mangelsdorff (eds), *Handbook of military psychology* (pp. 255–277). New York: Wiley.

Krueger, G.P. (1998). Military performance under adverse conditions. In C. Cronin, *Military psychology: An introduction* (pp. 89–111). New York: Simon & Schuster.

Kulka, R.A., Schlenger, W.E., Fairbank, J.A., Hough, R.L., Jordan, B.K., Marmar, C.R., & Weiss, D.S. (1990). *Trauma and the Vietnam War generation: Report of findings from the National Vietnam Veterans Readjustment Study*. New York: Brunner/Mazel.

Kumar & Mishra. (2006). A study of role stress of officers serving in field area. *Journal of Selection Centre*, 6, 18–21.

Labuc, S. (1991). Cultural and societal factors in military organizations. In R. Gal & A.D. Mangelsdorff (eds), *Handbook of military psychology* (pp. 471–490). New York: Wiley.

Laube, J., & Murphy, S.A. (eds). (1985). *Perspectives on disaster recovery.* Norwalk, CT: Appleton-Century-Crofts.

Lazarus, R.S., & Folkman, S. (1984). *Coping and adaptation*. In W.D. Gentry (ed.), *Handbook of behavioural medicine* (pp. 282–325). New York: Guilford.

Lazarus, R.S. (1991). *Emotion and adaptation.* New York: Oxford University Press.

Lazarus, R.S. (1999). *Stress and emotion: A new synthesis.* New York: Springer.

Lazarus, R.S., & Cohen, J.B. (1977). Environmental stress. In I. Altman & J.F. Wehlwill (eds), *Human behavior and environment* (Vol. 2). New York: Plenum.

Lazarus, R.S., & Folkman, S. (1991). The concept of coping. In A.M. Monat & R.S. Lazarus (eds), *Stress and coping: An anthology* (3rd ed., pp. 189–206). New York: Columbia University Press.

Lazarus, R.S., & Launier, R. (1978). Stress related transactions between person and environment. In L.A. Perrin & M. Lewis, *Perspectives in international psychology*. New York: Plenum.

Lazarus, R.S., Delongis, A., Folkman, S., & Gruen, R. (1985). Stress and adaptational outcomes: The problem of confounded measures. *American Psychologist*, 40, 770–779.

Lerman, Y. (1987). *Simulator sickness in a military tank driving simulator* (Israel Defence Forces Medical Corps Report). Tel Aviv, Israel: Israel Defence Forces.

Levi, L. (1984). *Stress in industry: Causes, effects, and prevention.* Geneva, Switzerland: International Labour Office.

Levi, L. (1990). *Four decades of Lennat Levi's research – A selection*. Stockholm, Sweden: Karolinska Institute.

Levi, L. (2002). Stress – An overview: International and public health perspective. In R. Ekman & B. Arnetz (eds), *Stress: Molecules, individuals, organization, society.* Stockholm, Sweden: Liber.

Levitan, S.A., & Alderman, K.C. (1977). *Warriors at work.* Beverly Hills, CA: Sage.

Litz, B. (1996). The psychological demands of peacekeeping for military personnel. *NCP Clinical Quarterly, Winter*, 6, 1–8.

Lively, S.E., Pisoni, D.B., van Summers, W., & Bernacki, R.H. (1993). Effects of cognitive workload on speech production: Acoustic analyses and perceptual consequences. *Journal of the Acoustical Society of America,* 93, 2962–2973.

Lundin, T., & Otto, U. (1989). Stress reactions among Swedish health care personnel in UNIFIL 1982–84. *Stress Medicine*, 5, 237–246.

MacDonough, T.S. (1991). Non-combat Stress in soldiers: How it is manifested, how to measure it, and how to cope with it. In R. Gal & A.D. Mangelsdorff, *Handbook of military psychology* (pp. 531–558). New York: John Wiley.

Major, B., Zubek, J.M., Cooper, M.L., Cozzarelli, C., & Richards, C. (1997). Mixed messages: Implications of social conflict and social support within close relationships for adjustment to a stressful life event. *Journal of Personality and Social Psychology*, 72, 1349–1363.

Manning, F.J., & Ingraham, L.H. (1987). *An investigation into the value of unit cohesion in peacetime.* In G. Belenky G (ed.), *Contemporary studies in combat psychiatry* (pp. 47–67). Westport, CT: Greenwood.

Manning, F.J. (1991). Morale, cohesion and Esprit de Corps. In R. Gal & A.D. Mangelsdorff (eds), *Handbook of military psychology* (pp. 453–470). New York: Wiley.

Marlowe, D.H. (1979). *Cohesion, anticipated breakdown, and endurance in battle: Considerations for severe and high intensity combat.* Unpublished monograph, Department of Military Psychiatry, Walter Reed Army Institute of Research. Washington, DC.

Marshall, S.L.A. (1947). *Men against fire.* New York. Morrow.

Martin, B.J., Bender, P.R., & Chen, H. (1986). Stress hormonal response to exercise after sleep loss. *European Journal of Applied Physiology*, 55, 210–214.

Martin, R.A. (1984). A critical review of the concept of stress in psychosomatic medicine. *Perspectives in Biology and Medicine*, 27, 443–64.

Maslach, C,, & Jackson, S.E. (1981). The measurement of experienced burnout. *Occupational Behaviour*, 2, 99–113.

Maslach, C., Jackson, S.E., & Leiter, M.P. (1996). *Maslach burnout inventory manual* (3rd ed.). Palo Alto, CA: Consulting Psychologists Press.

Maslach, C.J., & Leiter, M.P. (2000). *Burnout*, cited in Encyclopedia of stress (Vol. I) by Fink.

McEwen, B.S. (2000). Stress, definitions and concepts of. *Encyclopedia of Stress* (Vol. 3).

McGrath, J.E. (1970). A conceptual formulation for research on stress. In J.E. McGrath (ed.), Social *and psychological factors in stress* (pp. 10–21). New York: Holt Rinehart.

McGrath, J.E. (1976). Stress and behavior in organizations. In M.D. Dunnette (Ed.), *Handbook of industrial and organizational psychology* (pp. 1351–1395). Chicago: Rand McNally.

McGuire, F.L. (1990). *Psychology aweigh! A history of clinical psychology in the United States Navy, 1900–1988.* Washington, DC: American Psychological Association.

McLean, A. (1974). Occupational stress – A misnomer. In A. McLean (ed.), *Occupational stress* (pp. 98–105). Springfield, IL: C.C. Thomas.

Meehan, R.T., & Zavala, D.C. (1982). The pathophysiology of acute high-altitude illness. *American Journal of Medicine*, 73, 395–403.

Mehrotra. (2006). Stress and its management in armed forces. *Journal of Selection Centre*, 6, 63–66.

Miller, L.L., & Moskos, C. (1995). Humanitarians or warriors? Race, gender, and combat status in Operation Restore Hope. *Armed Forces & Society*, 21, 615–637.

Misra, N. (2006). Combat stress and its management in insurgency areas. *Journal of Selection Centre*, 6, 31–34.

Mitchell, B. (1993). *Women in the military: Flirting with disaster.* London: Brasseys.

Mitra, S.K. (1972). *A survey of research in psychology: Psychological research in India.* Mumbai: Indian Council of Social Science Research.

Mitra-Sinha, A. (1993). *Women in a changing society.* New Delhi: Ashish Publishing House.

Monat, A.M., & Lazarus, R.S. (eds). (1991). *Stress and coping: An anthology* (3rd ed.). New York: Columbia University Press.

Moore, B. (2006). *Monitor on Psychology.* Volume 37, No. 4.

Moore, T.J., & von Gierke, H.E. (1991). Military performance in acoustic noise environments. In R. Gal & A.D. Mangelsdorff (eds), *Handbook of military psychology* (pp. 295–311). New York: Wiley.

Morgan, D.J. (1993). *USAF mental health lessons learned during Operation Desert Shield/ Storm.* Maxwell AFB, AL: Air War College Associate Studies.

Moskos, C.C. (1977). From institution to occupation. *Armed Forces and Society*, 4, 41–50.

Moskos, C.C., Jr. (1973). The American dilemma in uniform: Race in the armed forces. *Annals of the American Academy of Political and Social Sciences, The Military and American Society,* 406, 94–106.

Moskos, C.C., & Wood, F.R. (eds). (1988). *The military: More than just a job?* Washington, DC: Pergamon-Brasseys.

Motowidlo, S.J., Lawton, G.W., & Dunnette, M.D. (1980). Factors in reenlistment decisions of first term enlisted personnel. In *Proceedings of the 22nd Annual Conference of the Military Testing Association* (pp. 679–690). Toronto: Canadian Forces Personnel Applied Research Unit.

Mountain, R.D. (1987). High-altitude medical problems. *Clinical Orthopedics and Related Research,* 216, 50–54.

Mukherjee, T. (2002). *Inside the Indian Army.* New Delhi: Manas Publications.

Munsey, C. (2006). Psychologists help troops handle the stresses of combat in Iraq and the anxieties of coming home. *Monitor of Psychology,* Vol. 37, No. 4.

Narian, R. (1979). *Military psychology.* Agra, India: National Psychological Corporation.

Nazareth, J. (1991). *The analysis and solution of military problems.* New Delhi: Central Electric Press.

Newman, A.S. (1992). Follow Me II: *More on the human element in leadership.* New York: Presidio Press.

Noy, S. (1987). Stress and personality as factors in the causation and prognosis of combat reaction. In G.L. Belenky (ed.), *Contemporary studies in combat psychiatry* (pp. 21–29). Westport, CT: Greenwood Press.

Noy, S. (1991). Combat stress reactions. In R. Gal & A.D. Mangelsdorff, *Handbook of military psychology* (pp. 507–530). New York: John Wiley.

Parmar, L. (1999). *Military sociology. Global perspectives.* Jaipur, India: Rawat Publications.

Payne, D. (1997). Can CSP enhance capability? *RAAF News,* 39, 14.

Pearlin, L.I. (1985). Social structure and processes of social support. In S. Cohen & S.L. Syme (eds), *Social support and health* (pp. 43–60). New York: Academic Press.

Pennebaker, J.W., & Beall, S.K. (1986). Confronting a traumatic event: Toward and understanding of inhibition and disease. *Journal of Abnormal Psychology,* 95, 274–281.

Pestonjee, D.M. (1987). Executive stress: Should it always be avoided? *Vikalpa,* 12, 23–30.

Pethybrigade, R.J. (1982). *Seasickness incidence in RN ships* (INM Report No. 37/82). Alverstoke, UK: Institute of Naval Medicine.

Pivar, I.L., & Field, N.P. (2004). Unresolved grief in combat veterans with PTSD. *Journal of Anxiety Disorders,* 18, 745–755.

Plumridge, N., & Brown, P. (2001). The hidden enemy: The contribution of negative affect to the experience of occupational stress in the RAAF. In G.

Kearney, M. Creamer, R. Marshall, & A. Goyne, *The management of stress in the Australian Defence Forces* (pp. 59–71). Canberra, Australia: Defence Publishing.

Rajan, R. (2004). *Stress management in counter insurgency operations.* Mhow, Indore, Madhya Pradesh, India: The Infantry (India), Infantry School.

Rana, R. (2005). Psychological warfare during Operation Iraqi Freedom. *War College Journal, Army War College,* 71–77.

Randhawa, D.S. (2004). *Women soldiers in counter insurgency operations.* Mhow, Indore, Madhya Pradesh, India: The Infantry (India).

Randhawa, D.S. (2005). Women soldiers in counter insurgency operations. *Pinnacle: The ARTAC Journal, Army Training Command, India.*

Raphael, B. (1986). *When disaster strikes: How individuals and communities cope with catastrophe.* New York: Basic Books.

Raphel, C. (1995). Current aspects of stress on foreign theaters of operations. *International Review of the Armed Forces Medical Services,* 1/2/3, 128–130.

Rawat. S. (2008). *Stress, coping and some related factors amongst serving combat veterans.* Unpublished doctoral research thesis submitted to University of Pune, India.

Rawat, S. (2011). *Stress and some related factors amongst serving combat veterans.* Paper Presented at the International Applied Military Psychology Symposium (IAMPS) in Vienna, Austria, May 2011.

Rawat. S. (2011a). *Stress amongst serving combat veterans.* Paper Presented at the International Military Testing Association (IMTA) in Bali, Indonesia.

Rawat. S. (2011b). Enhancing self-esteem of the soldier. *IDSA Journal,* 5, 2.

Rawat. S. (2013, May). *Stress and coping resources amongst serving combat veterans.* Paper Presented at the International Applied Military Psychology Symposium(IAMPS) in Berne, Switzerland.

Rawat. S. (2014). *Stress and other factors among combat soldiers.* Paper Presented at the International Military Testing Association (IMTA) in Hamburg, Germany.

Rawat, S., & Wadkar. A.J. (2012) *Positive outcomes of combat experience.* Paper Presented at the International Military Testing Association (IMTA) in Dubrovik, Croatia.

Rawat. S., & Wadker, A.J. (2009, January). *Stress amongst serving combat veterans.* Paper presented at 35th National Annual Conference of Indian Association of Clinical Psychologist (NACIACP-2009). Secunderabad, India.

Reimer, D.J. (1998). Combat stress control in a theater of operations: Tactics, techniques and procedures. *US Army Field Manual,* 8–51.

Rizzo, J., House, R., & Lirtzman, S.I. (1970). Role conflict and ambiguity in complex organizations. *Administrative Science Quarterly,* 15, 150–163.

Rolnick, A. (1985). *Seasickness incidence in the Israeli Navy* (Israel Navy Report C-101). Tel Aviv, Israel.

Rosenbaum, M., & Rolnick, A. (1983). Self-control behaviors and coping with seasickness. *Cognitive Therapy and Research,* 1, 93–98.

Salas, E., Jains, A., Cannon-Bowers, J.A., Payne, S.C., & Smith-Jentsch, K.A. (1998). Team and teamwork in the military. In C. Cronin, *Military psychology: An introduction* (pp. 71-87). New York: Pearson Education.

Schoene, R.B. (1987). High-altitude pulmonary edema. In J.R. Sutton, C. Houston, & G. Coates (eds), *Hypoxia and cold* (pp. 505–515). Westport, CT: Praeger.

Segal, D.R., & Segal, M.W. (1983). Change in military organization. *Annual Review of Sociology*, 9, 151–170.

Segal, D.R., Blair, J., Lengermann, J.J., & Thompson, R. (1983). Institutional and occupational values in the United States Military. In F. Margiotta, J. Brown, & M.J. Collins (Ed.), *Changing US Military manpower realities* (pp. 107–27). Boulder, CO: Westview.

Segal, M.W., & Harris, J.J. (1993). *What we know about army families* (Special Report # 21). Alexandria, VA: US Army Research Institute for the Behavioral and Social Sciences.

Selye, H. (1976). *The stress of life* (2nd ed.). New York: McGraw-Hill.

Selye, H. (1983). The stress concept: Past, present and future. In C.L. Cooper (ed.), *Stress research: Issues for the eighties* (pp. 1–20). Chichester: John Wiley.

Selye, H. (Ed.). (1980). *Selye's guide to stress research* (Vol. 1). New York: Van Nostrand.

Sharma, R. (2005). *Induction of women officers into infantry*. The Infantry, India.

Siebold, G.L. (1996). Small unit dynamics: Leadership, cohesion, motivation, and morale. In R.H. Phelps & B.J. Farr (eds), *Reserve component soldiers as peacekeeper.* Alexandria, VA: US Army Research Institute for the Behavioral & Social Sciences.

Singh, A.K. (2006a). *Unity is strength. Precis on behavioral and social science* (pp. 74–84). Pune, India: Institute of National Integration, College of Military Engineering Campus.

Singh, K.K. (1998). *Overcoming crisis in leadership: Indian Army*. New Delhi: Manas Publications.

Singh, M. (2006b). Has the Indian Army lost its sheen? *Journal of Selection Centre*, 6, 25–30.

Singh, M.K. (1985). *The Indian Army. A sociological study.* Pune: University of Poona.

Singh, R.S.N. (2006c). Fratricide incidents in the army. *Indian Defence Review*, 21, 49–52.

Sinha, A.K.P. (1972). Military psychology: A trend report. In S.K. Mitra (ed.), *A survey of research in psychology* (pp. 238–265). New Delhi: India.

Smelser, N.J. (1963). *Theory of collective behaviour*. New York: Free Press.

Smither, R.D., & Houston, M.R. (1991). Racial discrimination and forms of redress in the military. *International Journal of Intercultural Relations*, 15, 459–468.

Snelson, A., Ase, P., Bock, W., & Butler, R. (1983). *Characterization of combustion products of military propellants* (Final Report, Contract No. DAMD17-80-Cognitive-0019). Fort Detrick, MD: US Army Bioengineering Research and Development Laboratory.

Snow, R.E. (1984). Military motivation and morale: Questionnaire assessment of coherence of appraisal under stress. In L.E. Shaffer (Ed.), *European scientific notes* (pp. 599–603). London: US Office of Naval Research Branch Office.

Solomon, Z., Laror, N., & McFarlane, A. (1996). Acute post-traumatic reactions in soldiers and civilians. In B. van der Kolk, A. McFarlane, & L. Weisaeth (eds), *Traumatic stress: The effects of overwhelming experience on mind, body and society* (pp. 102–114). New York: Guilford.

Solomon, Z., Mikulincer, M., & Benbenishty, R. (1989). Combat stress reaction & Madash clinical manifestations and correlates. *Military Psychology*, 1, 35–47.

Solomon, Z., Openheimer, D., & Noy, S. (1986). Subsequent military adjustment of combat stress reaction casualties: A nine-year follow-up study. In N.A. Milgram (Ed.), *Stress and coping in time of war: Generalizations from the Israeli experience: Psychological stress series* (pp. 84–90). New York: Bruner/Mazel Publishers.

Sorley L. (1981). The leader as practicing manager. In J.H. Buck & L.J. Korb (eds), *Military leadership* (pp. 167–193). Beverly Hills, CA: Sage.

Southwick, S.M., Morgan, A., Nagy, L.M., Bremner, D., Nicolaou, A.L., Johnson, D.R., . . . Charney, D.S. (1993). Trauma-related symptoms in veterans of Operation Desert Storm: A preliminary report. *American Journal of Psychiatry*, 150, 1524–1528.

Srivastava, S.S. (2006). Stress on soldiers. *Asian Defence News, Journal of Asian Security Affairs*, 2, 24–25.

St. Pierre, M. (1991). Accession and retention of minorities: Implications for the future. *International Journal of Intercultural Reactions*, 15, 469–489.

Staal, M.A. (2004). *Stress, cognition and human performance: A literature review and conceptual framework* (NASA/TM-2004-212824). Moffett field, CA: National Aeronautics and Space Administration, Ames Research Center.

Steptoe, A. (1998). Psychophysiological bases of disease. In M. Johnston & D.W. Johnston (eds), *Comprehensive clinical psychology. Vol. 8: Health physiology* (pp. 39–78). New York: Elsevier.

Steptoe, A. (2000). Stress effects. Overview. *Encyclopedia of Stress* (Vol. 3, N-Z, Index).

Stewart-Watt, M.G.W. (1996). *Model base project on "Finals."* Canberra, Australia: Department of Defence, Directorate of Defence Publications and Visual Communications.

Stokes, J.W., & Jones, F.D. (1995). Combat stress control in joint operations. In F.D. Jones, L.R. Sparacino, V.L. Wilcox, J.M. Rothberg, & J.M. Stokes (eds), *War psychiatry (Textbook of military medicine, Part I. Warfare, weaponry and the casualty)*. Washington, DC: Office of the Surgeon General, US Army.

Taylor, A.J.W. (1989). *Disasters and disaster stress*. New York: AMS Press.

Taylor, H.L., & Alluisi, E.A. (1994). Military psychology. In V.S. Ramachandran (ed.), *Encyclopedia of human behavior* (Vol. 3, J-P, pp. 191–201). New York: Academic Press.

Taylor, S.E. (1991). Asymmetrical effects of positive and negative events: The mobilization-minimization hypothesis. *Psychological Bulletin*, 110, 67– 85.

Taylor, S.E. (2006). *Health psychology* (6th ed.). Los Angeles: University of California.

Thackray, R.I. (1981). The stress of boredom and monotony: A consideration of the evidence. *Psychosomatic Medicine*, 43, 165–176.

Tharion, W.J., Rauch, T.M., Strowman, S.R., & Shukitt, B.L. (1987). *The psychological attributes of ultra-marathon runners and factors which limits endurance* (USARIEM Technical Report No. T21-87). Natick, MA: US Army Research Institute of Environmental Medicine (DTIC No. AS: A185–015).

Thomas, E., & Barry, J. (1997). At war over women. *Newsweek*.

Thomas, E., & Vistica, G. (1997). At war in the ranks. *Newsweek*.

Thomas, J.A. (1988). *Race relations research in the US Army in the 1970s: A collection of selected readings*. Alexandria, VA: US Army Research Institute for the Behavioral and Social Sciences.

Thompson, K.E., Vasterling, J.J., Benotsch, E.G., & Brailey, K. (2004). Early symptom predictors of chronic distress in Gulf War Veterans. *Journal of Nervous & Mental Disease*, 192, 146–152.

Tillet, G. (1996). *Conflict resolution training for military peacekeepers*. Paper presented at the INCORE Conference on the Training and Preparation of Military and Civilian Peacekeepers, Aberfoyle House, Magee College, University of Ulster, Ireland.

Toner, M.M., White, R.W., & Goldman, R.F. (1981). *Thermal stress inside the XM-I Tank during operations in an NBC environment and its potential alleviation by auxiliary cooling* (Tech. Rep. No. T2/83). Natick, MA: US Army Research Institute of Environment Medicine.

Tucker, J.S., Sinclair, R.R., & Thomas, J.L. (2005). The multilevel effects of occupational stressors on soldier's well-being, organizational attachment, and readiness. *Journal of Occupational Health Psychology*, 10, 276–299.

Turner, M.A., Kiernan, M.D., McKechanie, A.G., & Finch, P.J.C., et al. (2005). Acute military psychiatric casualties from the war in Iraq. *British Journal of Psychiatry*, 186, 476–479.

Unwin, C., Blatchley, N., Coker, W., Ferry, S., Hotopf, M., Hull, L., & Ismail, K. (1999). Health of UK servicemen who served in Persian Gulf War. *The Lancet*, 353, 169–178.

Ursano, R.J., & Fullerton, C.S. (1990). Cognitive and behavioral responses to trauma. *Journal of Applied Social Psychology*, 20, 1766–1775.

US Army Field Manual. (2003). *Leaders manual for combat stress control* (FM 22–51).

Von Gierke, H.E., McCloskey, K., & Albery, W.A. (1991). Military performance in sustained acceleration and vibration environments. In R. Gal & A.D. Mangelsdorff (eds), *Handbook of military psychology* (pp. 335–364). New York: John Wiley.

Wakin, M.M. (1985). The professions: Wanted: Moral virtues on the military. *The Hastings Center Report*, 15, 25–26.

Wardak, A.W.H. (1993). The psychiatric effects of war stress on Afghanistan society. In J.P. Wilson & B. Raphel (eds), *International handbook of traumatic stress syndromes* (pp. 207–235). New York: Plenum.

Warm, J.S. (ed.). (1984). *Sustained attention in human performance.* New York: John Wiley.

Weisaeth, L., & Sund, A. (1982). Psychiatric problems in UNIFIL and the UN-Soldier's stress syndrome. *International Review of the Army, Navy and the Air Force Medical Services*, 109–116.

Weisaeth, L., Mehlum, L., & Mortensen, M.S. (1996). Peacekeeper stress: New and different? *NCP Clinical Quarterly, 6*, 12–15.

Weisenberg, M., Schwarzwald, J., & Solomon, Z. (1991). Effects of combat stress reaction and posttraumatic stress disorder on perceived self-efficacy in battle. *Military Psychology*, 3, 61–71.

Westcott, K.J. (2005). Modafinil, sleep deprivation and cognitive function in military and medical settings. *Military Medicine*, 170, 333–348.

Westman, M., & Etzion, D. (1995). Crossover of stress, strain and resources from one spouse to another. *Journal of Organizational Behavior*, 16, 169–181.

Wolff, H.G. (1953). *Stress and disease.* Springfield, IL: Charles G. Thomas.

Wong, P.T.P., & Wong, L.C.J. (2006). *Handbook of multicultural perspectives on stress and coping*. New York: Springer Science + Business Media, Inc. USA.

Yerkes, R.M. (1919). Report of the Psychology Committee of the National Research Council. *Psychological Review*, 26, 83–149.

3

Coping resources in the armed forces: a psychological perspective

Tintisha Basu

Introduction

Stress leads to persistent efforts by an individual to cope with it. Coping is thus a response to stress. Physical and environmental demands causing stressful taxation on person's resources are varied in nature. Besides personality factors, ability to cope with stress distinguishes one person from another.

Lazarus (1998) defined coping as 'constantly changing cognitive and behavioral efforts to manage specific external or internal demands that are appraised as taxing or exceeding resources of a person' (p. 201).

According to Taylor (2006), coping is a dynamic process and not a one-time action that an individual takes. It is a set of responses, occurring over a period of time, by which environment and person influence each other.

Magill (1996) defined coping resources as 'internal (such as knowledge) and external (such as social support) things that a person can utilise to cope with a stressful event' (p. 405). Hammer and Marting (1988) have stated that coping resources are 'those resources which are inherent in individuals that enable them to handle stressors more effectively, to experience fewer or less intense symptoms upon exposure or to recover faster in stressful situation' (p. 2).

de Ridder (2000) defined coping resources as personal (e.g. self-esteem and sense of control) and social (e.g. social support) resources an individual has to counter adverse effects of stress.

Coping behaviour incorporates a wide array of aspects. Coleman (1971) suggested that coping is either fight or flight response and identified two classes of coping behaviour: task-oriented and defence-oriented. Task-oriented coping is aimed at meeting requirements of adjustive demands. This covers reactions like attack (e.g. aggression, resistance) and withdrawal (e.g. escape, avoidance). Defence-oriented reactions of a person are aimed at protecting him/herself from psychological disorganisation.

Research has shown that people who rely more on effective coping resources tend to adapt to life stressors and experience fewer psychological problems (Folkman & Lazarus, 1991; Greenglass, 1993; Ray, Lindop, & Gibson, 1988).

During the past few decades, different forms of coping resources have been identified. Burke and Weir (1980) cited few of them: one may cope with stress by building work-group norms of cooperation and competition, devoting him or herself fully to what he or she is doing, developing peer support and so on.

Gruber (2004) stated coping resources from psychosocial point of view. Psychosocial aspects of coping resources include social support, mattering and self-efficacy that buffer effects of stress. Social support is the physical and psychological comfort provided by one's friends and family members (Antonucci, Lansford, & Ajrouch, 2000; Major et al., 1997; Sarason, Sarason, & Pierce, 1994). Mattering is defined as extent to which an individual considers oneself significant to others (Pearlin & LeBlanc, 2001; Rosenberg & McCullough, 1981; Schieman & Taylor, 2001). Self-efficacy is one's belief in own capabilities to have motivation and cognitive resources needed to meet given situational demands (Bandura, Cioffi, Taylor, & Brouillard, 1988; Chan, 2002). However, few studies indicate that social support can also be a source of stress (Cohen & Syme, 1985; Morgan, 1989).

According to Taylor (2006), coping resources are termed as stress moderators since they modify how stress is experienced as well as the effects of stress. Moderators of stress experience may have an impact on stress itself, on the relationship between stress and psychological responses, on the relationship between stress and illness, or on the degree to which a stressful experience intrudes into other aspects of life.

In conclusion, people may use problem-focused action, social support, negotiation skills, humour, altruism and religiosity in dealing with stress (Aldwin, 2000). Researchers have stated that coping with stress involves genetic predisposition, personality, prior experiences, social support, mattering and self-efficacy (Bandura et al., 1988; Bartone, 2006).

Military coping resources

Serving military personnel have a constant threat to life and bodily injuries. Persevering under stress of unfamiliar tasks and situational demands of combat, or alternately, mental breakdown under enemy fire, is determined by a complex interplay of many factors, coping resources being one such vital aspect (Milgram, 1991; Rawat, 2008). Hence, it is important to understand coping resources of military personnel operating under stressful conditions in military environment during peace times as well as during military operations.

In the present chapter, dimensions of coping resources which include cognitive, social, emotional, spiritual and physical coping resource are discussed.

Cognitive coping

Majority of studies have demonstrated that factors that help military personnel to adjust to stressors of combat include rigorous military life and training (Bartone, 1996; Csikszentmihalyi, 1975; Fontana and Rosenheck, 1998; Fotion and Elfstrom, 1986; Schnurr, Rosenberg, and Friedman, 1993), positive cognitive appraisal (Aldwin et al., 1994; Dohrenwend et al., 2004; Jennings et al., 2006) and higher cognitive skills (Rawat, 2008), keeping focused and fostering self-worth (King, King, Vogt, Knight, and Samper, 2006; Moore, cited in Munsey, 2006; Munsey, 2006), personality factors like ideological commitment (Kanagaratnam, Raundalen, and Asbjornsen, 2005), beliefs and attitude (Britt, Castro, and Adler, 2005; Day and Livingstone, 2001; Kraaij and Garnefski, 2006;

Marsella and Scheuer, 1995), fighting spirit (Hautamaki and Coleman, 2001), resilience and optimism about life (Seudfeld, 1997).

Unit cohesion has a moderating effect on relation of stress observed at individual soldier level (Bartone & Kirkland, 1991; Hunt & Phillips, 1991; Jacobs & Jaques, 1991; Lau, 1998; Manning, 1991; Salas et al., 1998). It is reported that soldiers in life-threatening situations are likely to gain solidarity and cohesiveness; shared danger enhances common bond and develops strong sense of belongingness among troops. Research has demonstrated that support from comrades protects in traumatic situation of combat, yet entails heavy cost when valued mates and friends are lost in battle (Elder & Clipp, 1988; Griffith, 2002).

There is research evidence stating that military personnel may have a tolerance for ambiguity and work overload due to nature of their postings and regular changes in job and geographical locations. It has been found that ambiguity is inherent in military way of life, which attracts certain type of people who thrive on active, dynamic and sometimes dangerous environment. It is reported that heavy workload is considered a challenge to military personnel who work as a team and a combination of positive affect, hard work, physical fitness and esprit-de-corps may well provide buffer against work stress (Beehr, 1976; Plumridge & Brown, 2001; Watson, Clark, & Tellegen, 1998).

Vickers, Kolur, and Hering (1990) studied personality correlates of coping resources in military personnel. It has been found that conscientiousness is related to problem-solving orientation to stress, while neuroticism is related to negative self-evaluation and wishful thinking in response to stress. However, Desmond and MacLachlan (2006) studied coping strategies of UK veterans and reported that coping styles were important predictors of psychological adaptation. It has been found that avoidance is strongly associated with psychological distress and poorer adjustment. The researchers reported that seeking social support is negatively associated with symptoms of depression and positively associated with social adaptation. Similarly, in a study by Peterson, Seligman, and Vaillant (1988) on difficulties experienced by Second World War combat veterans, it has been found that those with internal pessimistic style of coping with no apparent hope for escape resulted in poorer health than those veterans who described negative experiences of war with reference to external factors.

Social coping

Military research studies have demonstrated that social identity plays an important role in protecting group members from adverse reactions to stress since it provides a basis for group members to receive and benefit from social support. These research studies have reported that there is a strong positive correlation between social identification and both social support and lifestyle. There is also a strong negative correlation between social identification and stress (Bartone, 2006; Rawat, 2008).

An impressive body of evidence has found influence of leaders to be crucial in coping during military operations. It is found that military personnel showed high levels of coping, remaining healthy despite high stress levels. Research studies have identified leader's support as a factor of coping and reported that highly effective leaders can increase resilient coping responses to stressful circumstances within their units (Adler & Dolan, 2006; Bartone, 2003, 2006; Lambert, Lambert, & Yamse, 2003; McGonigle, Casper, Meiman, & Cronin et al., 2005; Paton, Violacti, & Smith, 2003).

Behaviour and support of unit and subunit leaders have been identified as crucial coping resource in stress control among military personnel (Gal, 1986; Kirkland, 1987; Kirkland, Furukawa, Teitelbaum, Ingraham, & Caine, 1987; Marlowe, 1985, 1986a, 1986b; Schneider, 1987; van Creveld, 1982).

Crossover effects of coping resources have, interestingly, been reported between military officers and their spouses; spouses' sense of control is an additional source of coping resource working to benefit military personnel (Davies, 2001; Figley, 2005; Hunt & Robbins, 2001a, 2001b; Teichman & Frischoff, cited in Selye, 1980; Westman & Etzon, 1995)

Gruber (2004) studied relationship between psychosocial coping resources, stress and task completion during military training. The researcher concluded that soldiers with high psychosocial coping resources of social support, mattering and self-efficacy were likely to perceive less stress than soldiers with less psychosocial coping resources.

Most of the studies reveal that primary source of courage to cope in combat is collective support of others, as near presence or presumed presence of comrades enables soldiers to keep going with their weapons.

Soldierly peer pride and confidence in each other, mutual respect and support sustain those in battlefield. These research studies found that in battle, no individual is alone by himself; there is shared danger, shared fear surmounting and shared courage (Badr, Acitelli, Duck, & Carl, 2001; Bowen, Mancini, Martin, & Ware et al., 2003; Coalson, 1993; Marshall, 1947; Newman, 1992).

However, it has been indicated that supportive relationships at work are not likely to emerge following combat if the framework is not built beforehand (Bartone, 1998; Reimer, 2003).

Research is consistent with the idea that unit cohesion and a soldier's relation with others are critical elements in mission accomplishment, individual survival and coping with stress in combat (Bartone, Johnsen, Eid, & Brun, et al., 2002; Bartone & Kirkland, 1991; Belenky, 1987; Gal & Mangelsdorff, 1991; Manning, 1991). These research studies found that social context variables of unit cohesion and leadership climate influence how stress gets processed in military environment. They also reported that person variables influence or moderate stress–outcome relationships which include past experience, pre-existing psychopathology and personality characteristics.

Support from home front has known to minimise negative psychological effects of combat among military personnel. Research studies have demonstrated enduring influence of combat and found stress reduction perspective among combat veterans wherein emotional adjustment difficulties that combat veterans probably experience get themselves resolved over time (Elder & Clipp, 1988; Figley, 1985; Laufer, 1985; Segal & Segal, 1976).

Few studies on psychological well-being among military personnel found that coping strategies that prevented soldiers from confronting situation were associated with least positive outcomes in terms of psychological well-being. It has been indicated that perceptions of social support are associated with psychological well-being (Bartone, Vaitkus, & Adler, 1994; Hotopf et al., 2003a, 2003b; Limbert, 2004; Terry, 1994).

Card (1983) reported residual stress perspective due to combat, which makes readjustment and adaptation difficult even later in life, probably in circumstances when social support is replaced by social rejection as seen by Vietnam Veterans.

Emotional coping

A large body of research on military personnel demonstrates that problem-focused and non-avoidant coping has been associated with better emotional functioning (Clemons, 1996; Watson and Pennebaker, 1989; Watson et al., 1998; Wolfe, Keane, Kaloupek, Mora, and Wine, 1993).

Numerous studies conducted in the area of cultural and societal factors in military organisations in UK, Israel and Soviet Russia have reported differences in morale as a cause of differences in coping resources and, consequently, stress casualties among military personnel. These research studies reported that morale of troops is an indicator of their adjustment and coping with combat. Results revealed that when morale is high, casualties are low and vice versa. By keeping soldiers occupied with purposeful activity like training, soldiers are better able to cope and see situation more objectively during stressful conditions. It is found that training as a coping resource to deal with stress reaction is also important in strengthening group cohesion (Gal, 1986; Labuc, 1991).

Hunt and Blair (1985) found that soldiers in battlefield accept inevitability of life and death, which, because of its calm effect, actually increases chance of better fighting and survival. The researchers reported that challenge is inherent in battlefields since there is a substantial discrepancy between demands of situation and capacity soldiers have to cope with it. The more successful soldiers are in reducing this discrepancy, better are their chances for survival under combat conditions.

However, contrary findings have been reported by Livingstone (2001), who examined moderating impact of positive and negative coping styles. The researcher reported that role ambiguity, overload and lack of job stimulation were associated with increased symptoms of stress. Only negative coping styles (i.e. venting of negative emotions and denial or disengagement) were uniquely associated with symptoms of stress. The researcher found that negative coping styles were associated with higher stress regardless of amount of stressor.

Few investigators have demonstrated effects of stressors on coping and found increased pathology in those combat veterans who cope with their traumatic memories primarily via emotion-focused and avoidance strategies (Bjorck & Klewicki, 1997; Green, Lindy, & Grace, 1988; Hyer, McCranie, Boudewyns, & Sperr, 1996).

Elder and Clipp (1990) studied combat experience and emotional health of veterans of Second World War and Korean conflicts. It has been found that veterans of heavy combat were at greater risk of emotional and behavioral problems in post-war years. However, it is reported that these combat veterans became more resilient and less helpless over time when compared with other military personnel without combat experience. Elder and Clipp (1988) also studied cultural differences in coping resources of US and Israeli combat veterans. It has been found that combat experience plays a major role in use of escape avoidance and emotional coping responses with combat veterans in both countries using more avoidance and emotional strategies than non-combat veterans.

Religious and spiritual coping

It has been indicated that meaning in one's life (Visotsky, Hamburg, Goss, and Lebovitz, 1961), sense of humor (Cousins, 1979; Moody, 1978), trust in others (Barefoot et al., 1998) and religion (Contrada et al., 2004; George, Ellison, and Larson, 2002) have all been suggested as internal coping resources that may deal with stress.

According to Albright and Ashbrook (2001), religion is among the most powerful of all social forces and has been in existence as long as there have been human beings. It is a powerful enduring institution and a critical socialising agent across cultures and societies (Sharot, 2001). However, it means different things to different people. It may vary across religious affiliations, particularly in the content of teachings about divine authority, power and God's will (Ellison, 1991; Ellison, Jason, David, & James, 2001; Ferraro & Kelley-Moore, 2000; Pargament, Sullivan, Balzer, van Haitsma, & Raymark, 1995; Schieman, Nguyen, & Elliott, 2003).

Researchers have shown increasing interest in studying religiosity in recent times (Miller, 1999). Research studies have been examining the link between religion and psychological, physical and interpersonal functioning (Emmons & McCullough 1999; Paloutzian & Kirkpatrick, 1995; Pargament, Koenig, & Perez, 2000).

According to Argyle and Beit-Hallahmi (1975), religiosity has been defined as 'a system of beliefs in a divine or superhuman power, and practices of worship or other rituals directed towards such a power' (p. 1).

Pargament (1997) found religiosity to be at intersection of the sacred and a search for the significant. According to the researcher, religiosity is defined as 'a process, a search for significance in ways related to the sacred' (p. 32). These definitions all recognise sacred quality of some mysterious and great power that is beyond humanity, yet related to it.

According to many researchers, studies relating to religious practices indicate that behavioral dimensions of religiosity preached almost commonly by different religions include: (a) observing prayers or worshipping God, (b) performing certain specific behavior from consideration of ethical good and bad, (c) observing rituals with faith that there is life beyond death or world beyond this reality and (d) observing sacrifice, tolerance, forgiveness, and so on as religious values (Beit-Hallahmi & Argyle, 1997; Stark, 2002).

In conclusion, religiosity indicates degree to which an individual can be identified as religious. Religiosity refers to having faith in a power beyond oneself whereby individual seeks to satisfy emotional need and gain stability of life, and which one expresses in acts of worship and service.

Connection between imminent death and religious fervor has been recognised by soldiers long before scholars and researchers began to construct models around religiosity (Watson, 1994). While most studies have been carried out that find a causal relationship between stress and religiosity among general population (Chen & Koeing, 2006), not many studies have been carried out on military personnel in this regard (Pargament, 1997). However, hardly any studies have been carried out to examine the effect of combat experience on patterning of religious experiences (Stouffer et al., cited in Pargament, 1997).

Shaw (2005) and colleagues reviewed 11 studies that reported links between religion, spirituality and posttraumatic growth. The researchers found religion to be beneficial to most individuals in dealing with the aftermath of stressful combat experience. Traumatic stressful experience can lead to deepening of religiosity. The studies demonstrated that positive religious coping, religious openness, readiness to face existential questions, religious participation and intrinsic religiousness are typically associated with posttraumatic growth.

Swank (2005) reported that religiosity helps soldiers find a sense of meaning in any and all circumstances in which their services may place them. It has been found that behavior of soldiers in hostile environments is more civil, humane, ethical and honorable if military leadership provides regular and consistent religious support for all soldiers.

Psychotherapeutic effects of religiosity in combat stress control and battle fatigue have been reported. It is found that negative effects of combat stress can be lessened when a soldier is prepared physically, emotionally and religiously, prior to combat. It has been observed that religiosity helps soldiers to draw upon religious strength and share strength and confidence during intensive combat. Soldiers' inner resources are often based on their religious and spiritual values. It is found that in combat, soldiers show more interest in their religious beliefs. When religious values are challenged during chaos of combat, soldiers may lose sight of inner resources that sustain them (Rudnick, 1997; US Army Field Manual, 2003).

Religion as a social function among soldiers is known to compensate for absence of families and friends. It has been reported that within army, religious devotion could replace worldly pleasures of camp and this sacrifice becomes evidence of a soldier's virtue and character. Faith and company of other soldiers gives the pious soldier a wholesome occupation for one's spare time and counters demoralising effects of loneliness, uncertainty and anxiety. Research studies have reported consolation as another understandable function religion has for soldiers at war – for fear, for killing, for watching other soldiers die. It has been reported that community, compensation and consolation take different shapes at different stages of a combatant's experience. All three aspects come into play before battle: compensation of a just cause and self-affirming rituals, enhanced cohesion produced by participation in these rituals and anticipation of a community of consolations. The effect of community religiosity contributes to unit morale and cohesion, while consolation explains events (i.e. deaths) and maintains discipline. This diagnostic-therapeutic process continues even after battle as soldiers attempt to understand why death spared them but took their colleagues (Linderman, cited in Watson, 1994; Watson, 1994).

According to Gordon, cited in Watson (1994), religiosity helps in infusing a spirit of endurance and determination in soldiers that no hardship, no suffering, can undermine or breakdown a soldier's morale. Research has demonstrated that religiosity is one of the most powerful agents sustaining morale of troops in battle.

However, Witvliet, Phipps, Feldman, and Beckham (2004) studied posttraumatic, mental and physical health correlates of forgiveness and religious coping in military veterans of combat. The researchers reported that difficulty forgiving oneself and negative religious coping is related to depression, anxiety and PTSD symptom severity, but not anxiety. Positive religious coping is associated with stress, including PTSD symptom severity.

Fontana and Rosenheck (2004) studied change in strength of religious faith and mental health service among combat veterans treated for stress. The researchers found that veterans' experience of killing others and failing to prevent death weakened their religious faith, both directly and as mediated by feelings of guilt. The researchers found that veterans' pursuit of mental health services appears to be driven more by their guilt and weakening of their religious faith than deficits in social functioning.

Studies have reported that religious coping activities are significant predictors of psychological stress in combat situations. Religious avoidant coping is associated with an increased stress. It is found that stressful experience serves as a religious coping mobiliser and that efficacy of religious coping methods may change over time. These studies reported that influence of religion declined significantly under strain of war (Fontana & Rosenheck, 2004; Wiley, cited in Watson, 1994).

However, Koing et al. (2006) examined effects of religious affiliation and religious coping on survival of injured combat veterans in the United States and found that religious coping was unrelated to survival. The researcher concluded that neither religious affiliation nor dependence on religion as a coping behaviour predicted survival among injured combat veterans. Similarly, Gallaway (1988) found that religiosity was not all powerful, be it bolstering or sapping soldiers willingness to fight in battle.

Stouffer and colleagues (1965) were perhaps the first researchers to study religiosity among soldiers in different theatres of operation during Second World War. The researchers found partial support for religion as stress moderator but no test of religion as a stress deterrent.

Research on religiosity of military personnel in India reported that successful military leadership in combat requires strong and positive interpersonal bond of interconnectedness between leaders and troops they take into battle. It has been reported that condition of selflessness and 'leader-led religiosity' can help reduce uncertainty, ambiguity and insecurity under condition of severe physical and psychological stress of battle. The researchers found that religiosity provides greater sense of meaning, purpose, connectedness, tolerance and understanding among combat veterans (Bhandal, 2007; Singh 1985).

Several research studies have indicated that soldiers have deep faith in religion. It has been noticed that any major unit activity in Indian army is preceded by a religious ceremony (Bhatia, 2005a; Chibber, 1986; Khan, 2006b; Parmar, 1999; Singh, 1985).

Govadia (2006a) studied religiosity among military personnel in Indian army and found that it is a unifying binding factor that motivates troops in combat. The researcher reported that religion builds character, moral rearmament and provides mental peace to military personnel.

A number of studies have shown an increase in religious practices and beliefs during and immediately following combat experience (Govadia, 2006a; Meisenhelder, 2002; Schumm & Rotz, 2001; Singh, 2006a).

An interesting coexistence of diverse religions among troops in India has been discovered. It has been reported that all religious occasions are celebrated together with national pride by all military personnel. Research studies have found that exploiting commonality in practices and customs of diverse religious and co-location of various religious institutions in close proximity brings religious harmony and tolerance leading to improved standard of national unity and integration in army units (Bhatia, 2005a; Govadia, 2006a).

However, studies on religiosity among combat veterans have also found that combat experience and death of close friends cause military personnel to lose faith that God has any power to help. It is found that young soldiers, potentially overwhelmed with fear, grief and guilt, control their vulnerability by hardening themselves to loss of friends killed by enemy fire and have emotional disturbances (Misra, 2006).

On the other hand, Rajan (2004) reported that military personnel place national pride above unit's prestige, own self-respect and religion. The researcher reported that fighting in name of religion is now an antiquated concept and found no correlation between religiosity and stressors of combat.

Thus, review of literature suggests that military personnel with combat experience are more likely to display religious inclination. From the studies, it is evident that religion helps military personnel to integrate their combat experience and give meaning to their life which helps them cope with stressors of military life.

Physical coping

Dolan, Adler, Thomas, and Castro (2005) focused on role of wellness behavior like physical exercise and sleep as coping resources and reported that both sleep and exercise moderately impact on health. The researchers demonstrated that physical exercise is a significant moderator of work hours for both psychological and physical health outcomes, whereas sleep moderated only psychological health outcomes.

An important focus of investigation has shown that in absence of social network, writing is a form of support which provides an outlet for solace, sense making, appraisal, and coping. It has been concluded that process of disclosing about stressful traumatic events like combat is essential for integration of experience by the soldier (Bartone, 1998; Bonck & Gray, 2005; Hunt, 2004; Pennebaker, Colder, & Sharp, 1990; Shalev, 1994; Shalev, Schrieber, & Galai, 1993; Smyth & Greenberg, 2001; Smyth & Helm, 2003). Other studies have found narrative therapy and art therapy among survivors of war and reported mediating effects of same (Tuval-Mashiach, Freedman, Bargai, & Boker et al., 2004; van der Velden & Koops 2005).

Researchers in India have reported that strong motivation and faith in oneself as a result of training, experience, and moral support provided by immediate superior and the military organisation acts as a coping resource (Bhatia, 2005b; Parmar, 1999; Singh, 1985; Srivastava, 2006).

A number of studies have shown that social support, especially from seniors at work, is an important factor related to good health under stress. It is reported that although support from friends and family is helpful, support from the boss far outweighs the value of support from other sources (Deusi, 2006; Kala, 2003; Kallai, 1983; Mehrotra, 2006; Singh, 1985).

A large body of research works have reported that other than individual coping resources, social support of family and significant others as well as unit cohesion, teamwork, training, and military leadership are significant factors in enhancing coping of serving combat veterans (Chibber, 1986;

Das, 1985; Deusi, 2006; Govadia, 2006b; Husain, 2006; Kshetrapal, 1999; Misra, 2006; Pasricha, 1983; Singh, 2006a).

In summary, it is seen that an increase in recent research on coping resources confirms that there is a strong relationship between stressful factors and events and adaptational outcomes among combat veterans (Bartone, 1998). From a review of literature, it can be concluded that effective use of coping resources is an integral aspect for psychological well-being and mental health of combat veterans. However, stress and coping resources among combat veterans need to be examined in more depth. It has been found that individual factors are not significantly associated with military performance. Individual differences in attribution style and in a propensity to dissociate significantly affect military performance during exposure to high-stress situations.

Review of above coping resources-related literature gives an insight in understanding behaviour among military personnel and forces that influence such behaviour. Deciphering why military personnel respond differently under similar circumstances of combat is a critical part of this endeavour.

Conclusion

This chapter explored how psychological literature on coping resources might enlighten military training programs to enhance 'mental readiness training' as a method to develop psychological resiliency of military personnel in dealing with unwanted stress. Accordingly, mental readiness training involves an integrated approach, infusing principles of emotional, cognitive, and behavioural control in the context of realistic military training. More explicitly, in selected training situations, military leaders would note psychological and cognitive responses to stress, how these responses may affect soldiers reactions, decisions made and course of action taken, as well as how these factors interact. Military leaders would do well to provide instruction in techniques of maintaining cognitive and emotional control in dealing with unwanted stress. In this way, valuable lessons and training in stress optimisation are more intrinsically applicable to soldiers, the techniques more contiguously practiced, and benefits accruing from these techniques experienced in operationally relevant contexts. Thus, integrating these principles of coping resources into relevant training opportunities may encourage application of mental readiness responses in the same way that tactical and technical competencies become reflexive in military contexts.

References

Adler, A.B., & Dolan, C.A. (2006). Military hardiness as a buffer of psychological health on return from deployment. *Military Medicine*, 171, 93–98.

Albright, C.R., & Ashbrook, J.B. (2001). *Where god lives in the human brain.* Naperville, IL: Sourcebooks.

Aldwin, C.M. (2000). *Stress, coping, and development: An integrative perspective.* New York: Guilford.

Aldwin, C.M., Levenson, M.R., & Spiro, A. Jr. (1994). Vulnerability and resilience to combat exposure: Can stress have lifelong effects? *Psychology and Aging*, 9, 34–44.

Antonucci, T.C., Lansford, J.E., & Ajrouch, K.J. (2000). Social support. *Encyclopedia of Stress*. Vol. 3.

Argyle, M., & Beit-Hallahmi, B. (1975). *The social psychology of religion.* London: Routledge & Kegan Paul.

Badr, H., Acitelli, L., Duck, S., & Carl, W.J. (2001). Weaving social support and relationships together. *Psychological Abstracts*, Vol. 88, No. 3, March 2001 (published by American Psychological Association, Washington DC; Abstract No. 7536, p. 966).

Bandura, A., Cioffi, D., Taylor, C.B., & Brouillard, M.E. (1988). Perceived self-efficacy in coping with cognitive stressors and opioid activation. *Journal of Personality and Social Psychology*, 55, 479–488.

Barefoot, J.C., Maynard, K.E., Beckham, J.C., Brummett, B.H., Hooker, K., & Siegler, I.C. (1998). Trust, health, and longevity. *Journal of Behavioral Medicine*, 21, 517–526.

Bartone, P.T. (1996). *Hardiness and resiliency in US peacekeeping soldiers.* Annual Convention of the American Psychological Association, Toronto, Canada.

Bartone, P.T. (1998). Stress in the military setting. In C. Cronin, *Military psychology: An introduction* (pp. 113–146). New York: Simon & Schuster.

Bartone, P.T. (2003). Hardiness as a resilience resource under high stress conditions. Promoting capabilities to manage posttraumatic stress: Perspectives on resilience (Vol. 22, pp. 59–73). *Psychological Abstracts*, Vol. 92, No. 7, July 2004 (published by American Psychological Association, Washington, DC; Abstract No. 19224, p. 2473).

Bartone, P.T. (2006). Resilience under military operational stress: Can leaders influence hardiness? *Military Psychology*, 18, S131–S148.

Bartone, P.T., & Adler, A.B. (1994). *A model for soldier psychological adaptation in peacekeeping operations.* Proceedings of the 36th Annual Conference of the International Military Testing Association (pp. 33–40), Rotterdam, Netherlands.

Bartone, P.T., & Kirkland, F.R. (1991). Optimal leadership in small Army units. In R. Gal & A.D. Mangelsdorff (eds), *Handbook of military psychology.* New York: Wiley & Sons.

Bartone, P.T., Johnsen, B.H., Eid, J., & Brun, W., et al. (2002). Factors influencing small-unit cohesion in Norwegian Navy Office cadets. *Military Psychology,* 14, 1–22.

Bartone, P.T., Vaitkus, M.A., & Adler, A.B. (1994). *Psychological issues in peacekeeping contingency operations.* Poster presented at the American Psychological Association Annual Convention, Los Angeles, CA.

Beehr, T.A. (1976). Perceived situational moderators of the relationship between subjective role ambiguity and role strain. *Journal of Applied Psychology,* 61, 35–40.

Beit-Hallahmi, B., & Argyle, M. (1997). *Religious behavior, belief, and experience.* New York: Routledge.

Belenky, G. (1987). Psychiatric casualties: The Israeli experience. *Psychiat. Ann., 17,* 528–531.

Bhandal, H.S. (2007). Changing the environment in workplace with spirituality. *Journal of College of Defence Management,* 6, 43–52.

Bhatia, M.K. (2005a). *Pamphlet on religiosity.* Pune, India: Institute of National Integration, College of Military Engineering Campus.

Bhatia, M.K. (2005b). *Pamphlet on behavioral and social science.* Pune, India: Institute of National Integration, College of Military Engineering Campus..

Bjorck, J.P., & Klewicki, L.L. (1997). The effects of stressor type on projected coping. *Journal of Traumatic Stress,* 10, 481–497.

Bonck, J.M., & Gray, N.D. (2005). Healing through ink on a page: Journal writing as a support intervention. *Psychology and Education: An Interdisciplinary Journal,* 42,1–9.

Bowen, G.L., Mancini, J.A., Martin, J.A., & Ware, W.B., et al. (2003). Promoting the adaptation of military families: An empirical test of a community practice model. *Family Relations: Interdisciplinary Journal of Applied Family Studies,* 52, 33–44.

Britt, T.W., Castro, C.A., & Adler, A.B. (2005). Self-engagement, stressors, and health: A longitudinal study. *Personality and Social Psychology Bulletin,* 31, 1475–1486.

Burke, R.J., & Weir, T. (1980). Coping with stress of managerial occupations. In C.L. Cooper & R. Payne (eds), *Current Concerns in Occupational Stress.* New York: John Wiley.

Card, J.J. (1983). *Lives after Vietnam: The personal impact of military service.* Lexington, MA: Lexington Press.

Chan, D.W. (2002). Stress, self-efficacy, social support, and psychological distress among prospective Chinese teachers in Hong Kong. *Educational Psychology,* 22, 557–569.

Chen, Y.Y., & Koeing, H.G. (2006). Do people turn to religion in times of stress? An examination of change in religiousness among elderly, medically ill patients. *Journal of Nervous and Mental Disease*, 194, 114–120.

Chibber, M.L. (1986). *Soldiers role in national integration*. New Delhi: Lancer International.

Clemons, E.P. (1996). Monitoring anxiety levels and coping skills among military recruits. *Military Medicine*, 161, 18–21.

Coalson, B. (1993). The trauma of war: Homecoming after Afghanistan. *Journal of Humanistic Psychology*, 33, 48–62.

Cohen, S., & Syme, S.L. (1985). Issues in the study and application of social support. In S. Cohen & S.L. Syme (eds), *Social support and health* (pp. 3–22). New York: Academic Press.

Coleman, J.C. (1971). *Psychology of effective behaviour*. Bombay: Taraporwala and Sons Co.

Contrada, R.J., Goyal, T.M., Cather, C.C., Rafalson, L., Idler, E.L., & Krause, T.J. (2004). Psychological factors in outcomes of heat surgery: The impact of religious involvement and depressive symptoms. *Health Psychology*, 23, 227–238.

Cousins, N. (1979). *Anatomy of an illness*. New York: Norton.

Csikszentmihalyi, M. (1975). *Beyond boredom and anxiety*. San Francisco, CA: Jossey-Bass.

Das, S.L. (1985). Courage in command, *Defence Management*, 12, 10–181.

Davies, S. (2001). The long-term psychological effects of traumatic wartime experiences on older adults. *Aging & Mental Health*, 5, 99–103.

Day, A.L., & Livingstone, H.A. (2001). Chronic and acute stressors among military personnel: Do coping styles buffer their negative impact on health? *Occupational Health Psychology*, 6, 348–360.

de Ridder, D. (2000). Social status and stress. *Encyclopedia of Stress*, Vol. 3.

Desmond, D.M., & MacLachlan, M. (2006). Coping strategies as predictors of psychosocial adaptation in a sample of elderly veterans with acquired lower limb amputations. *Social Science & Medicine*, 62, 208–216.

Deusi, S.S. (2006). Psychological growth of infantry soldier for combat. *Journal of Counter Insurgency & Jungle Warfare*, 2, CISW School, India.

Dohrenwend, B.P., Neria, Y., Turner, J.B., & Turse, N., et al. (2004). Positive tertiary appraisals and posttraumatic stress disorder in US male veterans of the war in Vietnam: The roles of positive affirmation, positive reformulation, and defensive denial. *Journal of Consulting & Clinical Psychology*, 72, 417–433.

Dolan, C.A., Adler, A.B., Thomas, J.L., & Castro, C.A. (2005). Operation tempo and soldier health: The moderating effect of wellness behavior. *Military Psychology*, 17, 157–174.

Elder, G.H., & Clipp, E.C. (1988). Combat experience, comradeship, and psychological health. In J.P. Wilson, Z. Harel, & B. Kahana, *Human adaptation to extreme stress* (pp. 131-156), Cleveland, OH: Cleveland State University.

Elder, G.H., & Clipp, E.C. (1990). Combat experience and emotional health: Impairment and resilience in later life. *Journal of Personality. Psychological Abstracts*, Vol. 77, No. 1, January 1990 (published by American Psychological Association, Washington, DC; Abstract No. 1436, p. 143).

Ellison, C.G. (1991). Religious involvement and subjective well-being. *Journal of Health and Social Behavior*, 32, 80–99.

Ellison, C.G., Jason, D.B., David, R.W., & James, S.J. (2001). Religious involvement, stress, and mental health: Findings from the 1995 Detroit Area Study. *Social Forces*, 80, 21–49.

Emmons, R.A., & McCullough, M.E. (eds). (1999). Religion in the psychology of personality. *J. Personal.* 67(6).

Faris JH. *The impact of basic combat training: The role of the drill sergeant.* In Goldman NL, Segal, DR, eds. The Social Psychology of Military Service. Beverly Hills, Calif: Sage; 1976: 11–24.

Ferraro, K.F., & Kelley-Moore, J.A. (2000). Religious consolation among men and women: Do health problems spur seeking? *Journal for the Scientific Study of Religion*, 39, 220–34.

Figley, C.R. (2005). Strangers at home: Comment on Dirkzwager, Bramsen, Ader, & van der Ploeg. *Journal of Family Psychology*, 19,227–229.

Figley, C.R. (ed.). (1985). *Trauma and its wake. The study and treatment of posttraumatic stress disorder. Psychological stress series.* New York: Brunner/Mazel.

Folkman, S., & Lazarus, R.S. (1991). Coping and emotion. In A.M. Monat & R.S. Lazarus (eds), *Stress and coping: An Anthology* (3rd ed., pp. 207–227). New York: Columbia University Press.

Fontana, A., & Rosenheck, R. (1998). Psychological benefits and liabilities of traumatic exposure in the war zone. *Journal of Traumatic Stress*, 11, 485–505.

Fontana, A., & Rosenheck, R. (2004). Trauma, change in strength of religious faith, and mental health service use among veterans treated for PTSD. *Journal of Nervous & Mental Disease*, 192, 579–584.

Fotion, N., & Elfstrom, G. (1986). *Military ethics: Guidelines for peace and war.* London: Routledge & Kegan Paul.

Gal, R. (1986). *A portrait of the Israeli soldier.* New York: Greenwood Press.

Gal, R., & Mangelsdorff, A.D. (1991). *A handbook of military psychology.* New York: John Wiley.

Gallaway, B. (1988). The ragged rebel: A common soldier. In W.H. Parsons, *Texas Cavalary, 1861–1865* (p. 53). Austin: University of Texas Press.

George, L.K., Ellison, C.G., & Larson, D.B. (2002). Explaining the relationships between religious involvement and health. *Psychology Inquiry*, 13, 190–200.

Govadia, D.J. (2006a). *Precis on Religion.* Pune, India: Institute of National Integration, College of Military Engineering Campus.

Govadia, D.J. (2006b). *Precis on national integration.* Pune, India: Institute of National Integration, College of Military Engineering Campus.

Goyne, A. (2001). The measurement of organisational stress in the Australian Regular Army. In G. Kearney, M. Creamer, R. Marshall, & A. Goyne, *The management of stress in the Australian Defence Forces* (pp. 21–33). Canberra, Australia: Defence Publishing.

Green, B.L., Lindy, J.D., & Grace, M.C. (1988). Long-term coping with combat stress. *Journal of Traumatic Stress*, 1, 399–412.

Greenglass, E.R. (1993). The contribution of social support of coping strategies. *Appl. Psychol.*, 42, 323–40.

Griffith, J. (2002). Multilevel analysis of cohesion's relation to stress, well-being, identification, disintegration, and perceived combat readiness. *Military Psychology*, 14, 217–239.

Gruber, K.A. (2004). *The relationship between psychological resources, stress, and task competition in elite military training*. University of Maryland.

Hammer, A., & Marting, S. (1988). *Manual for the coping resource inventory.* California: Consulting Psychologist Press.

Hotopf, M., David, A., Hull, L., Ismail, K., Palmer, I., & Unwin, C., et al. (2003a). The health effects of peace-keeping in the UK armed forces: Bosnia 1992–1996. Predictors of psychological symptoms. *Psychological Medicine*, 33, 155–162.

Hotopf, M., David. A., Hull, L., Ismail, K., Unwin, C., & Wessely, S. (2003b). The health effects of peacekeeping (Bosnia, 1992–1996): A cross-sectional study-comparison with nondeployed military personnel. *Military Medicine*, 168, 408–413.

Hunt, J.G., & Blair, J.D. (1985). *Leadership on the future battlefield.* Pergamon Brassey's International Defense Publishers.

Hunt, J.G., & Phillips, R.L. (1991). Leadership in battle and garrison: A framework for understanding the differences and preparing for both. In R. Gal & A.D. Mangelsdorff (eds), *Handbook of military psychology* (pp. 393–409). New York: Wiley & Sons.

Hunt, N. (2004). The contribution of all quiet on the Western Front to our understanding of psychological trauma. *European Psychiatry*, 19, 489–493.

Hunt, N., & Robbins, I. (2001a). World War II veterans, social support, and veterans associations. *Aging & Mental Health*, 5, 175–182.

Hunt, N., & Robbins, I. (2001b). The long-term consequences of war: The experience of World War II. *Aging & Mental Health*, 5, 183–190.

Husain, A. (2006). Managing psychological trauma of military personnel. In A. Husain & M.I. Khan (eds), *Recent trends in human stress management* (pp. 129–136). Global Vision Publishing House.

Hyer, L., McCranie, E.W., Boudewyns, P.A., & Sperr, E. (1996). Modes of long-term coping with trauma memories: Relative use and associations with personality among Vietnam veterans with chronic PTSD. *Journal of Traumatic Stress*, 9, 299–316.

Ingraham, L.H., & Manning, F.J. (1981). Cohesion: Who needs it, what is it, and how do we get it to them? *Milit Rev.*, 61, 2–12.

Jacobs, T.O., & Jaques, E. (1991). Executive: Leadership. In R. Gal & A.D. Mangelsdorff (eds), *Handbook of military psychology* (pp. 431–447). New York: Wiley & Sons.

Jennings, P.A., Aldwin, C.M., Levenson, M.R., Spiro, A., & Mroczek, D.K. (2006). Combat exposure, perceived benefits of military service and wisdom in later life. *Research on Aging*, 28, 115–134.

Kala, H.B. (2003). *Demystifying military leadership*. New Delhi: Manas Publications.

Kallai, E. (1983). *Trust in the commander*. Delivered in the Third International Convention of Psychological Stress and Coping in Times of War and Peace, Tel Aviv, Israel.

Kanagaratnam, P., Raundalen, M., & Asbjornsen, A.E. (2005). Ideological commitment and posttraumatic stress in former Tamil child soldiers. *Scandinavian Journal of Psychological*, 46, 511–520.

Kearney, G., Creamer, M., Marshall, R., & Goyne, A. (2001). *The management of stress in the Australian Defence Force: Human factors, families, and the welfare of military personnel away from the combat zone.*

Khan, J.A. (2006b). *Indian armed forces and society* (Vol. 2). New Delhi: Anmol Publications.

King, L.A., King, D.W., Vogt, D.W., Knight, J., & Samper, R.E. (2006). Deployment risk and resilience inventory: A collection of measures for studying deployment related experiences of military personnel and veterans. *Military Psychology*, 18, 89–120.

Kirkland, F.R. (1987). *Leading in COHORT companies* (WRAIR Report No. NP-88-13). Washington, DC: Walter Reed Army Institute of Research.

Kirkland, F.R., Furukawa, T.P., Teitelbaum, J.M., Ingraham, L.H., & Caine, B.T. (1987). *Unit manning system field evaluation*, (Technical Report No. 5). Washington, DC: Department of Military Psychiatry, Walter Reed Army Institute of Research (DTIC Report No. ADA 207193).

Koing, H.G., Larson, D.B., Hays, J.C., McCullough, M.E., George, L.K., Branch, P.S., . . . Kuchibhatila, H.G. (2006). Religion and the survival of 1010 hospitalized veterans. *Journal of Religion and Health*, 37, 15–30.

Kraaij, V., & Garnefski, N. (2006). The role of intrusion, avoidance, and cognitive coping strategies more than 50 years after war. *Anxiety, Stress, and Coping: An International Journal*, 19, 1–14.

Kshetrapal, R.M. (1999). *Team building*. Secunderabad, India: College of Defence Management.

Lambert, V.A., Lambert, C.E. Jr., & Yamase, H. (2003). Psychological hardiness, workplace stress, and related stress reduction strategies. *Nursing & Health Sciences*, 5, 181–184.

Lau, A. (1998). Military leadership. In C. Cronin, *Military psychology: An introduction* (pp. 49–69). New York: Simon & Schuster.

Laufer, R.S. (1985). War trauma and human development: The Vietnam experience. In S.M. Sonnerberg, A.S. Blank, Jr., & J.A. Talbott (eds), *The trauma of war: Stress and recovery in Vietnam veterans* (pp. 31–55). Washington, DC: American Psychiatric Press.

Lazarus, R.S., & Folkman, S. (1984). Coping and adaptation. In W.D. Gentry (ed.), *Handbook of behavioural medicine* (pp. 282–325). New York: Guilford.

Lazarus, R.S. (1998). *Fifty years of research and theory of R.S. Lazarus: An analysis of historical and perennial.* Mahwah, NJ: Lawrence Erlbaum Associates.

Limbert, C. (2004). Psychological well-being and job satisfaction amongst military personnel on unaccompanied tours: The impact of perceived social support and coping strategies. *Military Psychology*, 16, 37–51.

Livingstone, H.A. (2001). Chronic and acute stressors among military personnel: Do coping styles buffer their negative impact on health? *Occupational Health Psychology*, 6, 348–360.

Magill, F. (1996). *International encyclopedia of psychology* (Vol. 1). London: Filzroy.

Manning, F.J., & Ingraham, L.H. (1987). *An investigation into the value of unit cohesion in peacetime.* In G. Belenky (ed.), *Contemporary studies in combat psychiatry* (pp. 47–67). Westport, CT: Greenwood.

Manning, F.J. (1991). Morale, cohesion and esprit de corps. In R. Gal & A.D. Mangelsdorff (eds), *Handbook of military psychology* (pp. 453–470). New York: Wiley & Sons.

Marlowe, D.H. (ed.) (1985). *The new manning system field evaluation* (Technical Report No. 1). Washington, DC: Department of Military Psychiatry, Walter Reed Army Institute of Research (DTIC Report No. ADA 162087).

Marlowe, D.H. (ed.). (1986a). *New manning system field evaluation* (Technical Report No. 2). Washington, DC: Department of Military Psychiatry, Walter Reed Army Institute of Research.

Marlowe, D.H. (ed.). (1986b). *New manning system field department* (Technical Report No. 3). Washington, DC: Department of Military Psychiatry, Walter Reed Army Institute of Research (DTIC Report No. ADA 207026).

Marsella, A.J., & Scheuer, A. (1995). Coping: Definitions, conceptualizations and issues. *Integrative Psychiatry*, 9, 124–134.

Marshall, S.L.A. (1947). *Men against fire.* New York: Morrow.

Maslach, C., & Jackson, S.E. (1981). *The measurement of experienced burnout. Occup. Behav.*, 2, 99–113.

Maslach, C., Jackson, S.E., & Leiter, M.P. (1996). *Maslach burnout inventory manual* (3rd ed.). Palo Alto, CA: Consulting Psychologists Press.

Maslach, C.J. & Leiter, M.P. (2000). *Burnout*, cited in Encyclopedia of stress vol. I by Fink.

McGonigle, T.P., Casper, W.J., Meiman, E.P., & Cronin, C.B., et al. (2005). The relationship between personnel support programs and readiness: A model to guide future research. *Military Psychology*, 17, 25–39.

Mehrotra, (2006). Stress and its management in armed forces. *Journal of Selection Centre,* 6, 63–66.

Meisenhelder, J.B. (2002). Terrorism, posttraumatic stress, and religious coping. *Issues in Mental Health,* 23, 771–782.

Milgram, N.A. (1991). Personality factors in military psychology. In R. Gal & A.D. Mangelsdorff (eds), *Handbook of military psychology* (pp. 559–578). New York: Wiley & Sons.

Miller, W.R. (ed.). (1999). *Integrating spirituality into treatment: Resources for practitioners.* Washington, DC: Am. Psycol. Assoc.

Misra, N. (2006). Combat stress and its management in insurgency areas. *Journal of Selection Centre,* 6, 31–34.

Moody, R.A. (1978). *Laugh after laugh: The healing power of humor.* Jacksonville, FL: Headwaters Press.

Morgan, D.L. (1989). Adjusting to widowhood: Do social networks really make it easier? *Gerontologists,* 29, 101–107.

Munsey, C. (2006). Psychologists help troops handle the stresses of combat in Iraq and the anxieties of coming home. *Monitor of Psychology,* Vol. 37, No. 4.

Newman, A.S. (1992). Follow Me II: *More on the human element in leadership.* California: Presidio Press.

Paloutzian, R.F., & Kirkpatrick, L.A. (eds). (1995). Religious influences on personal and societal well-being. *J. Soc.* Issues 51(2), Whole issue.

Pargament, K.I. (1997). *The psychology of religion and coping.* New York: Guilford

Pargament, K.I., Koenig, H.G., & Perez, L.M. (2000). The many methods of religious coping: Development and initial validation of the RCOPE. *J. Clin. Psychol., 56,* 519–543

Pargament, K.I., Sullivan, M.S., Balzer, W.E., van Haitsma, K.S., & Raymark, P.H. (1995). The many meanings of religiousness: A policy capturing approach. *Journal of Personality,* 63, 953–983.

Parmar, L. (1999). *Military sociology. Global perspectives.* Jaipur: Rawat Publications.

Pasricha, P.M. (1983). Modernisation of leadership in the armed forces. *Strategic Analysis,* 7, 513–527.

Paton, D., Violaati, J.M., & Smith, L.M. (2003). Resilience and growth in high-risk professions, reflections and future directions. *Promoting Capabilities to Manage Posttraumatic Stress: Perspectives on Resilience,* Vol. 22, pp. 204–209. *Psychological Abstracts,* Vol. 91, No. 7, July 2004 (published by American Psychological Association, Washington, DC; Abstract No. 20939, p. 2691).

Pearlin, L.I., & LeBlanc, A.J. (2001). Bereavement and the loss of mattering. In T. J. Owens, S. Stryker, & N. Goodman (eds), *Extending self-esteem theory and research* (pp. 285–300). Cambridge: Cambridge University Press.

Pennebaker, J.W., Colder, M., & Sharp, L.K. (1990). Accelerating the coping process. *Journal of Personality and Social Psychology,* 58, 528–537.

Peterson, C., Seligman, M.E.P., & Vaillant, G.E. (1988). Pessimistic explanatory style is a risk factor for physical illness: A thirty-five year longitudinal study. *Journal of Personality and Social Psychology*, 55, 23–27.

Plumridge, N., & Brown, P. (2001). *The hidden enemy: The contribution of negative affect to the experience of occupational stress in the RAAF*. In G. Kearney, M. Creamer, R. Marshall, & A. Goyne, *The management of stress in the Australian Defence Forces* (pp. 59–71). Canberra, Australia: Defence Publishing.

Rajan, R. (2004). Stress management in counter insurgency operations. Mhow, MP, India: The Infantry (India), Infantry School.

Rawat, S. (2008). *Stress, coping and some related factors amongst serving combat veterans*. Unpublished doctoral research thesis submitted to University of Pune, India.

Rawat. S. (2011). Enhancing self-esteem of the soldier. *IDSA Journal*, Vol. 5, No. 2.

Rawat. S. (2011). *Stress and some related factors amongst serving combat veterans*. Paper Presented at the International Applied Military Psychology Symposium(IAMPS) in Vienna, Austria, May 2011.

Rawat, S. (2011). *Stress and some related factors amongst serving combat veterans*. Paper Presented at the International Military Testing Association (IMTA) in Bali, Indonesia.

Rawat, S. (2013). *Stress and some related factors amongst serving combat veterans*. Paper Presented at the International Applied Military Psychology Symposium (IAMPS) in Vienna, Austria.

Rawat, S., & Wadker, A.J. (2009). *Stress amongst serving combat veterans*. Paper presented at 35th National Annual Conference of Indian Association of Clinical Psychologist (NACIACP-2009). Secunderabad, India.

Ray, C., Lindop, J., & Gibson, S. (1988). The concept of coping. *Psychology and Medicine*, 12, 385–395.

Reimer, D.J. (2003). *Combat stress control in a theater of operations: Tactics, techniques, and procedures*. Washington, DC: Department of the Army.

Rosenberg, M., & McCullough, C. (1981). Mattering: Inferred significance and mental health. *Research in Community and Mental Health*, 2, 163–182.

Rudnick, A. (1997). Psychotherapeutic effects of religion. *Psychosomatics*, 38, 576–577.

Salas, E., Jains, A., Cannon-Bowers, J.A., Payne, S.C., & Smith-Jentsch, K.A. (1998). Team and teamwork in the military. In C. Cronin, *Military psychology: An introduction* (pp. 71–87). New York: Simon & Schuster.

Sarason, I.G., Sarason, B.R., & Pierce, G.R. (1994). Social support: Global and relationship-based levels of analysis. *Journal of Social and Personal Relationships*, 11, 295–312.

Schieman, S., & Taylor, J. (2001). Statuses, roles, and the sense of mattering. *Sociological Perspectives*, 44, 469–484.

Schieman, S., Nguyen, K., & Elliott, D. (2003). Religiosity, socioeconomic status and the sense of mastery. *Social Psychology Quarterly*, 66, 202–221.

Schneider, R.J. (1987). Stress breakdown in the Wehrmact: Implications for today's Army. In G.L. Belenky (ed.), *Contemporary studies in combat psychiatry.* Westport, CT: Greenwood Press.

Schnurr, P.P., Rosenberg, S.D., & Friedman, M.J. (1993). Change in MMPI scores from college to adulthood as a function of military service. *Journal of Abnormal Psychology,* 102, 288–296.

Schumm, W.R., & Rotz, P.L. (2001). A brief measure of intrinsic religiosity used with a sample of military veterans. *Psychological Reports,* 88, 351–352.

Segal, D.R., & Segal, M.W. (1976). The impact of military service on trust in government, international attitudes and social status. In N.L. Goldman & D.R. Segal (eds), *The social psychology of military service* (pp. 114–139). Beverly Hills, CA: Sage.

Seudfeld, P. (1997). Reactions to societal trauma: Distress and or eustress. *Political Psychology,* 18, 849–861.

Shalev, A. (1994). Debriefing following traumatic exposure. In R.J. Ursano, B.G. McCaughey, & C.S. Fullerton (eds), *Individual and community responses to trauma and disaster* (pp. 201–219). Cambridge: Cambridge University Press.

Shalev, A., Schrieber, S., & Galai, T. (1993). Early psychological responses to traumatic injury. *Journal of Traumatic Stress,* 6, 441–450.

Sharot, S. (2001). *A comparative sociology of world religions: Virtuosos, priests and popular religion.* New York: New York University Press.

Shaw, A., Joseph, S., & Linley, A. (2005). Religion, spirituality, and posttraumatic growth: A systematic review. *Mental Health, Religion & Culture,* 8, 1–11.

Singh, A.K. (2006a). *Unity is strength. Precis on behavioral and social science* (pp. 74–84). Pune, India: Institute of National Integration, College of Military Engineering Campus.

Singh, M.K. (1985). *The Indian army. A sociological study.* Poona, India: University of Poona.

Smyth, J., & Helm, R. (2003). Focused expressing writing as self-help for stress and trauma. *Journal of Clinical Psychology,* 59, 227–235.

Smyth, J.M., & Greenberg, M.A. (2001). Scriptotherapy: The effects of writing about traumatic events. *Psychological Abstracts,* Vol. 88, No. 3, March 2001 (published by American Psychological Association, Washington, DC; Abstract No. 8592, p. 1100).

Sorley, L. (1981). The leader as practicing manager. In J. H. Buck & L. J. Korb (eds). *Military leadership* (167–193). Beverly Hills, CA: Sage.

Srivastava, S.S. (2006). Stress on soldiers. *Asian Defence News, Journal of Asian Security Affairs,* 2, 24–25.

Stark, R. (2002). Physiology and faith: Addressing the *universal* gender differences in religious commitment. *Journal for the Scientific Study of Religion,* 41, 495–507.

Swank, J. (2005). Logotherapy in the life of a US Army Chaplain: Serving those who serve. *International Forum for Logotherapy,* 28, 43–46.

Taylor, S.E. (2006). *Health psychology* (6th ed., pp. 184–186). Los Angeles, CA: University of California.

Terry, D. (1994). Determinants of coping: The role of stable and situational factors. *Journal of Personality and Social Psychology*, 66, 895–910.

Tuval-Mashiach, R., Freedman, S., Bargai, N., & Boker, R., et al. (2004). Coping with trauma: Narrative and cognitive perspectives. *Psychiatry: Interpersonal & Biological Processes*, 67, 280–293.

US Army Field Manual. (2003). *Leaders manual for combat stress control*. FM 22–51.

van Creveld, M. (1982). *Fighting power*. Westport, CT: Greenwood Press.

van der Velden, I., & Koops, M. (2005). Structure in word and image: Combining narrative therapy and art therapy in groups of survivors of war. *Interventions: International Journal of Mental Health, Psychosocial Work & Counseling in Areas of Armed Conflict*, 3, 57–64.

Vickers, R.R., Kolur, D.W., & Hering, L.K. (1990). Personality correlates of coping with military basic training. *Psychological Abstracts*, Vol. 77, No. 1, January 1990 (published by American Psychological Association, Washington, DC; Abstract No. 3177, p. 305).

Visotsky, H.M., Hamburg, D.A., Goss, M.E., & Lebovitz, B.Z. (1961). Coping behavior under extreme stress. *Archives of General Psychiatry*, 5, 423–428.

Wardak, A.W.H. (1993). The psychiatric effects of war stress on Afghanistan society. In J.P. Wilson & B. Raphel (eds), *International handbook of traumatic stress syndromes* (pp. 207–235). New York: Plenum.

Watson, D., & Pennebaker, J.W. (1989). Health complaints, stress and distress: Exploring the central role of negative affectivity. *Psychological Review*, 96, 234–254.

Watson, D., Clark, L.A., & Tellegen, A. (1998). Development and validation of brief measures of positive and negative affect: The PANAS Scales. *Journal of Personality and Social Psychology*, 54, 1063–1070.

Watson, S.J. (1994). Religion and combat motivation in the confederate armies. *The Journal of Military History*, 58, 29–55.

Weisaeth, L., & Sund, A. (1982). Psychiatric problems in UNIFIL and the UN-Soldier's Stress Syndrome. *International Review of the Army, Navy and the Air Force Medical Services*, pp. 109–116.

Weisenberg, M., Schwarzwald, J., & Solomon, Z. (1991). Effects of combat stress reaction and posttraumatic stress disorder on perceived self-efficacy in battle. *Military Psychology*, 3, 61–71.

Westman, M., & Etzion, D. (1995). Crossover of stress, strain and resources from one spouse to another. *Journal of Organizational Behavior*, 16, 169–181.

Witvliet, C.V.O., Phipps, K.A., Feldman, M.E., & Beckham, J.C. (2004). Posttraumatic mental and physical health correlated of forgiveness and religious coping in military veterans. *Journal of Traumatic Stress*, 17, 269–273.

Wolfe, J., Keane, T.M., Kaloupek, D.G., Mora, C.A., & Wine, P. (1993). Patterns of positive readjustment in Vietnam combat veterans. *Journal of Traumatic Stress*, 6, 179–193.

4

Resilience among military spouses during soldier deployment in operational areas

Vrashali Patil

Introduction

Research indicates that a critical consideration in family's positive functioning in the military environment is the well-being of military spouse; poorer well-being was associated with more difficulty in family interactions among military families (Barker and Berry, 2009; Chandra, Lara-Cinisomo, et al., 2010; Flake, et al., 2009; Morris and Age, 2009; Park, 2011; Rawat 2013). Despite the challenges they face when a soldier is deployed, many military spouses appear to be resilient during deployment and continue to provide their children the support they may need (Morris and Age, 2009; Rawat, 2013, 2016). Under given circumstances, resilience may be linked to regular scheduled deployment cycle of military personnel during peacetime.

A large body of research indicates that deployment status is not associated with social functioning (Chandra, Lara-Cinisomo, et al., 2010; Rawat, 2013); however, additional research is needed before clear conclusions can be drawn regarding differences between military spouses and non-military spouses in terms of resilience. In interviews, some military spouses report that friends are a meaningful source of support while others report that friends do not or cannot understand what they are going through (Mmari, et al., 2009; Rawat, 2012). Military spouses with a deployed soldier reported being more comfortable discussing problems they are having with other military spouses rather than civilian friends or psychologists and counsellors (Mmari, et al., 2009; Rawat, 2013). Additional research is needed to help draw clear conclusions regarding the effect of deployment on the resilience of military spouse.

Resilience studies among soldiers appear to have got the attention that they deserve, as literature is replete with research carried out on military personnel (Aldwin, Levenson, & Spiro, 1994; Antonovsky, 1987; Bartone, 1996; Bartone, 2003; Bartone, 2006; Hughes, et al., 2005; Rawat, 2012). However, despite the need to understand the impact of deployment on military spouses and provide the requisite support, resilience studies on military spouses are lacking and yet to gain momentum, despite being significant, especially since resilience plays a crucial and determining role in not just stabilising the soldier's home front and minimising unwanted stress but also in soldier retention/reducing attrition in the armed forces (Park, 2001; Rawat 2013). Military spouses have displayed a great capacity for adaptation and resilience since long. An increased frequency and multiplicity of deployments in operational areas has posed multiple challenges for the military spouse; the present study seeks to determine evidence-based resilience levels among military spouses and compares them with those of non-military spouses. Specifically, military spouses were asked how they dealt with the stress of military life stemming from soldier deployment in operational areas where threat to life and loss of limbs is a stark reality, given that deployments in such areas have increased in intensity, multiplicity, and duration. An additional goal was to examine the relationship between their resilience and the military environment using the Resilience Scale of Wagnild and Young (1987) and customise the same to suit the Indian norms.

Defining resilience

Resilience is sustained competence or positive adjustment in the face of adversity.

It allows people to recover successfully from trauma or maintain appropriate or healthy functioning even when they are under considerable stress (Lerner, 2012). The relationship between an individual and his or her context produces resilience; in other words, resilience involves a fit between a person's individual characteristics (e.g. health or talents) and supportive features of his or her environment (e.g. family, school, or community).

How humans respond to adversity can vary tremendously. If we understand the processes that underlie this variability, we can better support efforts to help military spouse to adapt and thrive; the processes of resilience operate in the same way for military spouse as they do in the civilian population, although the stresses that military spouses face, and the contexts in which they face them, may sometimes be unique.

Resilience as a relationship

Resilience comes from interactions between an individual and their environments as part of an 'evolutionary developmental system' and as such should neither be construed as a personal attribute or trait nor as something that is present in a person's environment (Rawat, 2013). Thus, resilience is dynamic; it can change across time and situations. For example, a military spouse who is dealing with a soldier's deployment may show resilience at school where she teaches, participating and maintaining school activities, and yet may suffer emotionally, with symptoms of anxiety and depression in her dealings with the maid at home. Furthermore, a military spouse may demonstrate resilient functioning during one instance of soldier deployment yet may struggle with the next one.

Statement of the problem

The present research is aimed at studying resilience among military spouses. To assess these aspects, difference in perception of military spouses and civilian spouses (who will be referred to as non-military spouses) will be found in the present study. The present research also attempts to find difference among groups with reference to number of years of marriage (0–10 years and 11–20 years of marriage, respectively).

Objectives of the study

The study is based on following objectives:

1. To find out whether military spouse and non-military spouse differ with respect to their resilience levels.
2. To find out whether military spouses and non-military spouses having spent 0–10 years of married life differ with respect to their resilience levels from those in both categories who have spent 11–20 years of married life.
3. To find out whether military spouse and non-military spouse differ in personal competence factor in relation to their resilience levels.
4. To find out whether military spouse and non-military spouse differ in acceptance-of-life factor in relation to their resilience levels.

Method

Independent variable: Category of spouse (military spouse and non-military spouse); years of marriage (0–10 and 11–20 years)

Dependent variable: Resilience

Research design

The present research is designed to study certain important psychological aspects of military spouses. Wives of civilian personnel (non-military spouses) have been selected as a comparison group.

The present research is a 2 x 2 (Types of married spouse x Number of years of marriage) between-subjects design.

The subgroups of military and non-military spouses under study are compared on variables of resilience under two sub-factors, namely, 'personal competence' and 'acceptance of life and self'.

Hypotheses and rationale

Certain hypotheses are formulated regarding differences between military and non-military spouses on resilience. These were based on relevant literature on military spouse's experiences and perceptions with reference to variables considered in the present study.

Main hypotheses of the study are as follows:

1. Military spouse and non-military spouses differ in their resilience levles.
   1a. Military spouses with 0–10 years of marriage have better resilience levels compared to non-military spouse with 0–10 years of marriage .
   1b. Military spouses with 11–20 years of marriage have better resilience levels compared to non-military spouses with 11–20 years of marriage.
2. Military and non-military spouses with 0–10 years of marriage have lesser resilience than military and non-military spouses with 11–20 years of marriage
3. Military spouse and non-military spouses differ in personal competence factor in relation to resilience.
   3a. Military spouses have better personal competence factor in relation to resilience compared to non-military spouses.
   3b. Military spouses with 11–20 years of marriage have better personal competence factor in relation to resilience compared to military spouses with 0–10 years of marriage.
4. Military spouses and non-military spouses differ in acceptance of self and life factor in relation to resilience.
   4a. Military spouses have better acceptance of self and life factor in relation to resilience compared to non-military spouses.
   4b Military spouses with 11–20 years of marriage have better acceptance of self and life factor in relation to resilience compared to military spouses with 0–10 years of marriage.

Rationale behind hypotheses stemmed from the reasoning that gradual exposure to demanding military environment changes an individual's viewpoint. Military spouses benefit immensely from shouldering additional responsibility as has been suggested by review of related literature. With this background, above hypotheses of differences between military and non-military spouse on the variables under study have been framed.

Sample

- Total sample included 60 military spouses and 60 non-military spouses.
- Each group has a further split:
- 30 military spouses with 0–10 years of marriage and 30 military spouses with 11–20 years of marriage
- 30 non-military spouses with 0–10 years of marriage and 30 non-military spouses with 11–20 years of marriage.

Tools

- Personal data sheet (Developed By Researcher)
- Resilience Scale by Wagnild and Young (1987).

Resilience Scale

The Resilience Scale has 25 items on a 7-point rating scale from 1 (*disagree*) to 7 (*agree*) representing two factors, namely, personal competence (17 items) and acceptance of self and life (8 items). It is used to identify degree of individual resilience, considered a positive personality characteristic that enhances individual adaptation. Respondents are asked to state the degree to which they agreed or disagreed with each of the 25 items on a 7-point rating scale from 1 = *disagree* to 7 = *agree*. All items are worded positively. Possible scores range from 25 to 175 with higher scores reflecting higher resilience. Cronbach's alpha of the Resilience Scale is 0.89.

Procedure

Data were collected from military spouses staying in Pune Military Cantonment and from non-military spouses staying in various civilian residential colonies in Pune using purposive sampling method to include 60 military spouses (30 with 0–10 years of marriage and 30 with 11–20 years of marriage) and 60 non-military spouses (30 with 0–10 years of marriage and 30 with 11–20 years of marriage), all residing in Pune city itself. Participation was voluntary, and importance of sincere responses was stressed. Initially, participants filled personal data sheet. Later, they were given clear instructions on how to answer. Doubts were personally clarified to ensure everyone understood procedure. No time limit was imposed. Administration of the test was carefully done.

Results

Table 1. Differences between military and non-military spouses (0–10 years of marriage) in resilience levels

Variable	Category	*N*	*M*	*SD*	*t* value	*df*
Resilience	Military spouse, 10 years of marriage	30	140.20	18.11	6.50*	58
	Non-military spouse, 10 years of marriage	30	110.03	17.82		

Note: *N* = total number of sample participants; *M* = mean; *SD* = standard deviation; *t* = Student's *t* test value; *df* = degree of freedom.
*significant at 0.01 level.

Table 2. Differences between military and non-military spouses (11–20 years of marriage) in resilience levels

Variable	Category	*N*	*M*	*SD*	*t* value	*df*
Resilience	Military spouse, 20 years of marriage	30	140.70	12.83	13.89*	58
	Non-military spouse, 10 years of marriage	30	96.83	11.58		

Note: *N* = total number of sample participants; *M* = mean; *SD* = standard deviation; *t* = Student's *t* test value; *df* = degree of freedom.
*significant at 0.01 level.

Table 3. Differences in resilience levels between military and non-military spouses with 0–10 years of marriage and military and non-military spouses with 11–20 years of marriage

Variable	Category	*N*	*M*	*SD*	*t* value	*df*
Resilience	Military and non-military spouse, 10 years of marriage	60	125.11	23.42	1.43 (*ns*)	118
	Military and non-military spouse, 20 years of marriage	60	118.76	25.22		

Note: *ns* = non-significant; *N* = total number of sample participants; *M* = mean; *SD* = standard deviation; *t* = Student's *t* test value; *df* = degree of freedom.

Table 4. Differences on personal competence factor of resilience between military spouses and non-military spouses

Variable	Category	*N*	*M*	*SD*	*t* value	*df*
Personal competence factor of resilience	Military spouse	60	97.33	8.31	14.22*	118
	Non-military spouse	60	71.96	11.03		

Note: *N* = total number of sample participants; *M* = mean; *SD* = standard deviation; *t* = Student's *t* test value; *df* = degree of freedom.
*significant at 0.01.

Table 5. Differences on personal competence factor of resilience between military spouses with 0–10 years of marriage and military spouses with 11–20 years of marriage

Variable	Category	*N*	*M*	*SD*	*t* value	*df*
Personal competence factor of resilience	Military spouse, 10 years of marriage	30	96.46	8.50	0.80 (*ns*)	58
	Military spouse, 20 years of marriage	30	98.20	8.17		

ns = non-significant.

Table 6. Differences on acceptance of self and life factor of resilience between military spouses and non-military spouses

Variable	Category	*N*	*M*	*SD*	*t* value	*df*
Acceptance of self and life factor of resilience	Military spouse	60	42.25	5.86	9.93*	118
	Non-military spouse	60	31.46	6.02		

Note: *N* = total number of sample participants; *M* = mean; *SD* = standard deviation; *t* = Student's *t* test value; *df* = degree of freedom.
*significant at 0.01 level.

Table 7. Differences on acceptance of self and life factor of resilience between military spouses with 0–10 years of marriage and military spouses with 11–20 years of marriage

Variable	Category	*N*	*M*	*SD*	*t* value	*df*
Acceptance of self and life factor of resilience	Military spouse, 10 years of marriage	30	42.00	5.78	0.33 (*ns*)	58
	Military spouse, 20 years of marriage	30	42.50	6.03		

Note: N = total number of sample participants; M = mean; SD = standard deviation; t = Student's t test value; df = degree of freedom.
ns = non-significant.

Discussion

Military spouses and non-military spouses differ in resilience.

1. Military spouses with 0–10 years of marriage have better resilience levels compared to non-military spouses with 0–10 years of marriage

Table-1 shows t value = 6.50 is significant at 0.01 level. Mean score of military spouse is 140.20, which is higher than the mean score of non-military spouse, which is 110.03. Hence, the hypothesis that military spouses with 0–10 years of marriage have better resilience levels as compared to non-military spouse with 0–10 years of marriage is *accepted*.

2. Military spouses with 11–20 years of marriage have better resilience levels compared to non-military spouses with 11–20 years of marriage.

Table-2 shows t value = 13.89 is significant at 0.01 level. Mean score of military spouse (11–20 years of marriage) is 140.70, which is higher than that of non-military spouse (11–20 years of marriage) mean score, which is 96.83. Hence, the hypothesis military spouses with 11–20 years of marriage have better resilience levels compared to non-military spouses with 11–20 years of marriage is *accepted*.

3. Military and non-military spouses with 0–10 years of marriage have lesser resilience than military and non-military spouses with 11–20 years of marriage.

Table-3 shows *t* value = 1.43 is not significant at 0.01 or 0.05 levels. Mean score of military and non-military spouses with 10 years of marriage is 125.11, which is higher than the mean score of military and non-military spouses with 20 years of marriage, which is 118.76. Hence, the hypothesis military and non-military spouses with 0–10 years of marriage have lesser resilience than military and non-military spouses with 11–20 years of marriage is *rejected.*

Military spouses and non-military spouses differ in personal competence factor in relation to resilience.

4. Military spouses have better personal competence factor in relation to resilience compared to non-military spouses.

Table-4 shows *t* value = 14.22 is significant at 0.01 level. Mean score of military spouse is 97.33, which is higher than non-military spouse's mean score at 71.96. Hence, the hypothesis that military spouses have better personal competence factor in relation to resilience compared to non-military spouses is *accepted.*

5. Military spouses with 11–20 years of marriage have better personal competence factor in relation to resilience compared to military spouses with 0–10 years of marriage.

Table-5 shows *t* value = 0.80 is not significant at 0.01 or 0.05 levels. Mean score of military spouse with 20 years marriage is 96.46, which is higher than military spouses with 10 years of marriage whose mean score is 98.20. Hence, the hypothesis that military spouses with 11–20 years of marriage have better personal competence factor in relation to resilience compared to military spouses with 0–10 years of marriage is *rejected.*

6. Military spouses have better acceptance of self and life factor in relation to resilience compared to non-military spouses.

Table-6 shows *t* value = 9.93 is significant at 0.01 level. Mean score of military spouse is 42.25, which is higher than the mean score of non-military spouse at 31.46. Hence, the hypothesis that military spouses have better acceptance of self and life factor of resilience compared to non-military spouse is *accepted*.

7. Military spouses with 11–20 years of marriage have better acceptance of self and life factor in relation to resilience compared to military spouses with 0–10 years of marriage.

Table-7 shows *t* value = 0.33 is not significant at 0.01 or 0.05 levels. There is little difference between the mean score 42.00 of military spouses with 10 years of marriage and mean score of 42.50 of military spouses with 20 years of marriage. Hence, the hypothesis that military spouses with 11–20 years of marriage have better acceptance of self and life factor in relation to resilience compared to military spouses with 0–10 years of marriage is *rejected*.

Implications

Research studies and programs on resilience on not just the soldier but the military spouse as well need to move beyond prevention or reduction of their problems and recognise their assets as well as strengths and to promote them for the benefit of others in the demanding military environment as well as the general population at large. To a large extent, military spouses go unsung for the sacrifices that they make on a regular basis, the crucial role that they play in optimal soldier well-being, psychological functioning and performance; they are critical to mission effectiveness and success and deserve far greater attention from researchers, psychologists, the military and society.

Limitation and future analyses

This study may have a number of limitations, which should be considered when reviewing the findings, including the following:

a. Lack of research, both branch-specific and inclusive of all Arms/ branches, limits our ability to draw conclusions about the positive impact of soldier deployment on military spouse either within Army, Navy, or Air Force across different Arms of branch or across branches.

b. Neither pre-deployment assessment nor examining military spouse's resilience levels over time was done, as either of these strategies would shed light on the direction of associations between variables and help rule out alternative explanations for findings due to confounding variables.
c. Matching techniques could have been used on important demographic variables like family composition as well as age to ensure that the different groups under study do not have critical pre-existing differences that may influence the results.
d. Limited number of available research works examining the positive impact of soldier deployment on military spouse is too small to consider for drawing empirical conclusions, which limits our ability to fully understand the positive impact of soldier deployment on military spouse.
e. Selected or participating military spouses may differ from non-participating military spouses in ways that are not measured but affect the outcome variables. For example, military spouses who agreed to participate in our study may be more or less resilient than those military spouses who chose not to participate.

Conclusion

A large body of literature indicates that while soldier deployment is directly associated with an increased family functioning problem for the military spouse, at the same time other researchers have reported 'successful adaptation' to the challenges in overcoming adversities inherent in military life.

Attempts to promote and enhance resilience levels in military spouses accentuate the following guiding principle, which are highly congruent with the acquired knowledge about the military community and resilience in the face of military deployment:

- An optimally functioning and resilient military spouse has powerful protective effects on the soldier and his family as well as other members and families in the military unit.
- Strategies that work are well-timed developmentally and customised to the military spouse, the immediate military environment, and the situation at hand.

- Safeguarding the well-being of military spouse promotes their resilience, and, consequently the resilience of the soldier as well as the military community
- Resilience in military spouse can be strengthened in several ways at different system levels.

Many factors such as spouse age, ethnicity and cultural background, and length and multiplicity of soldier deployments have been shown to either buffer or exacerbate the association between soldier deployment and military spouse outcomes.

Understandably, these conclusions cannot be generalised across the military population and further research needs to be done before drawing any conclusions. Nevertheless, it is evident that deployment imposes stress on both the soldier and the spouse. Furthermore, both deployment and reintegration disrupt family roles and functioning; however, the soldier and the spouse are able to come out of this 'deployment challenge' yet stronger.

The evidence and findings from the study substantiate the need for additional scientific, evidence-based research to gather more and higher-quality data. Moreover, the potential benefits for the military community as a whole are gripping. Finding what works among military spouses to promote resilience may have a profound significance for the future in nation building through strengthening the military community at large.

To further explore resilience among military spouses, we need to further refine resilience attributes to include those that are in sync with resilience across the military setting. Finally, we intend to evaluate resilience attributes among the entire military family to include the soldier, parents, spouse, and children during deployment in operational areas as well as peace locations.

References

Aldwin, C.M., Levenson, M.R., & Spiro, A. Jr. (1994). Vulnerability and resilience to combat exposure: Can stress have lifelong effects? *Psychology and Aging*, 9, 34–44.

Antonovsky, A., & Bernstein, J. (1986). Pathogenesis and salutogenesis in war and other crises: Who studies the successful coper? In N.A. Milgram (Ed.), *Stress and coping in time of war: Generalizations from the Israeli experience* (pp. 52–56). New York: Brunner/Mazel.

Antonucci, T.C., Lansford, J.E., & Ajrouch, K.J. (2000). Social support. *Encyclopedia of Stress* (Vol. 3).

Bahr, H.M., & Bahr, K.S. (2001). Families and self-sacrifice: Alternative models and meanings for family theory. *Social Forces*, 79, 1231–1258.

Barker, L., & Berry, K. (2009). Developmental issues impacting military families with

Bartone, P.T. (1996). *Hardiness and resiliency in US peacekeeping soldiers.* Annual Convention of the American Psychological Association, Toronto, Canada.

Bartone, P.T. (1999). Hardiness protects against war-related stress in army reserve forces. *Consulting Psychology Journal: Practice and Research*, 51, 72–82.

Bartone, P.T. (2003). Hardiness as a resilience resource under high stress conditions. Promoting capabilities to manage posttraumatic stress: Perspectives on resilience (Vol. 22, pp. 59–73). *Psychological Abstracts*, 92, No. 7, July 2004. published by American Psychological Association, Washington, DC. (Abstract No. 19224, p. 2473)

Bartone, P.T. (2006). Resilience under military operational stress: Can leaders influence hardiness? *Military Psychology*, 18, 131–148.

Bonanno, G.A. (2004). *Loss, trauma, and human resilience: Have we underestimated the human capacity to thrive after extremely aversive events? American Psychologist*, 59, 20–28.

Bonanno, G.A. (2005). Resilience in the face of potential trauma. *Current Directions in Psychological Science*, 14, 135–138.

Bonanno, G.A., Galea, S., Bucciarelli, A., & Vlahov, D. (2006). *Psychological resilience after disaster: New York City in the aftermath of the 11 September terrorist attack. PsycholSci*, 17, 181–186.

Bowen, G.L. (1981). Family patterns of US military personnel. In J.S. Parry & K.L. Parhinson (eds), *Proceedings of the National Association of Social Workers Pre-Conference Institute on Social Work Services for Military Families* (pp. 34–56). Springfield, VA: Military Family Resources Center.

Bowen, G.L., Mancini, J.A., Martin, J.A., Ware, W.B., et al. (2003). Promoting the adaptation of military families: An empirical test of a community practice model. *Family Relations: Interdisciplinary Journal of Applied Family Studies*, Vol. 52, 33–44.

Brace, N., Kemp, R., & Snelgar, R. (2003). *SPSS for psychologists.* New York: Palgrave Macmillan.

Chandra, A., Lara-Cinisomo, S., Jaycox, L., Tanielian, T., Burns, R., Ruder, T., & Han, B. (2010). Children on the home front: The experience of children from military families. *Pediatrics*, 125, 16. doi:10.1542/peds.2009-1180

Cozza, S.J., Chun, R.S., & Polo, J.A. (2005). Military families and children during operation Iraqi freedom. *Psychiatric Quarterly*, 76, 371–378.

Elder, G.H., & Clipp, E.C. (1989). Combat experience and emotional health: Impairment and resilience in later life. *Journal of Personality*, 57, 311–341.

Elder, G.H., & Clipp, E.C. (1990). Combat experience and emotional health: Impairment and resilience in later life. *Journal of Personality. Psychological Abstracts*, Vol. 77, No. 1, January 1990; published by American Psychological Association: Washington, DC. (Abstract No. 1436, p. 143)

Faber, A.J., Willerton, E., Clymer, S.R., MacDermid, S.M., & Weiss, H.M. (2008). Ambiguous absence, ambiguous presence: A qualitative study of military reserve families in wartime. *Journal of Family Psychology*, 22, 222–230.

Flake, E., Davis, B., Johnson, P., & Middleton, L. (2009). The psychosocial effects of deployment on military children. *Journal of Developmental & Behavioral Pediatrics*, 30, 271.

Gimbel, C., & Booth, A. (1994). Why does military combat experience adversely affect marital relations? *Journal of Marriage and the Family*, 56, 691–703.

Hughes, J.H., Cameron, F., Eldridge, R., Devon, M., et al. (2005). Going to war does not have to hurt: Preliminary findings from the British deployment to Iraq. *British Journal of Psychiatry*, 186, 536–537.

Kelly, T.M. (2005). Natural resilience and innate mental health. *American Psychologist*, 60, 265.

Lerner, R.M. (2012). Resilience and positive youth development: A relational developmental systems model. In S. Goldstein & R. Brooks (eds), *Handbook of Resilience in Children* (pp. 293–298; 2nd ed.). New York: Springer.

Lerner, R.M. (2012). Resilience across the Lifespan. In B. Hayslip Jr., & G. C. Smith (eds), *Emerging perspectives on resilience in adulthood and later life* (pp. 275–299). New York: Springer.

Limbert, C. (2004). Psychological well-being and job satisfaction amongst military personnel on unaccompanied tours: The impact of perceived social support and coping strategies. *Military Psychology*, 16, 37–51.

Litz, B.T. (2005). Has resilience to severe trauma been underestimated? *American Psychologist*, 60, 262.

McCubbin, H.I., & McCubbin, M.A. (1988). Typologies of resilient families: Emerging roles of social class and ethnicity. *Family Relations*, 37, 247, 254.

Mmari, K., Roche, K., Sudhinaraset, M., & Blum, R. (2009). When a parent goes off to war: Exploring the issues faced by adolescents and their families. *Youth & Society*, 40, 455–475.

Morris, A., & Age, T. (2009). Adjustment among youth in military families: The protective roles of effortful control and maternal social support. *Journal of Applied Developmental Psychology*, 30, 695–707.

Rawat, S. (2012). Resilient military training for Commanding Officers. *Guest lecture for Senior Command Course*, Army War College, Mhow, India.

Rawat, S. (2013). Stabilising the home front for the soldier: Building resilient military families. *Guest lecture for Senior Command Course*. Army War College, Mhow, India

Rawat. S. (2016, May). *Resilience among military spouses during soldier deployment in operational areas.* Paper presented at the International Applied Military Psychology Symposium (IAMPS) in Porto, Portugal.

Rawat. S. (2015). *Absent leadership on homefront and its challenges to military families.* Paper Presented at the International Military Testing Association (IMTA) in Stockholm, Sweden.

Rutter, M. (2012). Resilience as a dynamic concept. *Development and Psychopathology,* 24, 335–344.

Schwarz, R., MacDermid, S., & Weiss, H. (2007). *Military families on the move.* National Council on Family Relations 69th Annual Conference. Pittsburgh, Pennsylvania.

Tedeschi, R.G., & Kilmer, R.P. (2005). Assessing strengths, resilience, and growth to guide clinical interventions. *Professional Psychology, Research and Practice,* 36, 230–237.

VanBreda, A.D. (2001). Resilience theory: A literature review with special chapters on deployment resilience in military families & resilience theory in social work.

Vogt, D.S., Pless, A.P., King, L.A., & King. D.W. (2005). Deployment stressors, gender, and mental health outcomes among Gulf War I veterans. *Journal of Traumatic Stress,* 18, 115–127.

Wagnild, G.M., & Young, H.M. (1993). Development of psychometric evaluation of the resilience scale. *Journal of Nursing Measurement,* 1, No. 2, 1993.

Walsh, F. (2007). Traumatic loss and major disasters: Strengthening family and community resilience. *Family Process,* 46, 207–227.

Young children during single and multiple deployments. *Military Medicine,* 174, 1033–1040.

5

Competency-based human resources management: selecting future leaders in the Indonesian Army

Eri Radityawara Hidayat

The early Roman practiced a form of competency profiling in attempts to detail the attributes of a good Roman soldier.

— Kierstad (1998)

Introduction

The Indonesian Army (*Tentara Nasional Indonesia Angkatan Darat* or TNI AD) has set a vision to become a world-class army by the next two decades. Traditionally, however, the priority of the Indonesian government's budget is for supporting the country's economic growth, and as a consequence, the TNI AD must work with less than optimum budget. As a consequence, in 2010 the Ministry of Defence of the Republic of Indonesia officially adopted a defence strategy called Minimum Essential Force (MEF), which outlined the country's future strategic defence requirements (Marbun, 2009). With the MEF, the focus of the TNI AD was to build an army capable of facing potential threats yet at the same time within the budget requirements.

As an organisation that relies on 'men who are armed', MEF means the TNI AD must have competent soldiers who can perform their job. Consequently, to achieve its future vision, the focus of the TNI AD should be to develop its human resources. In short, the recruitment and development of world-class soldiers is the basis of its human capital advantage. Therefore, it is very important for the TNI AD to adopt the most current and effective human resource management system so that its challenging vision can be realised.

Following advances in the behavioural sciences, many civilian and military organisations all over the world have adopted the so-called Competency-Based Human Resource Management System or CBHRM (Hidayat, 2005). As the Indonesian government is not immune to the dynamics in the HR world, the Ministry of Administrative and Bureaucratic Reform has declared that all government ministries must implement CBHRM in order to create professional government bureaucrats and use the Assessment Centre method to assess their top echelon (Kusumaningsih, 2013). Consequently, the Ministry of Defense, through Regulation 65 of 2014, has stated that it will adopt CBRHM as well as implement the Assessment Centre method (Sumardi, 2016). This chapter will discuss the concept of CBHRM and Assessment Centre and their application in military organisation, then elaborate on its implementation in the TNI AD.

Meaning of competency

Apparently there are so many descriptions of what competency is and what it is not, that one wonders whether people are talking about the same concept or whether there are in fact many different concepts of competency? Therefore, it would be useful if one tries to discuss first the different types of competencies.

People-based competencies

The modern competency movement was actually born in the 1970s (Adams 1996), when David McClelland, a Harvard University psychology professor, argued that competencies, or the characteristics of superior performing individuals, would be better at predicting performance than traditional psychometric test results derived from academic-type intelligence. Richard Boyatzis (1982), a McClelland disciple, who used a method called behavioural event interviews, attempted to create a generic managerial competency framework by studying more than 2000 managers from various organisations and focused on individual characteristics that could differentiate superior performers. HR practitioners then developed competency models, based on the belief that it is possible to identify the behaviours of employees who exhibited excellent performances so that it will provide a thread which links to all other human resource processes – hence CBHRM (Thompson, Lemaire, Jacob, & Gubman, 1996).

From what was originally an American phenomenon, the competency movement took a different route in Europe. Here, Constable and McCormick (1987) criticised the state of management training in Britain and called for the establishment of a standardisation process for Competency-Based Training (CBT). The British Training Standards Agency (Horton 2000b) defined 'competence' as 'an action, behaviour, or outcome, which the person should be able to demonstrate'. Unlike the American version, this definition refers to an output-oriented standard of performance, based on the accomplishment of the jobholder and derives from formal training (Heffernan & Flood, 2000). These so-called threshold competencies equate less with superior performance but, instead, are concerned more with establishing an acceptable minimum performance level (Spencer & Spencer, 1993).

To accommodate these conceptual differences, as well as to minimise confusion as to the nature of 'competencies', Spencer and Spencer (1993) sought to characterise competencies in terms of an 'iceberg model'. In this model, the 'visible' skill and knowledge aspect of competencies, which is the focus of the British-based approach, is represented as comprising 'above-the-water-line' competencies. On the other hand, the hidden elements of traits, motive, attitudes, values, and self-concept, which are the focus of the US approach, are depicted as hidden or 'submerged' competencies.

Later practices in both countries, however, seemed to suggest that a combination of both approaches might offer a better solution. For example, American authorities, by creating the National Skills Standards Board – an entity consciously modelled on the British system, have shown a willingness to experiment with output-oriented competency models on European lines (Wilcox, 2002). On the other hand, spearheaded by the British subsidiaries of American multinational companies, many UK-based organisations have been benchmarking against the American competency version and focusing on ways to identify person-based competencies (Horton, 2000b). And Rodriguez et al. (2002) found that the US Office of Personnel Management, which is responsible for managing human resources for the federal government, have reportedly used both approaches in developing their competency.

Organisation-based competencies

Organisational competencies are a more recent phenomenon and refer to core competencies that an organisation requires in order to have competitive advantage over its competitors, which include particular sets of skills and resources or organisational characteristics related to effective behaviour or performance (Pralahad & Hamel, 1990). In order to define the competencies, the starting point should be to analyse the unique organisational vision, which subsequently will be broken down into business strategy, structure, culture, and values that the organisation aspires (Treen, 2000). In short, a competency model is based on the business process that comes from the mission of the business or the organisation's ideology and on how it will perform and survive in the competitive future.

Competency-based human resources management system

Assessing the competencies

After an organisation has agreed on the competencies that it requires, the next issue that must be resolved is assessing the competencies of its people. Competency assessment can be defined as the process of identifying the underlying characteristics of employees that can lead to successful performances (McNerney & Briggins, 1995). There are two different approaches concerning competency assessment that one must consider prior to discussing any methods of assessment. For job- or role-related competencies, especially when it is related to selection, placement, and promotion, validity, reliability, and accuracy issues are of paramount concern because there would be issues of procedural justice that must be taken care of (Klein, 1996). However, for organisational competencies, in which the competencies are considered more as tool to communicate a new set of values, rather than to specifically focus on the individual job holder, the validity of competency assessment is not the main concern ('The state of competencies', 1997).

Although there are many different tools to assess competencies, the most common method used in CBHRM is the Assessment Centre method. Assessment Centre was found to be very valuable in identifying management potential because their use of external assessors can provide an independent view free of subjective biases commonly related to internal assessor (Dulewicz, 1991). In addition, apart from the high construct and content validity, the utilisation of behavioural simulations enabled the provision of standardised method for observing behaviour (Thornton & Byham, 1982). Finally, Assessment Centre can uncover hidden strengths that are not needed, and therefore not demonstrated, in a current position but would be very useful in higher-level positions, which can facilitate early identification of senior management potentials (Ritchie, 1994).

Competency-based performance management

In the United States, Thompson et al. (1996) have found that performance management is the most popular area of application of a competencies approach, followed by training and development. In essence, performance management is concerned with how individual employees can align their capabilities, behaviours, and results more closely with organisational objectives and success factors (Storey & Sisson, 1993). Consequently, effective performance management requires the establishment of a goal setting process, regular performance evaluation, and the corresponding development and reward practices, in which for underperformances training and development would be targeted to cover the specific competencies that require improvements (Stone, 2005).

Competency-based development

It is widely assumed that competencies may be developed over time (Athey & Orth, 1999). While it would seem to be easier to train for above-the-surface competencies, many argue that below-the-surface competencies can also be developed, provided they are 'behaviourised'; that is, provided it is possible to identify and observe behaviours associated with particular submerged competencies (Wusteman, 2000). Thus, the development method must be dependent on the specific competency that is to be developed (Byham, 1982). For instance, a 'strategic thinking' competency could be best developed through case study discussion and analysis, while interpersonal skills are best learned with role-playing and modelling (Peterson, 1996).

CBHRM in the military

Similar to their civilian counterparts, today's military organisations must be able to adapt to the increasingly complex environment characterised by continuously changing missions, technologies, sociocultural norms, and new forms of organisations. Although there is no known record available, implementation of CBHRM in the military may have started with the publication of the US Army Field Manual 22–100 'Be-Know-Do' competency framework (Cronin et al., 2003). The competency framework probably inspired other military organisations, such as the Canadian Forces (Walker, 2006).

From website of the International Military Testing Association (IMTA) (http://www.imta.info/home.aspx) – a grouping of military psychologists from around the globe, one can see that since the early 2000, many militaries have adopted CBHRM, although the motives are quite varied. For example, following the major reorganisation after the conclusion of their African operations, the Portuguese Army adopted the competency approach because they needed a method to 'evaluate the performance of the military officers in a simple and clear manner, and to identify potential development opportunities' (Leitao et al., 2001). Another implementation is the Competency-Based Human Resources Information System presented by the New Zealand Defence Force. With a total of 36 competencies spread over 13 competency groups, it was indicated that there would be measurement and development program for each competency and that the whole system would be integrated through an information technology system (Davis, 2007). A more recent phenomenon is the competency dictionary of Canadian Armed Forces, which can be used for a wide range of HR applications (Karin & Williams, 2015).

Institutional competencies

Surely, implementing CBHRM in the military can be very appealing because with its performance appraisal system and the related developmental and mentoring guidelines CBHRM can create highly prescriptive template of desired behaviour that in the end will produce members who can think and act in similar fashion (Townley, 1999). Yet the challenge of implementing such a system in a military organisation is, of course, the business orientation of the CBHRM system.

One of the unique feature of a military organisation is that it demands the ultimate sacrifice of its members, that is, laying down their life if necessary for the sake of the country. Consequently, the main difference between military competency framework and its business counterpart is the existence of institutional competencies related to military values – much like organisational competencies in the civilian world (Hidayat, 2005). For example, the Canadian Forces competency framework includes a competency cluster that is called Professional Ideology that they claimed will differentiate them from other industrial/business-related institutions (Walker, 2006). Therefore, adopting a values-based institutional competency is very important to ensure that military members remain true to their calling. Comprising unique organisational values that reflect the organisational culture, these values are important for members of military organisations who often join the military for some abstract reason such as patriotism (Shen, 2002).

Military technical competencies

Related to the American and European divide on competency definition, it is interesting to note that some military organisation used both types of competencies but then applied it for the different ranks. For example, in the Australian Army technical competencies is deemed more relevant for junior officers who need familiar solutions to solve familiar problems in a familiar terrain (Doctrine Wing, 2002). However, when experienced commanders and senior officers have to cope with the 'chaos and friction of modern warfare', where they have to face unfamiliar problems in an unfamiliar environment, then these leaders must be equipped with higher-level capabilities such as analytical and lateral thinking. This is due to the fact that depending solely on a conventional mindset is no longer adequate for today's military. The asymmetric approach – defined as 'a conflict spectrum dominated less by large, force-on-force battles and more by disorganised, civilianised, and primitive warfare, conducted by individuals and non-state actors, which offers limitless opportunities to employ niche capabilities with potentially crippling effects' (Applegate, 2001) – seems to be increasingly common and 'can be applied at all levels of warfare – strategic, operational, and tactical – across the spectrum of military operations' (Joint Chiefs of Staff, 1999).

Consequently, military thinkers have concluded that there should be two platforms which can balance the need for uniformity and traditional hierarchy in the conventional combat arena, with the need for creativity and adaptability in the more fluid asymmetric warfare (Borchert & Jones, 1999). US Army Colonels McCausland and Martin (2001), from the US Army War College, argue that traditional career-based military courses, fashioned along the lines of Cold War confrontation, are inadequate to answer today's problems. Officers learn tactical levels of warfare at basic training in the military academy, progressing to operational level at Command and General Staff College, and finally to strategic level at Army War College. The spectrum of leadership competencies progresses from the mostly technical to mostly personal and values-based, with the Command and General Staff College as the crossover point. Considering these new developments, Williams (2003) has argued that the dimensions of creativity and risk taking should be included into the taxonomy of officer's competencies, either embedded as additional competencies or by creating new leadership competencies altogether.

Competency-based centre

The Assessment Centre method actually was developed by the military, when in the 1930s Dr Max Simoneit from the University of Berlin was contracted by the German Army to develop new method to select their officers (Rowe, 2006). He found that the results of traditional paper-and-pencil test showed differences in what the officer candidates said they would do if they are promoted with the actual behaviours that they did when they became officers – a term that psychologists now called as 'faking good.' Simoneit and his team then developed a series of behavioural tests which he called assessments, one of which is *Fuehrerprobe* (leadership simulation).

During the Second World War, when the British Office of Strategic Services attempted to select their intelligence officers, their psychologists started to re-evaluate Simoneit's Assessment Centre (Morgan, 1955). The British Armed Forces then established the English War Office Selection

Assessment Board to select candidates for intelligence services by using several individual and team simulations which were called Groupstacle – similar to *Fuehrerprobe*. Afterwards, US Army General William Donovan from the US Office of Strategic Services (OSS), which was responsible for espionage activities during the Second World War, went to England to study how the British Army selected their spies (Mackinnon, 2005). When he returned from Britain, he built Station S, the first modern Assessment Centre in the world, which was manned by psychologists from Harvard. From then on, the Assessment Centre method has been used by many organisations all over the world.

Competency-based performance management

Although there is not much research showing direct linkage between performance management and development, Cooper et al. (1998) found integrated CBHRM to be most appropriate for a centralised military-style career management system, where members spend most of their career in the same organisation. The main advantage is that it could give a military organisation a consistent and 'common language' to discuss a whole range of HR functions from recruitment and selection to performance management, training, and development (Horton, 2000a).

Competencies development

Competencies development deals mainly with people-based competencies in which military organisations try to develop people skills and competencies that are lacking in a person (Hidayat, 2005). As such, coaching intervention was found to be 'the most useful means of teaching human relations skills' (Sperry 2004) because it could develop the officer's 'private self-consciousness', which would make them more aware of 'the causes and meaning of their behaviour, thoughts and feelings', especially when they interact with other people (Grant, 2001, p. 52). In fact, leadership coaching is formally used in many military organisations to improve the leadership performance of their officers, such as the Australian Defence Force (Carroll 2004), the German Bundeswehr (Scherm and de Jonge, 2012), the Singaporean Armed Forces (Tan and Ang 2015), the Swiss Army (Annen, 2009), and the US Navy (Hedge *et al.*, 2004).

CBHRM in the Indonesian Army

As mentioned in beginning of this writing, the TNI AD must implement the CBHRM as mandated by the Ministry of Defence. The fact to the matter is that the TNI AD has partially implemented this system in 2004, when the Psychological Service of the Indonesian Army, together with other army institutions, conducted a mapping of the competencies needed for Indonesian Field Commanders such as Resort Military Commanders, District Military Commanders, and Battalion Commanders. The resulting competency framework can be seen in Figure 1 as follows.

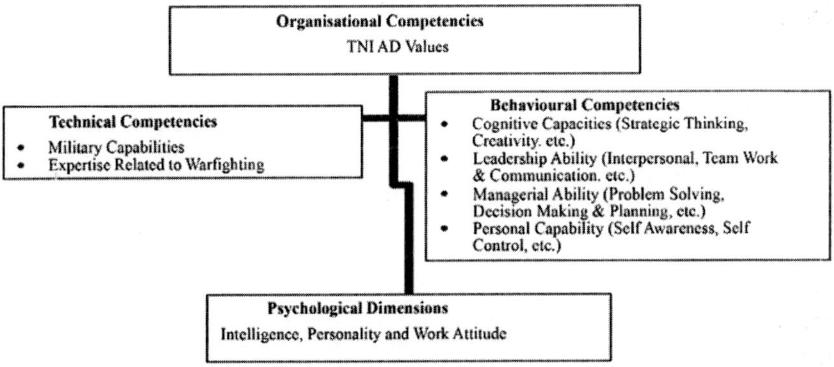

Figure 1. Competency Framework of TNI AD Field Commanders

After the framework was approved by the Chief of Army, a Position Competencies Assessment Program (PCAP) was launched to select the candidates.

Position Competencies Assessment Program (PCAP)

As shown in Figure 1, the behavioural competencies consisted of four main competencies: cognitive capacities, leadership abilities, managerial abilities, and personal capabilities. In turn, each of these core competencies consists of several sub-competencies. On the other hand, the psychological potentials that are being observed are intelligence, personality, and work attitude. To assess these competencies, a field simulation which was a legacy from the Psychological Service of the Dutch Colonial Army was used. In fact, they are very similar to the original German and British Assessment Centres that were used during the World War periods. In terms of technical competencies, for field commanders such as battalion commanders, the Infantry Training Centre is responsible for designing the test materials, while the Territorial Training Centre is responsible for would-be territorial commanders. For values-based organisational competencies, as there is no known method for evaluating these competencies yet, more subjective evaluation from the superior officers is used to determine the fitness of a candidate.

Competencies developmental program

Competency development programs are done at the Army's Training Centres, integrating all the curricula that have been designed by the related institutions. Based on the competency framework, a competency-based development matrix can be formulated, in which different development programs can be designed for each competency. Afterwards, different army units will be able to develop a curriculum for developing competencies in specific areas. For instance, the Corps and Branch responsible for technical competencies will develop a curriculum similar to the British CBT, while Army Psychology is responsible for the development of the behavioural competencies and the psychological dimensions, much like the American competencies development. On the other hand, the Mental Guidance Service of the Army is responsible for developing programs to inoculate soldiers with the institutional values of the army, which mostly were derived from Indonesia's War of Independence with the Dutch.

Integrated CBRHM

Since the implementation of PCAP more than a decade ago, the Army is finally interested in implementing an integrated CBHRM system. As can be seen from Figure 2, the competency framework will be used for a full-fledged HR system, starting from recruitment, assessment, development, performance management, career management to separation. For instance, career management and separation would be based on the competencies of the individual soldiers. Based on a talent management system, an officer's competencies would be matched against future job target. On the other hand, the Army's Personnel Officer would be responsible to find second career opportunities based on the competencies of those officers who must be separated early.

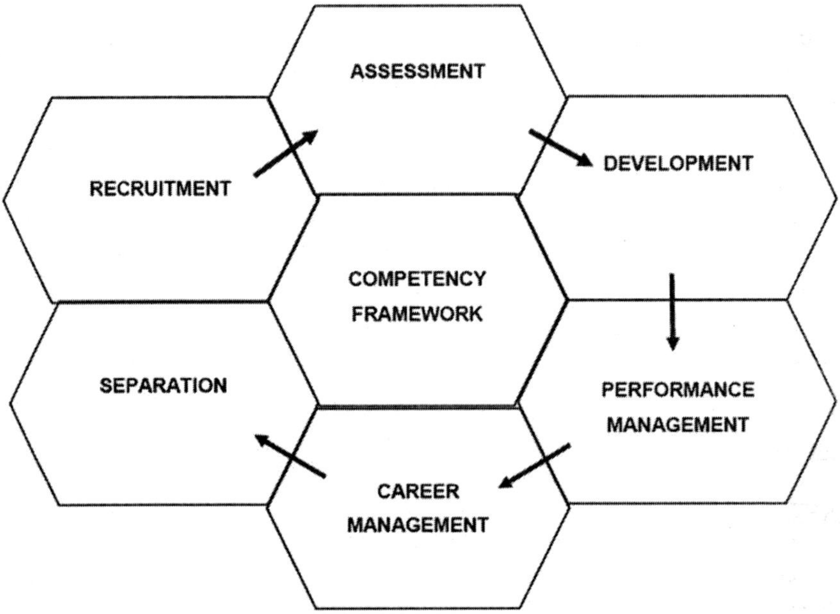

Figure 2. CBRHM in the Indonesian Army

Conclusion

In this ever-changing world, competency frameworks have been found to be a promising tool for improving organisational performance. Military organisations, which face similar problems to those in the business world, have also attempted to adopt competency frameworks to improve their organisational performance, including in the battlefield. As no nation can live in a vacuum, the Indonesian government has also declared that it will adopt CBHRM and the Assessment Centre Method to strengthen its human capital. In line with the government's reform agenda, the Indonesian Army has implemented CBHRM and used the Assessment Centre Method to select and develop its future leaders. Although the jury is still out there to determine whether this is indeed the best method to be adopted, effort should still be continued in creating more competent soldiers in the face of change.

References

Adams, K. (1996). Competency's American origins and the conflicting approaches in use today. *Competency*, 3, 44–48.

Annen, H. (2009). *Coaching for military personnel – From the idea to the implementation*. Presentation material at the 51st International Military Testing Association Conference, 2–5 November 2009, Tartu, Estonia.

Applegate, M. (2001). *Preparing for asymmetry: As seen through the lens of Joint Vision 2020* (Monograph for the US Army War College, Strategic Studies Institute). Carlisle Barracks, PA: US Army War College.

Athey, T.R., & Orth, M.S. (1999). Emerging competency methods for the future. *Human Resource Management*, 38, 215–225.

Borchert, A., & Jones, C.R. (1999). *Organizational fitness of a proposed network-centric organization*. Presentation material at the 29 June–1 July 1999 Command and Control Technology Symposium at the US Naval War College, Newport, RI.

Boyatzis, R.E. (1982). *The competent manager: A model for effective performance*. New York: John Wiley.

Byham. W.C. (1982). Applying a systems approach to personnel activities part II: Developing job-related, legally defensible personnel subsystems for training, selection and appraisal. *Training and Development Journal*, 36, 70–75.

Carroll, L. (2004). Coaching and mentoring in the Australian Army Senior Leader Development Program, *Australian Defence Force Journal*, 164, 3–30.

Cooper, S., Lawrence, E., Kierstead, J., Lynch, B., & Luce, S. (1998). *Competencies – A brief overview of development and application to public and private sectors*. Research Directorate, Policy, Research and Communications Branch, Public Service Commission of Canada, Gatineau, Quebec, Canada.

Cronin, B., Morath, R., & Smith, J. (2003, 3–6 November). *Army leadership competencies: Old wine in new bottles?* Presentation material at the 45th International Military Testing Association Conference, Pensacola, FL, USA.

Davis, E. (2007, 8–12 October). *New Zealand Defence Force Competency Framework On-Line Reporting Tool*. Presentation material at the 49th International Military Testing Association Conference, Gold Coast, Australia.

Day, M. (1989). Management competence and the charter initiative. *Personnel Management*, 21, 30–34.

Doctrine Wing. (2002). *Australian Army land warfare doctrine* (LWD 0–2, Leadership). Training and Doctrine Group, Land Warfare Development Centre: Tobruk Barracks, Puckapunyal, Victoria, Australia.

Dulewicz, V. (1991). Improving assessment centres. *Personnel Management*, 23(6), 50–54.

eitao, M.A.L.S., Thomaz, J.P.C.F., & Freire, F.J.V. (2001). *Performance evaluation of the Portuguese Army officers*. Presentation material at the 23–25 October 43rd International Military Testing Association (IMTA) conference, Canberra, Australia.

Grant, A.M. (2001). *Towards a psychology of coaching. The impact of coaching on meta cognition, mental health and goal attainment*. Phd Dissertation, Department of Psychology, Macquarie University, Sydney, Australia.

Hedge, J.W., Borman, W.C., Bruskiewicz, K.T., & Bourne, M.J. (2004). The development of an integrated performance category system for supervisory jobs in the US Navy. *Military Psychology*, 16, 231–243.

Heffernan, M.M., & Flood, P.C. (2000). An exploration of the relationships between the adoption of managerial competencies, organisational characteristics, human resource sophistication and performance in Irish organizations. *Journal of European Industrial Training*, 24, 128.

Hidayat, E.R. (2005). *A case study of the use of a competency framework in the Australian Army for performance management and development*. Unpublished Master of Human Resources Management and Coaching Research Thesis, University of Sydney, Sydney, Australia.

Horrocks, P. (1993). A case for developing generic management standards in Australia. *The Practising Manager*, 14, 18–23.

Horton, S. (2000a). Competency management in the British Civil Service. *The International Journal of Public Sector Management*, 13, 354–368.

Horton, S. (2000b). Introduction – The competency movement: Its origins and impact on the public sector. *The International Journal of Public Sector Management, 13*, 306–319.

Joint Chiefs of Staff. (1999). *Joint strategy review 1999*. Washington, DC: Author.

Kierstead, J. (1998). *Competencies and KSAOs*. James Kierstead Research Directorate. Retrieved from http://www.hrma-agrh.gc.ca/research/personnel/comp_ksao_e.pdf on 10 March 2005.

Klein, A. (1996, July/Augusty). Validity and reliability for competency-based systems: Reducing litigation risks. *Compensation and Benefits Review*, 31–38.

Kusumaningsih, S. (2013). *Implementasi kebijakan Assessment Center di lingkungan pegawai negeri Sipil* [Implementation of Assessment Center policy for civilian state employee]. Presentation material at the 3rd National Congress. Assessment Center Indonesia, 21–23 May 2013, J.W. Marriot Hotel, Jakarta, Indonesia.

MacKinnon, D. (1974). *How assessment centers were started in the United States*. Pittsburgh, PA: Development Dimensions International.

Marbun, H. (2009). *Menata Postur TN AD Sesuai Dengan Kebijakan Minimum Essential Forces Guna Mewujudkan Daya Tangkal Aspek Darat Yang Tangguh* [Developing Army Posture in Accordance with the Minimum Essential Forces Policy to Create Strong Land Defence Deterrence Power]. *Yudhagama*, 83, 11.

McCausland, J.D., & Martin, G.F. (2001). Transforming strategic leader education for the 21st-century army. *Parameters, US Army War College Quarterly*, 17–33.

McNerney, D.J., & Briggins, A. (1995). *Competency assessment gains favor among trainers. HRFocus*, 72, 19.

Morgan, W. (1955). *Spies and saboteurs*. London: Victor Gollancz Ltd.

Peterson, D.B. (1996). Executive coaching at work: The art of one-on-one change. *Consulting Psychology Journal: Practice & Research*, 48, 78–86.

Pralahad, C.K., & Hamel, G. (1990). The core competence of the corporation. *Harvard Business Review*, 68, 79–91.

Ritchie, R.J. (1994). Using the Assessment Center Method to predict senior management potential. *Consulting Psychology Journal: Practice and Research*, 46, 16–23.

Rodriguez, D., Patel, R., Bright, A., Gregory, D., & Gowing, M.K. (2002). Developing competency model to promote integrated human resource practices. *Human Resource Management*, 41, 309–324.

Rowe, T.L. (2006). *A preparation guide for the Assessment Centre Method*. Springfield, IL: Charles C. Thomas.

Scherm, M., & de Jonge, J. (2012, 5–8 November). *Coaching German Bundeswehr's military leaders: Results of an empirical evaluation*. Presentation material at the 54th International Military Testing Association Conference, Dubrovnik, Croatia.

Shen, S.P. (2002). A culture for transformational change: Strategies for the Singapore Armed Forces. *Pointer: Journal of the Singapore Armed Forces*, 28(3).

Spencer, LM., & Spencer, S.M. (1993). *Competence at work*. New York: John Wiley.

Sperry, L. (2004). *Executive coaching: The essential guide for mental health professionals*. New York: Brunner-Routledge.

Stone, R. (2005). *Human resource management* (5th ed.). Milton, Australia: John Wiley.

Storey, J., & Sisson, K. (1993). *Managing human resources and industrial relations*. Buckingham, UK: Open University Press.

Sumardi. (2016, 17 March). *Pemanfaatan Assessment Center di Kementerian Pertahanan Republik Indonesia* [The use of Assessment Center at the Ministry of Defense, Republic of Indonesia]. Presentation material at the 2nd National Seminar on Military Psychology, Grand Royal Panghegar Hotel, Bandung, Indonesia.

Tan, M., Ng, K., & Ang, S. (2015, 21–25 September). *Leadership development through executive coaching*. Presentation material at the 57th International Military Testing Association Conference, Stockholm, Sweden.

The state of competencies: ACA's research one year later. (1997). *ACA Journal*, 6, 54–61.

Thompson, M.A, Lemaire, K.C., Jacob, T.W., & Gubman, E. (1996). The role of competencies in an integrated HR strategy. *ACA Journal*, 5, 6–22.

Thornton, G.C., III, & Byham, C.C. (1982). *Assessment centers and managerial performance*. New York: Academic Press.

Townley, B. (1999). Nietzsche, competencies and Übermensch: Reflections on human and inhuman resource management. *Organization*, 6, 285–305.
Treen, D. (2000). Strategic human resources. *Ivey Business Journal*, 64, 62–67.
Walker, R. (2006). *The professional development framework: Generating effectiveness in Canadian Forces leadership*. Kingston, Ontario, CA: Canadian Forces Leadership Institute.
Wilcox, D.E. (2002, 17–19 October). *Developing a system of skill standards for the United States*. Paper presented at the International Conference on Technical and Vocational Education and Training, Winnipeg, Manitoba, Canada.
Williams, T.J. (2003). Strategic leader readiness and competencies for asymmetric warfare. *Parameters: US Army War College Quarterly*, 33, 19–36.
Wustemann, L. (2000). New dimensions to competencies: An interview with Bill Byham. *Competency & Emotional Intelligence Quarterly*, 8, 15–19.

6

Character strengths and their relevance for military officers

Ole Boe

Introduction

War is for participants a test of character. It makes bad men worse and good men better.

(Chamberlain, 1915, p. 295)

Serving in the military is for most people a challenging task. Military personnel must be able to handle situations that occur suddenly and surprisingly, with an unknown content, where outcomes of actions are characterised by a low degree of predictability (i.e. the unforeseen; Kvernbekk, Torgersen, & Moe, 2015). This requires a type of leadership often referred to as 'in extremis leadership' (Kolditz, 2010). Previous attempts to identify suitable personnel and to predict performance in the military and in other high-risk organisations have usually been based on measurements of personality (Elsass, Fiedler, Skop, & Hill, 2001: Picano & Roland, 2012; Picano, Williams, & Roland, 2006). One challenge with this is that personality is about differences between individuals when it comes to how one reacts to circumstances, while character is about the values that govern the actions and behaviour (Boe, 2013, 2015a,b,c).

Changes, uncertainty, complexity, and ambiguity characterise many modern military operational environments. These types of situations are also referred to as VUCA, an acronym used to describe the volatility, uncertainty, complexity, and ambiguity of different conditions and situations (Stiehm, 2002). An additional challenge is 'asymmetric' warfare, that is, a type of war characterised by terrorism, guerrilla warfare, and ideological manipulation (Matthews, 2014). This forces the military leader to constantly rethink the role, norms, and values in the chosen military profession (Snider & Matthews, 2012). What personal attributes does it take to be a successful soldier or officer? According to Matthews (2014), successful military personnel must be of high character, and they also need to be fair and honest in dealing with others. They also need to be both physically fit and morally courageous and be loyal to their country and to their units. Matthews (2007) had found that those who manage to get through the education at the US Military Academy well scored higher on certain character strengths as compared to those who did not perform so well. Continuing this line of thinking, Matthews (2014) also states that military personnel, more than anything else, must be tough-minded and unwilling to give up when they face difficult situations. For instance, looking at West Point candidates at the US Military Academy, it was found they scored higher than civilians did on character strengths such as bravery, honesty, leadership, teamwork, self-regulation, and persistence (Matthews, Eid, Kelly, Bailey, & Peterson, 2006). Persistence bears a close resemblance to the concept of grit as grit refers to the quality of persistence (Matthews, 2014). Building resilience through character strengths has been stated to be a very important factor when it comes to selection and education of military leaders (Boe, 2016).

Relevance of character strengths for military officers

Leadership is a potent combination of strategy and character. But if you must be without one, be without the strategy.

(General H. Norman Schwarzkopf Jr., in Kruse, 2012)

Starting around the year 2000, a new trend emerged within psychology. This new trend was the positive psychology paradigm, and since its birth, it has grown a lot as a new psychology paradigm (Weiten, 2007). Embedded within the positive psychology paradigm one will find a lot of research on different character strengths. In 2004, a character strength classification system was developed. The result was the book *Character Strengths and Virtues*. This book classifies 24 specific character strengths sorted under 6 virtues (Peterson & Seligman, 2004). Research on Peterson and Seligman's (2004) classification system has flourished over the past ten years (see Niemiec, 2013, for an overview of the research). The six virtues – wisdom and knowledge, courage, humanity, justice, temperance, and transcendence – each has a corresponding set of character strengths, which serve as psychological ingredients or pathways to these virtues. In addition, each strength needs to meet most of the following ten criteria: 'fulfilling, morally valued, does not diminish others, has non-felicitous opposites, trait-like, distinctive from other strengths, have paragons who exemplify it, has prodigies, selective absence of it in some situations, and has institutions/ rituals to celebrate or express it' (Niemiec, 2013, p. 12). For instance, the virtue *courage* entails emotional strengths that involve the exercise of one's will to accomplish goals in the face of opposition, external or internal. Included in this virtue are the character strengths *bravery* (valour), *persistence* (perseverance, industriousness), *integrity* (authenticity, honesty), and *vitality* (zest, enthusiasm, vigour, energy). Courage is a fundamental aspect for every military officer when it comes to leading others in dangerous contexts (Matthews, 2014). Elements of courage have been said to include self-volition, a worthy goal, and a significant personal risk (Lester & Pury, 2011). A person can express his or her values through one's character. This has been shown to play an important role in aspects such as leadership, adaptability, and achievement (Matthews, Eid, Kelly, Bailey, & Peterson, 2006; Gayton & Kehoe, 2015a; Picano & Roland, 2012). One way to describe character is that character is a pattern of qualities of an individual which are distinct from other human beings. This is especially in relation to moral values and mental qualities. One description of personality is that it is a set of qualities that make an individual unique. Thus, personality may be seen as generally associated with the outer appearance and behaviour of an individual. Until 2012, an empirical report of associations between the Big Five personality traits and specific character strengths has not been put forth (Littman-Ovadia,

2012). This may be seen as evidence that character strengths are something different from personality traits. Furthermore, individual character strengths have proven to be able to predict success when it comes to the selection of personnel by so-called high-risk organisations (Matthews, 2008). A recent study investigating character strengths at work revealed that curiosity, zest, hope, gratitude, and spirituality were associated with work satisfaction. This was found across different occupations (Peterson, Stephens, Park, Lee, & Seligman, 2010). In another study, specifically zest was found to be associated with both greater quality of life and work satisfaction (Peterson, Park, Hall, & Seligman, 2009).

Defining character strengths

According to the VIA Institute on Character (VIA Institute on Character, 2016), character strengths are psychological ingredients that one uses to display virtues or human goodness. They are seen as positive traits and are referred to as the capacities humans have for thinking, feeling, and behaving in such ways that benefit self and others. The character strengths all have individual differences, and they are distinct from each other. At the same time, character strengths interact and influence each other. They are seen as quite stable, but they can also change over time. In addition, character strengths are shaped by the context in which one finds oneself. Character strengths can also be seen as multidimensional. They are made up of a group of positive traits manifested in an individual's thoughts, emotions, and behaviours (Park & Peterson, 2008). Character strengths can be developed through increased vigilance and effort, and it is a phenomenon that exists along with objectives, interests, and values (Biswas-Diener, Kashdan, & Minhas, 2011).

Measuring character strengths subjectively

A self-report 240-item questionnaire has been created based on the strength classification system developed by Peterson and Seligman in 2004. This questionnaire is referred to as the Values in Action Inventory of Strengths (VIA-IS). It was constructed in 2003 and has been used by over 3 million people around the world (VIA Institute on Character, 2016). It is a well-known questionnaire for assessing character strengths. It is known to be a reliable and valid measure of character. The VIA-IS has yielded satisfactory psychometric properties in relation to all of its 24 character strengths. Cronbach's alphas were found to be generally higher than .70 (Park, Peterson, & Seligman, 2004). These results suggest that the VIA-IS is a reliable instrument to measure individual differences in character strengths. The most common method for measuring character strengths is thus the VIA-IS, but no measurement of objective character strengths was developed until around this time. Then, in an on-going research project on character strengths at the Norwegian Military Academy (NMA; Boe, 2014), such an instrument was developed (Boe, Bang, & Nilsen, 2015a) and field-tested (Bang, Boe, Nilsen, & Eilertsen, 2015; Bang, Eilertsen, Boe, & Nilsen, in press). The aim of this instrument is to obtain a measure of observable character strengths under stressful and difficult situations.

However, not all of the 24 character strengths derived by Peterson and Seligman (2004) seem to be important for military officers. One may question whether a character strength such as appreciation of beauty has any relevance for military officers. Studies have shown that this character strength scored very low on the ranking regarding which character strengths are important (Boe & Bang, 2016; in press-a; Boe, Bang, & Nilsen, 2015b; 2015c, Matthews, Eid, Kelly, Bailey, & Peterson, 2006). On the other hand, in relation to facing unforeseen situations, 12 character strengths have been found to be important for military officers (Bang & Boe, 2016; Boe, Bang, & Nilsen, 2015b; 2015c; Boe & Torgersen, 2015).

Gayton and Kehoe (2015b) asked applicants to the Australian Army Special Forces to rank themselves on 24 character strengths at the start of their selection process. The most frequently assigned character strength was integrity followed by team worker, persistence, and love of learning. Successful applicants assigned top four rank to 'team worker', which was significantly higher compared to the ranking assigned for this item measure by unsuccessful applicants. The likelihood of passing when 'team worker' was highly ranked was 2.6 times greater than without 'team worker' listed in the top ranks. Self-ratings of 'hardiness' revealed no discernible differences between successful and unsuccessful applicants, either alone or in combination with 'team worker' rankings. These results were largely consistent with the results of a previous study with a cohort of applicants for a different Australian Special Forces unit (Gayton & Kehoe, 2015a). In this study, applicants were asked to rank themselves on 24 character strengths at the beginning of their selection process. The successful applicants assigned top ranks to the following three character strengths: team worker, integrity, and persistence. Applicants who did not include any of those three character strengths in their top ranks all failed to complete the selection process. It was also found that both successful and unsuccessful applicants did not differ on physical assessments and a written test. Intelligence, combined with character and commitment, was proven to be successful in the selection of Special Forces units (Boe, 2011; Boe, Woolley, & Durkin, 2011).

The 12 most important character strengths for military officers

A series of studies conducted in the NMA´s research project on character may shed some light on which character strengths to look for in military officers or candidates (Boe & Bang, 2016; in press-a; Boe, Bang, & Nilsen, 2015b; 2015c; Boe, and Torgersen, 2015). In a study by Boe, Bang, and Nilsen (2015a), effort was made to ascertain which character strength(s) was most important for military officers to qualify. Two groups of participants, one expert group and one military group, were given a list of 24 character strengths to select from (Peterson & Seligman, 2004). It was found that the following nine character strengths were most important to both groups: leadership, integrity, persistence, bravery, teamwork, open-mindedness, social intelligence, self-regulation, and creativity. In addition, perspective, fairness, and love of learning were chosen by the military group, totalling 12 character strengths in all.

In the conducted NMA studies, military officers were asked to rate each of the 24 character strengths on a 5-point scale ranging from 1 (*not at all important*) to 5 (*very important*) as to whether the character strength was important or not for a military officer. In order to differentiate between important and less important character strengths, a cut-off score of 4.00 was used in the analyses. The 12 character strengths were given a score of 4.00 or higher by the military officers (Boe & Bang, 2016; in press a; Boe, Bang, & Nilsen, 2015b; 2015c; Boe & Torgersen, 2015). Table 1 gives an overview of the 12 most important character strengths chosen by the military officers in the previously mentioned NMA studies. The character strengths were given numbers from 1 to 24 indicating their importance in relation to other character strengths. This descending order was dependent on the mean values that the military officers assigned to each of the character strengths.

Table 1. Mean[1] values given to the 24 character strengths by military officers[2]

Character strengths	Mean (*N* = 100) Study 1	Mean (*N* = 27) Study 2	Mean (*N* = 25) Study 3	Mean (*N* = 21) Study 4
1. Leadership	4.92[3]	4.89	4.92	4.86
2. Integrity	4.82	4.85	4.76	4.76
3. Open-mindedness	4.78	4.56	4.76	4.81
4. Bravery	4.76	4.63	4.76	4.62
5. Teamwork	4.74	4.59	4.46	4.81
6. Persistence	4.58	4.78	4.76	4.71
7. Social intelligence	4.55	4.52	4.20	4.43
8. Love of learning	4.53	4.33	4.24	4.43
9. Fairness	4.47	4.59	4.52	4.42
10. Self-regulation	4.42	4.19	4.32	4.00
11. Perspective	4.22	4.26	4.08	4.29
12. Creativity	4.20	4.00	4.00	4.14
13. Hope	4.11	3.96	3.88	4.00
14. Vitality	4.11	3.85	3.68	3.76
15. Kindness	4.08	3.93	3.80	3.90
16. Forgiveness and mercy	4.02	3.93	3.72	3.90
17. Curiosity	3.99	3.89	3.84	4.58
18. Humour	3.86	3.44	3.64	3.71
19. Capacity to love	3.86	3.33	2.84	3.57
20. Gratitude	3.81	3.33	3.36	3.57
21. Humility/modesty	3.82	3.63	3.72	3.85
22. Prudence	3.79	3.56	3.52	3.90
23. Appreciation of beauty and excellence	2.90	2.81	2.76	2.76
24. Spirituality	1.85	1.85	2.16	1.90

[1] Scale ranging from 1 (*not important*) to 5 (*very important*).
[2] Standard deviations are reported in the respective studies.
[3] Character strengths in Study 2, 3, and 4 are based on the descending order of the character strengths chosen for Study 1.

As can be seen from Table 1, in the study with 100 military officers (Study 1: Boe, Bang, & Nilsen, to be submitted), 16 character strengths were given a score of 4.00 or higher. These were in descending order: leadership, integrity, open-mindedness, bravery, teamwork, persistence, social intelligence, love of learning, fairness, self-regulation, perspective, creativity, hope, vitality, kindness, and forgiveness and mercy. In Study 2 (Boe, Bang, & Nilsen, 2015b) and Study 3 (Boe, Bang, & Nilsen, 2015c), only 12 out of the 16 character strengths chosen in Study 1 were given a score of 4.00 or higher and thereby chosen to be the most important. The character strengths hope, vitality, kindness, and forgiveness and mercy were not chosen as important in the other studies. In Study 4 (Bang, Eilertsen, Boe, & Nilsen, in press), the character strength 'curiosity' was chosen as an important measure. However, in total, 'curiosity' was ranked as number 17 out of the 24 character strengths used in the larger study (Study 1).

A common theme found in all studies is that the chosen 12 character strengths are mainly related to justice, wisdom and knowledge, and courage. Leadership, teamwork, and fairness are three character strengths that belong to the virtue 'justice'. Open-mindedness, love of learning, perspective, and creativity are character strengths found under the domain of the virtue 'wisdom and knowledge'. Bravery, persistence, and integrity are related to the virtue 'courage'. One of the character strengths, social intelligence, is related to the virtue 'humanity', whereas no character strengths were chosen by the study participants as important under the virtue 'transcendence' for military officers. One character strength, self-regulation, was chosen under the domain of the virtue 'temperance'. It is thus interesting to note that the 12 selected character strengths cover 5 out of 6 core virtues included in Peterson and Seligman's (2004) taxonomy.

Another common finding in all studies has been that the two character strengths – appreciation of beauty and excellence, and spirituality – were clearly regarded as not important by military officers. Appreciation of beauty and excellence and spirituality scored, respectively, as character strength 23 and 24 out of the 24 character strengths. Regarding spirituality, it is important that the low importance given to this character strength may simply reflect the tendency for Norwegian military officers to be very secularised. Religion does not seem to play any role in the Norwegian society, and as military officers are drawn from the civilian society they simply are not very spiritual. As also can be seen from Table 1, there are only minor differences between the four NMA studies when it comes to the ranking of the 12 most important character strengths. In all four studies, the same 12 character strengths were among the chosen ones.

Matthews (2011) surveyed US Army captains who just had returned from combat rotations in Iraq and Afghanistan. He was interested in finding out which character strengths these officers had used to deal effectively in combat situations. In descending order from the most used character strengths, the character strengths used were teamwork, bravery, capacity to love, persistence, and honesty ('honesty' is labelled 'integrity' in the NMA studies referred to earlier). When life is on the line, either your own life or that of your fellow soldiers, or when you are forced to take lives, these character strengths seemed to matter most. Contrasting this, the least used character strengths in combat were prudence, spirituality, curiosity, creativity, and appreciation of beauty. Matthews's findings corroborate well with the NMA studies. In addition, several of the character strengths found to be used by combat leaders as reported in Matthews' study (2011) were also chosen by the NMA officers to be important. However, in contrast to Matthew´s study, the character strength 'capacity to love' was not chosen as important as reported in the NMA studies. The reason for this may be that the NMA cadets did not think specifically of combat when deciding on which character strengths were important for military officers. In contrast, it is very likely that the character strength 'capacity for love' might be more important in combat situations for Norwegian military officers. 'Capacity for love' in combat refers to the ability to love and to take care of the men and women in your unit. Looking at combat situations, Park (2005) investigated the content analysis of the narratives accompanying US Congressional Medal of Honor recipients. Park found that 100 per cent of the recipients were brave, and their next highest character strengths were self-regulation, persistence, leadership, and teamwork. The character strengths chosen as the most important in the abovementioned NMA studies corroborate well with Park's study.

Measuring character strengths objectively

An observational instrument measuring character strengths has been developed (Boe, Bang, & Nilsen, 2015a) based on the results from the

NMA studies. The instrument is referred to as OBServation of Character in Field (OBSCIF; Bang, Boe, Nilsen, & Eilertsen, 2015: Bang, Eilertsen, Boe, & Nilsen, in press). OBSCIF uses the 12 character strengths previously chosen in the NMA studies by military officers to be important (Boe, Bang, and Nilsen, to be submitted; 2015b; 2015c; Bang, Eilertsen, Boe, & Nilsen, in press). In addition, an assessment study of the NMA's chosen methods of measuring character strengths has been conducted (Boe, Heiskel, Grande, & Bang, in press). In this study, data were collected during a field exercise with high physical and psychological stress. Military cadets from the NMA filled out self-reports and were observed by both fellow cadets and experienced instructors during the field exercise. Both categories of cadets, that is, fellow cadets and the experienced instructors, used the OBSCIF developed by Boe, Bang, and Nilsen (2015a). The results showed significant correlations within the used methods, which can mean some character strengths are best suited for measurement through self-report and others through observation. The combination of the methods self-reporting and observation was found to be likely a correct choice for the NMA in order to assess the performance of military officers in VUCA situations. However, more research should be carried out to reduce different sources of error associated with the measurement of character (Boe, Heiskel, Grande, & Bang, in press). Two other studies have been conducted using the OBSCIF, and the results will be reported shortly (Bang, Boe, Nilsen, & Eilertsen, to be submitted-a-b). Scores on the 12 character strengths measured by self-evaluations on VIA-IS and OBSCIF have been found to correlate significantly with each other, indicating that OBSCIF is a valid measure of the 12 character strengths. In addition, reliability coefficients (Cronbach's alphas) estimated for the 12 scales in OBSCIF are all within acceptable levels, indicating that OBSCIF provides reliable measures of the 12 character strengths.

Conclusion

This chapter has dealt with character strengths and their relevance for military officers. In addition, a discussion on subjective and objective measures of character strengths was done. The conducted NMA studies show considerable consistency at least among Norwegian military officers as to which character strengths are considered to be the most important for military officers. Most of the findings from the NMA studies described in this chapter correlate to a high degree with other conducted studies, indicating that certain character strengths are more relevant and important for military officers than other character strengths.

In sum, a promising perspective on selecting personnel to the military and educating personnel who already are in the military are emerging. As such, it may also have applicability for other high-risk organisations. However, more work will be needed as the number of participants in the NMA studies until now has been quite low. Future research on character strengths should focus upon the whole spectrum of leadership, from small unit leadership to high command in the military. This may reveal if there are certain clusters of character strengths or specific character strengths required for successful leaders at different levels of leadership.

References

Bang, H., Boe, O., Nilsen, F.A., & Eilertsen, D. E (2015). Evaluating character strengths in cadets during a military field exercise: Consistency between different evaluation sources. *EDULEARN Proceedings*, 7076–7082.

Bang, H., Boe, O., Nilsen, F.A., & Eilertsen, D.E. (to be submitted a). Testing an observational instrument (OBSCIF) for evaluating character strengths in army cadets during military field exercises. Oslo, Norway: Norwegian Military Academy.

Bang, H., Boe, O., Nilsen, F.A., & Eilertsen, D.E. (to be submitted b). *Which character strengths are the best predictors of army cadets' performance in military field exercise?* Oslo, Norway: Norwegian Military Academy.

Bang, H., Eilertsen, D.E., Boe, O., & Nilsen, F.A. (in press). Development of an observational instrument (OBSCIF) for evaluating character strengths in army cadets. *EDULEARN Proceedings*.

Biswas-Diener, R., Kashdan, T.B., & Minhas, G. (2011). A dynamic approach to psychological strength development and intervention. *Journal of Positive Psychology, 6*, 106–118.

Boe, O. (2011). *How to find leaders that will be able to face and solve problematic decisions in an operational context?* Proceedings of the 13th International Military Health Conference (13IMMHC), 35–42.

Boe, O. (2014). Prosjektbeskrivelse for KS FoU-prosjekt: Karakter hos militære offiserer [Project description for NMAs research and development project: Character in military officers]. *Research Project Applied for to the Norwegian Military Academy*, 1–39.

Boe, O. (2015a). Developing leadership skills in Norwegian military officers: Leadership proficiencies contributing to character development and officer competency. *Procedia-Social and Behavioral Sciences*, 186, 288–292.

Boe, O. (2015b). Character in military leaders, officer competency and meeting the unforeseen. *Procedia-Social and Behavioral Sciences*, 190, 497–501.

Boe, O. (2015c). Selecting personnel for high-risk and security jobs. Why character and character strengths matters. International Military Testing Association Presentations 2004–2015. file:///C:/Users/olboe/Downloads/2015112P.pdf

Boe, O. (2016). Building resilience: The role of character strengths in the selection and education of military leaders. *International Journal of Emergency Mental Health and Human Resilience*, 17, 714–716.

Boe, O. (2013). *Leadership development in Norwegian junior military officers: A conceptual framework of building mission-solving competency.* Proceedings of the 16th International Military Mental Health Conference (16IMMHC).

Boe, O., & Bang, H. (2016, 23–26 May). *The big 12: The most important character strengths for officers*. Psychology Abstracts: Tenth Annual International Conference on Psychology, Athens, Greece, Athens Institute for Education and Research (ATINER), p. 22.

Boe, O., & Bang, H. (in press-a). Assessing the correlation between character strengths and mental toughness in military officers. *Procedia-Social and Behavioral Sciences.*

Boe, O., & Torgersen, G.-E. (2015). *When encountering the unforeseen, which character strengths are most important for military leaders?* 24th SRA-E Programme and Proceedings, p. 108.

Boe, O., Bang, H., & Nilsen, F.A. (2015a). The development of an observational instrument in order to measure character strengths. *Procedia-Social and Behavioral Sciences*, 197, 1126–1133.

Boe, O., Bang, H., & Nilsen, F.A. (2015b). Selecting the most relevant character strengths for Norwegian Army officers: An educational tool. *Procedia-Social and Behavioral Sciences*, 197, 801–809.

Boe, O., Bang, H., & Nilsen, F.A. (2015c). Experienced military officer's perception of important character strengths. *Procedia-Social and Behavioral Sciences*, 190, 339–345.

Boe, O., Bang, H., & Nilsen, F.A. (to be submitted). *Investigating the 12 most important character strengths for military officers*. Oslo, Norway: Norwegian Military Academy.

Boe, O., Eldal, L., Hjortmo, H., Jensen, A.L., Holth, T., Kjørstad, O., & Nilsen, F. (2014). *Offisersutvikling: NMA konsept for lederutvikling* [Officer development: NMAs concept of leadership development]. Oslo, Norway: Norwegian Military Academy.

Boe, O., Heiskel, B.-A., Grande, Ø.M., & Bang, H. (in press). *Measuring character strengths*. International Military Testing Association Presentations 2016.

Boe, O., Woolley, K., & Durkin, J. (2011). Choosing the elite: Examples of the use of recruitment, assessment, and selection programs in Law Enforcement Tactical Teams and Special Forces. In P. Sweeney, M. Matthews, & P.B. Lester (eds), *Leading in dangerous contexts* (pp. 333–349). Annapolis, MD: Naval Institute Press.

Chamberlain, J.L. (1915). *The passing of armies: An account of the final campaign of the army of the Potomac.* New York: G.P. Putnam.

Elsass, W.P., Fiedler, E., Skop, B., & Hill, H. (2001). Susceptibility to maladaptive responses to stress in basic military training based on variants of temperament and character. *Military Medicine,* 166, 884–888.

Gayton, S.D., & Kehoe, E. J (2015a, February). A prospective study of character strengths as predictors of selection into the Australian Army Special Forces. *Military Medicine,* 180, 151–157.

Gayton, S.D., & Kehoe, E.J. (2015b). Character strengths and hardiness of Australian Army Special Forces applicants. *Military Medicine,* 180, 857–862.

Kolditz, T.A. (2010). *In extremis leadership: Leading as if your life depended on it.* San Francisco, CA: Jossey Bass.

Kvernbekk, T., Torgersen, G-E., & Moe, I.B. (2015). Om begrepet det uforutsette [About the concept of the unforeseen]. In G.-E. Torgersen (ed.), *Pedagogikk for det uforutsette* [Pedagogics for the unforeseen; pp. 28–55]. Bergen, Norway: Fagbokforlaget.

Lester, P.B., & Pury, C. (2011). What leaders should know about courage. In P. Sweeney, M. Matthews, & P.B. Lester (eds), *Leading in dangerous contexts* (pp. 21–39). Annapolis, MD: Naval Institute Press.

Littman-Ovadia, H., & Lavy, S. (2012). Character strengths in Israel: Hebrew adaptation of the VIA Inventory of Strengths. *European Journal of Psychological Assessment,* 28, 41–50.

Matthews, M.D. (2014). *Head strong: How psychology is revolutionizing war.* New York: Oxford University Press.

Matthews M.D., Eid, J., Kelly, D., Bailey, J.K., & Peterson, C (2006). Character strengths and virtues of developing military leaders: An international comparison. *Military Psychology,* 18, 557–568.

Matthews, M.D. (2007, August). *Where eagles soar: Positive character and success at West Point.* Paper presented at the Annual Meeting of the American Psychological Association, San Francisco, CA.

Matthews, M.D. (2008). Positive psychology: Adaptation, leadership, and performance in exceptional circumstances. In P.A. Hancock & J.L. Szalma (eds), *Performance under stress* (pp. 163–180). Aldershot, UK: Ashgate.

Matthews, M.D. (2011, August). *Character strengths and post-adversity growth in combat leaders.* Paper presented at the Annual Meeting of the American Psychological Association, Washington, DC.

Niemiec, R. (2013). VIA character strengths: Research and practice (the first 10 years). In H.H. Knoop & A. Delle Fave (eds), *Well-being and cultures: Perspectives from positive psychology*. Dordrecht, Netherlands: Springer.

Park, N. (2005, August). *Congressional Medal of Honor recipients: A positive psychology perspective*. Paper presented at the Annual Meeting of the American Psychological Association, Washington, DC.

Park, N., & Peterson, C. (2008). Positive psychology and character strengths: Application to strengths-based school counseling. *Professional School Counseling*, 12, 85–92.

Park, N., Peterson, C., & Seligman, M.E.P. (2004). Strengths of character and well-being. *Journal of Social and Clinical Psychology*, 2, 603–619.

Peterson, C., & Seligman, E.P. (2004). *Character strengths and virtues: A handbook and classification*. Oxford, UK: Oxford University Press.

Peterson, C., Park, N., Hall, N., & Seligman, M.E.P. (2009). Zest and work. *Journal of Organizational Behavior*, 30, 161–172.

Peterson, C., Stephens, J.P., Park, N., Lee, F., & Seligman, M.E.P. (2010). Strengths of character and work. In P.A. Linley, S. Harrington, & N. Page (eds), *Handbook of positive psychology and work* (pp. 221–231). New York: Oxford University Press.

Picano, J., & Roland, R.R. (2012). *Assessing psychological suitability for high-risk military jobs*. In J.H. Laurence & M.D. Matthews (eds), *The Oxford handbook of military psychology* (pp. 148–157). New York: Oxford University Press.

Picano, J., Roland, R.R., Rollins, K.D., & Williams, T.J. (2002). Development and validation of a sentence completion test measure of defensive responding in military personnel assessed for non-routine missions. *Military Psychology*, 14, 279–98.

Snider, D., & Matthews, L.J. (2012). *The future of the army profession* (2nd ed.). Boston: McGraw-Hill.

Stiehm, J.H. (2002). *The US Army War College: Military education in a democracy*. Philadelphia, PA: Temple University Press.

VIA Institute on Character. (2016). *Frequently asked questions*. Retrieved from http://www.viacharacter.org/www/About-Institute/FAQs

Weiten, W. (2007). *Psychology: Themes and variations*. New York: Thomson/ Wadsworth.

7

Cyber-psychology and the soldier of the future

Cristian Dobre

Introduction

The chapter identifies and discusses certain aspects related to influence which cyber-warfare will play against emotions and behaviour of the world's future soldiers. Most of these aspects can be explained with help of cyber-psychology.

Cybernetic warfare – a new dimension of security

Humanity's fight for resources has always been a violent one and represented a confrontation between people, countries, empires, and non-governmental entities which never ceased to exist.

However, with time, this fight slowly became more humane and sensible. Regardless of this, in essence, the fight still carries the same purpose: to gather as many resources as possible. Not only the world or local wars, civil wars, invasions, revolutions but also diplomatic and financial conflicts all represent ways that have been used to achieve the main purpose of the war on resources.

War, as an extreme manifestation of political will, has gradually extended its boundaries of confrontation from the ground, to the sea, air, subaquatic, social, economic, diplomatic, and last but not least, cybernetic environments. Based on this, the ways through which enemies can be hurt have expanded from close-range physical objects such as swords and axes, to objects which can hit from a distance such as bullets, rockets, and bombs, and later to virtual objects which have an unlimited rate of fire, and action, such as cybernetic software.

The legal framework meant for carrying out wars has also gradually changed with history. The legal conditions of warfare have diversified as well throughout history. With this in mind, we can identify, by multiple criteria, various forms of wars, such as those of conquest/invasion, defence, ideological, religious, imposing democracy, rescue, reunion, punitive, winning power, liberation, independence, and so on.

The ethics of war also had multiple changes throughout history. While hundreds of years ago, killing tens of thousands of people with the help of cruel methods, without discrimination represented proof of bravery; with time, wars have begun targeting combatants who are clearly defined with the help of sophisticated international conventions.

While moratoriums on development of new weapons (e.g. nuclear, biological and chemical) or escalation of the arms race in certain environments (e.g. space) are considered illegal and strongly frowned upon by international conventions, other forms of warfare are quickly developing. We are talking of course about psychologic, economic and cybernetic warfare. These forms of aggression are not contained in international treaties, but their ethic principles are confusing and these types of warfare do not have to be publicly declared, before being triggered by a state or non-state entity against another. Moreover, these forms of violence can also be used during times of peace.

In the following sections, we'll talk about cyber-warfare and its psychological effects on the combatants and on the public.

The end of the second millennium and the beginning of this millennium brought a development without precedent, especially in the past 30 years, given the advances made in electronics, telecommunication and information technology. In turn, this brought in the revolution of cybernetics, which gave people from all around the world almost unlimited access to the virtual environment.

If at first this new virtual environment was the exclusive prerogative of super-secret laboratories of the great powers, gradually, the civil society was given access to this new space. The virtual environment can now be read and used by just about anyone with basic tech knowledge and internet access.

This virtual environment, immaterial by its nature, can be viewed as a new dimension accessible by the human kind. The virtual environment was quickly integrated into the human psychology and gradually created cyber-culture and cyber-psychology.

Cyber-psychology: definition and role

The definition of cyber-psychology is intrinsically linked to the manifestation of the human environment in the cyberspace. Thus, we consider that cyber-psychology is a branch of psychology that studies general multidimensional manifestation of personality in the virtual environment defined earlier.

Research in this area was timidly started in the early 2000s but expanded rapidly with the explosion of social networks and the web of online communication in cyberspace.

This manner of communication on the internet has quickly become a genuine 'necessity' and created millions of dependents, which is manifested by behavioural and emotional changes.

The cyberspace is also used for tasks such as storing data, design new products, circulation of information, and so on.

Cyber-psychology research has focused on several areas, including the following:

Impact of virtual environment on the human personality

It is estimated that the cyberspace has opened a new dimension of human perception, which enables one to move more freely than in the other three physical dimensions (length, width and height), already known and described as 'too restrictive'. The size of the virtual-cybernetic provides a mechanism through which one may achieve more freedom and derive satisfaction and contentment in different forms, in a manner more pronounced than we're already used to.

Accessibility of cyberspace

This approach is related to studying the mechanisms of human adaptation in general but especially in relation to the impact that cyberspace has on people depending on their age. For example, younger generations feel great when navigating in cyberspace in order to quickly process information, which allows them to adapt well. It has also been demonstrated that the tools that can be accessed through the cyberspace – computers, laptops, phones, tablets, TVs, and gaming consoles – are becoming increasingly more accessible to the general public, thanks to friendly interfaces on cyberspace, which allows people, regardless of their race, age, sex, religion, level of education, and so on, to join the cyberspace.

Research has also shown that an increasing number of children are capable of fluently using electronic devices prior to being able to speak and walk.

Changes in the personality traits and cognitive performance in individuals while browsing in the cyberspace

The analysis of this issue has revealed that the thought processes, memory, imagination, emotions, attitudes, opinions, concepts, and so on radically change when people browse the internet. The main changes are related not only to the increasing the speed of data processing but also the content being accessed. While contact with the traditional physical environment decreases, the mind tends to adapt to the new virtual environment.

The fundamental differences between the real world, which is full of all sorts of limitations, and the virtual world, which has no limitations imposed upon it, have also been taken into consideration by researchers.

The virtual world allows each user to define their status and role, which can play a positive role in personal development and increasing self-confidence. However, it is not clear to what extent. The increase in cyberspace users' cognitive performance is explained by the amplified speed of data processing that contributes to solving problems often met in the virtual environment. Thus, cyberspace allows the use of programs that provide humans with solutions to all types of problems. This favours a shortening in the analysis that stimulates the decision and, thus, the dynamics of the individual cognitive processes.

Redefining of the ego

Traditionally, the ego each person builds is reported to the system of reference within which he or she lives. Thus, it is estimated that individuals who live and think in the physical world are connected to the realities of this world, be it good or bad, pleasant or not. For example, a carpenter who is a family man defines reality in relation to the everyday projects that he works on, the financial gain that allows him to support his family, and his loved ones. The same mechanism works in other trades and occupations.

The mechanisms for Ego building are restructured to the new reality perceived by the individual, even if it is one that doesn't have much in common with the physical world in which the subject lives. The individual learns thus to live with his avatar and to satisfy all its needs, the physical body, relationships with parents, family, and friends, alongside the real social obligations dictated by the laws of society, and so on, thus becoming a non-adaptive, or as experts call it, a 'cyber-addict'.

Preventing and treating cyber-addiction

The opening of a number of increasingly large portals for access to cyberspace and the increase in product quality considerably increase the attractiveness of the virtual environment. When compared to the hardships of the real world, more people tend to focus on the latter, thus forgetting about their real world needs and only satisfying those in the online environment. Based on this, a deepening detachment from reality takes place and the virtual world gradually forms.

Psychological consequences of this slide are comprehensive and complex. At this moment, this kind of personality disorder is not caught yet in the code of psychiatric disorders, although an increasing number of specialists strive to help those detached from the real world to re-join it.

Typical manifestations of this addiction are: neglecting one's body (they do not eat and drink), bystanders (family, friends, colleagues, etc.), and social functions (work, study, relief other peers, etc.), while also taking part in substance abuse (drugs) and losing the notion of time.

The emergence of optical illusions and/or hallucinations includes the adoption of unnatural behaviour such as social isolation, radical change of emotions, and adopting a new language. Another strong effect is giving up their identity in favour of the virtual character, which has an identity that is often better in every way when compared to the real identity of the person affected by cyber-addiction.

The main forms of recovery are targeted at reducing and offering controlled access to the internet, redefining social motivations of the person and also the development of a personal inventory of activities that prove to be imperative, and progressing connections between the affected individual and other people around him.

Mechanisms of interaction between an individual and computer

This field of cyber-psychology seeks to identify the most appropriate technical means to connect to the virtual world human psyche. One thing that can be said about this area of activity is that it has much in common with the principle of ergonomics, as it aims to create the most appropriate human–machine interfaces for networking. Developments in recent years, illustrated by the creation of new tools to access the cyberspace, alongside friendly and adaptable software that takes account of human psychological needs, can bring in success in this area.

The electronic games championships, which bring together millions of fans and hundreds of performers, is only one of many examples of success in the prevention of cyber-addiction and improving the means of interaction between humans and computer.

Other devices such as virtual reality headsets further facilitate the access to the virtual environment. Such devices can be used for gaming purposes, but there are also functionalities which allow virtual actions to have effects in the physical environment, thus once again defying the boundary of interaction between humans and machines.

Using the virtual environment for the benefit of humans

This area of research seems inexhaustible and continues to be developed with consistently. It was encouraged by the growing access of people to the virtual environment, and thus, the increasing number of internet users. The areas of development are different, but, for example, we can mention the following: distance learning through virtual platforms, developing cheap and high speed communication systems, the ability to connect simultaneously to more than one person, the possibility of simulations in all fields, developing 'e-therapy and counselling'; developing programs for fun and relaxation; appearance of virtual libraries; execution of financial transactions; design of new products; development of intuitive search engines; broadcasting news and other online media; storage, directing, and controlling technical equipment; viewing images/movies from specific target areas; and trading, buying, and more.

Architecture of interpersonal relationships in cyberspace

This field of study seeks ways of allowing people to interact in the virtual space.

The appearance of social media platforms such as Facebook constitute real evidence of the development in this field of study. As more and more people get access to such platforms, cyber-psychology and organisational psychology become even more important in these fields.

Studying human behaviour, comparatively, in cyberspace and in real life

This area of interest arose from empirical observations and is currently being based with the help of research studies. Understanding more about the psychology of the modern fighter when put into a relationship with the virtual environment is essential for getting a better understanding of people's limits while also seeing what traits the modern fighter should have. For example, a fighter can adopt a behaviour characterised by increased safety and precision when using the keys of a computer compared to the situation when you press the trigger of a firearm. However, exposure to physical hazards and disturbances are much lower.

Comparative study of emotions in cyberspace with emotions in the physical environment

This has highlighted significant differences in the emotions of the subjects when carrying out the same activity in both the virtual environment and the real environment.

The differences vary depending on several factors, among which we can mention: the personality characteristics of the individual, his or her familiarity with the real world versus the virtual environment, situational context to perform a certain activity, the consequences of the action, and so on.

Some subjects were completely detached from real world; however, they have shown intense emotions in the virtual world (e.g. love for virtual characters and sensations such as pleasure, pain, panic, anger, joy, etc.).

When the soldiers were asked to execute combat missions in cyberspace, with real-life consequences, researchers have found a reduction in the negative emotions (guilt), absence of PTSD, more concentration on the mission along with a low level of negative emotions, and encouragement arising from being happy for having achieved the goal.

Studying the ways through which access to cyber world can be limited

The entry into the cyberspace gives access to the 'residents' of that environment to great deal of information which is often extremely important. This could change the balance of power so that human entities will be better informed ascendancy over the other. For this reason, organisations controlling certain segments of cyberspace may try to limit unauthorised access to certain areas. The limitation, conditioning, or prohibition of access to certain areas of cyberspace is most often through systems of codes and passwords. These actions generate offensive reactions, boosting efforts to break the codes or passwords and thus enter into prohibited areas. These actions are based on psychological mechanisms which have been studied by researchers before.

The relationship between the cyber world and the real world in terms of security may be that people often choose passwords which have actual meanings for them outside the virtual environment, such as their birth date, name of children, spouse, other relatives, or pets.

Disruption of navigation in the cyberspace

This step is aggressive because through the use of cyber viruses navigation in cyberspace is negatively affected. Viruses penetrate unwilling 'inhabitants' of cyberspace through different ways and end up causing destruction of programming elements and also slow down operating systems, steal information, and so on.

These consequences are reflected directly in the mental stability of the person or entity which becomes the target in cyberspace. Often, the consequences of cyber-attacks is reflected in all physical environments (land, sea, underwater, space) and can produce dramatic consequences of all kinds. Some subjects feel devastated, as they lose their online persona, online wealth, and so on. The destructive actions of viruses shall be counteracted by antiviruses to take care of the device being used to access the internet.

Using cyberspace as a battlefield/theatre of military operations

This approach aims, as in any military confrontation, to obtain cyber supremacy, and of course, to win. The purpose of winning this confrontation is explained in large part by imposing the interests of an entity, to others and to facilitate access to resources, including virtual ones. Fighting means used in cyberspace are different, stretching from a wide array of methods, from the destruction of hardware support to actions of subtlety which allow the attackers to access the secret files, steal valuable information and cause disruptions in the operation of equipment in the physical space (nuclear, weapons systems, financial flows, precision machinery, space systems etc.). As you can practically control anything in the physical world through the use of a mouse and keyboard, the costs are much lower, while the psychological impact that the user gets is also a lot more controllable.

Cyber-psychology versus the psychology of cybernetics

While these two terms do seem similar, there is a clear difference between the two fields of study.

Thus, while cyber-psychology is suited to the elements that have been described in the article, the psychology of cybernetics is much older, being born with the appearance of the first cybernetics. The parents of Cybernetics are Romanian scientist Stefan Odobleja, who published 'Psychologie Consonantiste', Publishing Maloine, Paris (1938) and the

American scientist Norbert Wiener, who wrote the book 'Cybernetics or Control and Communication in the Animal and the Machine' (1948).

The psychology of cybernetics was first developed under the premise of introducing scientific methods to assess psychological manifestations. Thus, gradually, other ideas have developed in this area, such as psychometry (linked to the name of Lee Loevinger), ergonomics (related to study human-machine of Colin Topper), computer psychology (the idea of focusing on the human being as a cybernetic system, which processes cybernetic information), and more.

Psychological implications of cyberspace on the emotions and behaviour of military personnel

Cyber-psychology, as shown, has become an environment of military confrontation.

News such as 'Company X website has been blocked by hackers ...,' 'Z country has undergone a major cyber-attack ...,' 'intelligence networks have been revealed Y of ...,' 'debit/credit cards of a number of citizens from the city were cloned,' 'electricity network in the town fell due to a cyber-attack,' 'W Nuclear Plant could not be started due to a cyber-attack ...,' 'a military satellite was hijacked due to the action of a hacker ...,' 'a virus has entered a nuclear missile control system ...' have become mainstream in the last couple of years.

All these are the result of combat actions organised by various state or non-state entities in cyberspace.

To counter such acts of aggression, governments and companies allocate annual budgets, and, in some military institutions, cyber-defence departments were set up and given the role of fighting hackers in the cyberspace.

Considering that cyberspace is now directly linked with physical space, and a distortion of it is reflected almost immediately in the lives of millions of people, the cyber environment has also become crucial in the security environment.

Because of the issues that have been outlined above, people have started asking many more questions, including how the future looks like for soldiers, what should soldiers to do protect themselves in the cyberspace, how are soldiers emotionally affected when using the internet to attack and eliminate targets, should pre- and post-mission training be offered, what should be the ethical code of using cyberspace for military operations, what does the legislative framework in this area state, how much freedom should people have in the cyberspace, and so on.

The answers of all these questions are going to offer the configuration of future soldier.

The aim of this article is not to answer the questions mentioned above but rather to signal some of the issues that we'll have to deal with in the near future.

The extent to which armies from all around the world train their officers and soldiers to perform in the cyberspace will most likely reflect the future hold on the Earth's most important resources.

Reference

Barlow, J.P. (1990). *Crime and puzzlement.* Available from: http://www.eff.org/~barlow/

Berger, P., & Luckmann, T. (1967). *Social construction of reality.* New York: Anchor Books.

Dobre, C. (2013). *Diplomatic psychology (Psihologie diplomatic□).* Bucharest, Hungary: National Defense University Print House.

Geertz, C. (1993). *The interpretation of cultures.* London: Fontana Press.

Kitchin, R. (1998). *Theoretical perspective: Approaching cyberspace. Cyberspace: The world in the wires.* New York: Wiley.

Leary, T., & Horowitz, M. (Ed.). (1994). *Chaos and cyberculture.* Berkeley, CA: Ronin Publishing.

Lévy, P. (2000). *Kyberkultura.* Praha: Karolinum.

Macek, J. (2004). *Defining Cyberculture,* http://macek.czechian.net/defining_cyberculture.htm.

Suler, J. (1996). *The psychology of cyberspace.* Available from: http://truecenterpublishing.com/psycyber/psycyber.html

Whittle, D.B. (1997). *Cyberspace: The human dimension.* New York: W.H. Freeman.

8

Research and teaching of military psychology at the Swiss Military Academy

Hubert Annen

Introduction

The Chair of Military Psychology of the Swiss Military Academy at the Swiss Federal Institute of Technology in Zurich (in German: Eidgenössische Technische Hochschule or ETH Zurich; academy abbreviation: MILAK/ETHZ) conducts research on the psychological aspects of selection, training, motivation, and leadership of military personnel. The respective research activities are the foundation of the lectures on the different levels of education for prospective and experienced career officers. In order to bridge the gap between theory and practice the relevant contents must be taught with a clear focus on application and using methods, which foster critical thinking and individual processing of the lesson content.

Holistic model of military psychological

the Swiss Armed Forces' experience in war or war-like operations is sparse and, as a consequence, a general and prevention-oriented approach is needed for military psychological activities, which led to a holistic model (Annen, 2014; see Figure 1) that is based on the following hypotheses (Annen, Nakkas, & Gehring, in press):

- Stress is a result of perceived excessive demands. With scientifically sound and professionally conducted selection procedures one should be able to ensure that military personnel and specifically military cadres are not overstrained by the demands of their job.
- Motivated people are less stressed. Thus, with continuous research on motivation, the relevant motivators in everyday military life as well as in more demanding situations can be identified. This results in valuable suggestions to personnel management and the training and education of leaders.
- Bad leaders can be a huge stressor. Thus, various measures to foster the self-reflection of military cadre on every hierarchical level have been initiated as this has a pivotal role in their development and advancement as credible and competent leaders.

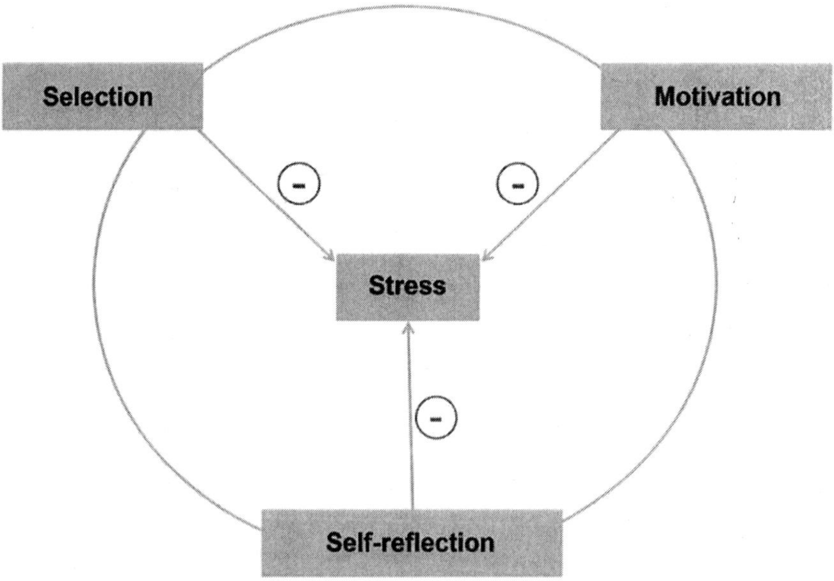

Based on this model and largely regardless of the current tasks and missions of the Swiss Armed Forces, it is possible to conduct purposeful research, to create meaningful content for lectures in military psychology and to give useful advice.

This includes for instance the operational responsibility for several selection procedures, with an emphasis on the assessment centres for prospective professional officers and professional NCOs respectively (Annen, Eggimann, & Ebert, 2012). These instruments are routinely evaluated, and the results of these scientific evaluations are used to optimise the assessment centres themselves and are also presented to the scientific community through publications and conference presentations (e.g. Melchers & Annen, 2010; Merkulova, Melchers, Kleinmann, Annen, & Szvircsev Tresch, 2014). When considering leadership issues the topics of motivation, self-awareness, and stress are of paramount importance. With regard to motivation, researches in Organisational Citizenship Behaviour as well as cadre motivation are of the greatest significance for the Swiss Armed Forces as a militia organisation (Annen, Goldammer, & Szvircsev Tresch, 2015). The willingness and ability for systematic and recurrent self-reflection is a pivotal attribute of a good leader; thus, recent research projects have focused on the accuracy and motivational aspects of self-appraisal, the effects of coaching, and the importance of military values and virtues on various hierarchal levels. Stress and stress management in basic military training is part of a comprehensive research project that will lead into a subsequent study on the benefits of resilience training in cadre schools. Regarding combat stress and war-related stress disorders, the lessons learned by military organisations with more experience in combat deployments, such as the US Army and Israel Defense Forces, have proven especially helpful (e.g. Matthews, 2014). This scientific research forms the foundation of teaching military psychology at the Swiss Military Academy.

Education of professional officers in the Swiss Armed Forces

The Military Academy at ETH Zurich (MILAK/ETHZ) is the educational institution for the professional officers of the Swiss Armed Forces. The educational objectives are directed such that prospective professional officers can acquire and develop the following abilities:

- to perform as didactically skilled and technically competent instructors;

- to act as goal-oriented and effective leaders applying principles of management by objectives;
- to adopt a committed stance on military matters based on expertise in military sciences;
- to offer scientifically based views on non-military issues of a political, social, economic, and ecological nature.

Prospective professional officers holding an upper-secondary degree first complete the Bachelor Study Course (BSC) lasting 3.5 years or, if they already hold a university degree, the 18-month Diploma Study Course (DSC). On completion of their course, the professional officers assume their duties as company commanders, mentors of the militia cadre, or instructors at recruit and cadre schools. After five to eight years practice most of these officers attend specific Supplementary Training Courses, which prepare them for functions such as school commandants or heads of organisational units; in addition, Advanced Training Courses provide mission-related training.

MILAK aims to keep pace with the rapid developments and changes in military and civilian life through the provision of a broad and comprehensive education and through scientifically based research. The latter involves the six departments of Military History, Strategic Studies, Economics of Defense, Leadership and Communication Studies, Military Sociology, and Military Psychology. Together with the Chair of Leadership and Communication Studies, the Chair of Military Psychology seems to have the strongest relationship to the everyday military life a professional officer encounters after completing his basic education. Accordingly, based on a sound theoretical foundation the relevant topics are presented with a focus on practical application.

Military psychology in basic and continuing education of professional officers

In the first semester of the BSC as well as of the DSC the objective for the students is to become acquainted with the scientific basics of psychology with specific reference to military practice. Since military psychology is defined as the application of psychological theories, methods, instruments, and findings to the military sphere (Taylor & Alluisi, 1994), consequently, selected aspects of various school of thoughts, such as behaviourism, humanistic psychology, and cognitive psychology, and psychological principles, such as content and process theories of motivation, are covered. Building on this knowledge acquired during the first semester, in the second semester the students will be sensitised for psychological aspects and dynamics of military formation, education, and leadership, for example, sensitised to the dangers of group processes or abuse of authority and power in a hierarchical setting. Finally, special attention is directed to the phenomenon of 'stress', and different models of stress and stress management are discussed, specifying symptoms of stress-related disorders and their prevention and common treatments. Topics of current relevance are further explored in a seminar that takes place in the fourth and fifth semester of the BSC; recently, the seminar's subject matter focused on job satisfaction and retention of military professionals.

During the Supplementary Training Course, a refresher of basic findings and achievements of military psychology and insights from recent research projects is provided. Against this backdrop, the participants bring their practical experiences and problems in their individual everyday military life and explore how psychological knowledge could or should respectively contribute to solutions and general improvements. Due to the explicit reference to the realm of practice this course serves also as an indicator for relevant problems in the respective period of time. In recent years topics such as values and virtues in military organisations as well as detecting and training of resilience were key components of this course.

It has become clear that the courses in military psychology are characterised by interaction and discourse in order to make the link between a sound theoretical basis and the perspective of the practitioner. The students are being asked to participate actively in class; therefore, established methods such as essays, case studies, and group discussions are common (Annen, 2010). This may not be very innovative, but it is nevertheless a logical consequence of the courses' aim. More exceptional is the method of testing, which follows strictly the main characteristics of the lecture in military psychology and therefore takes the learning process and reflection into account.

Portfolio assessment – reflection instead of reproduction

The classical approach of ensuring that students retain and memorise a given subject matter is to require a written text at the end of the semester. In study courses and academic fields that mainly rely on processing information and gaining knowledge this kind of assessment may be appropriate. However, when we look at educational areas that teach psychological principles and insights and focus on providing students with soft skills, this approach has its shortcomings. As the objective of these educational fields is to cultivate in students a characteristic mindset and to instil them with an appropriate attitude, the technique of examining more or less disparate nuggets of knowledge alone will not suffice.

In particular, within the framework of leadership training, psychological topics should be examined with a focus on the processes that are effective in everyday life rather than solely on content. Accordingly, if (self-)reflection, interaction, and discourse are the central emphasis in the teaching, then the performance appraisal should be congruent with this principle – *instruction drives testing*.

Therefore, the so-called portfolio-assessment (Jones, 1994, or for a broader view, refer to Dochy, Segers, Gjibels, & Struyven, 2006) emerges as an appropriate way to assess students' performance. This means that students document their learning process during the semester on a continuous basis. They are compelled to assume responsibility for their own learning, recognise coherence and interconnections, and through this critically deal with the subject matter in such a way that the practical usefulness of the knowledge is brought to the fore. In the portfolio interview at the end of the semester, it is then discussed *what* has been entered into the individual portfolio, *why* it was selected, how one rates one's own performance and learning process, and what *practical consequences* one thinks should be drawn. In addition, the lecturer can pose questions designed to evaluate the student's knowledge.

The experiences with this appraisal instrument are systematically evaluated and analysed (see Nakkas & Annen, 2010). Regarding this, the acceptance and the perceived fairness of this method are of particular interest; that is, the specific aims of the portfolio assessment should be recognised by the students and the resulting grades should be seen as fair and comprehensible. Therefore, a survey has been sent to 122 graduates who were assessed with the portfolio method between 2007 and 2010.

They were asked to view their individual experience with the portfolio from their current perspective as professional officers in everyday military life. The response rate of 77 per cent and the fact that over 40 per cent of the respondents added partially comprehensive comments suggest a good degree of interest in the topic. The majority (85 per cent) indicated that they became more aware of their learning process and reflected more on their learning behaviour. Almost all of the former students (95 per cent) considered their grades to be fair and reasonable. They viewed the portfolio interview as an equitable and pleasant experience and regarded the procedure of assessing their performance as transparent and comprehensible. More than 90 per cent believed that their standard of knowledge was enhanced by the use of the portfolio and even 94 per cent of the respondents regarded the tool, in comparison with other exam types, as beneficial in transferring their knowledge into practice. Although the responses inevitably included some less favourable comments, these findings show evidence of the potential value of portfolio assessments in the education and training of professional officers.

Conclusion

Leadership development is the development of character and personality. In the career of a professional officer of the Swiss Armed Forces this becomes tangible at an early stage insofar as the time they spend at the assessment centre, during which period personality traits and social behaviour are systematically observed and assessed, and the observation process at the centre is the most decisive hurdle for admission to the Military Academy. Subsequently, (military) psychology is one of the main elements of the courses in basic and continuing education of professional officers. There, within the framework of the holistic model of military psychology, the relevant topics stem from the basics of psychological theories and principles, established insights of military psychology, lessons learned of other armed forces, as well as current research projects. In order to foster the critical analysis of the subject matter of the course and to bridge the gap between theory and practice interaction during the lessons is essential. The principle of 'reflection instead of reproduction' should also be applied when it comes to testing. Regarding this, the Portfolio Assessment is an important and recommendable component in the teaching of military psychology and has proven successful in achieving sustainability in the education of officers.

References

Annen, H. (2010). Current challenges of Swiss military pedagogy. In H. Annen & W. Royl (eds), *Educational challenges regarding military action* (pp. 109–122). Frankfurt, Germany: Peter Lang.

Annen, H. (2014). Tätigkeitsfelder der Militärpsychologie – ein holistisches Modell [Fields of activities in military psychology – A holistic model]. In G. Kreim, S. Bruns, & B. Voelker, *Psychologie für den Einsatz und Notfall* [Psychology for deployment and emergency] (pp. 23–31). Bonn, Switzerland: Bernard & Graefe.

Annen, H., Eggimann, N., & Ebert, J. (2012). Testing of social behaviour – On the use of the assessment centre method in a military organisation. In G. Kaur, S. Awasthy, & M.K. Mandal (eds), *Psychometric testing in armed forces* (pp. 56–74). New Delhi: Pentagon Press.

Annen, H., Goldammer, Ph., & Szvircsev Tresch, T. (2015). Longitudinal effects of OCB on cadre selection and voluntariness of expending extra effort in the Swiss Armed Forces by pursuing a career as militia cadre. *Military Psychology*, 27, 9–21.

Annen, H., Nakkas, C., & Gehring, Th. (in press). 'What if ...' – The Swiss Armed Forces' approach to military psychology. In St. Bowles & P. Bartone (eds), *Military psychology: Clinical and organizational practice*. New York: Springer.

Dochy, F., Segers, M., Gjibels, D., & Struyven, K. (2006). *Assessment engineering: Breaking down barriers between teaching and learning, and assessment*. In D. Carless (ed.), *Excellence in university assessment* (pp. 87–100). New York: Routledge.

Jones, J.E. (1994). Portfolio assessment as a strategy for self-direction in learning. *New Directions for Adult and Continuing Education*, 64, 23–29.

Matthews, M.D. (2014). *Head strong. How psychology is revolutionizing war.* New York: Oxford University Press.

Melchers, K.G., & Annen, H. (2010). Officer selection for the Swiss army: An evaluation of validity and fairness issues. *Swiss Journal of Psychology*, 69, 105–115.

Merkulova, N., Melchers, K., Kleinmann, M., Annen, H., & Szvircsev Tresch, T. (2014). *Effects of individual differences on applicant perceptions of an operational assessment center. International Journal of Selection and Assessment*, 22, 355–370.

Nakkas, C., & Annen, H. (2010). Portfolio assessment – Achieving sustainability in officers' education. In H. Annen & W. Royl (eds), *Educational challenges regarding military action* (pp. 227–234). Frankfurt, Germany: Peter Lang.

Taylor, H.L., & Alluisi, E.A. (1994). Military psychology. In V.S. Ramachandran (Ed.), *Encyclopedia of human behavior* (Vol. 3, pp. 191–201). New York: Academic Press.

9

Health beyond symptoms: multidimensional approach to functional fitness in military organisations

Merle Parmak

Introduction

In the military, failures can be measured in loss of lives, and consequences are often irreversible and errors difficult to correct. Well-functioning staff are required across the military hierarchy as the toll of mistakes tends to increase with the rank of a decision-maker. To serve their purpose well service members have to be in good functional condition. Service-related functionality can decline relative to the occurrence of performance-restrictive physical symptoms. While distressing and painful, those symptoms are not always consistent with identifiable pathophysiology. Medical checks may result in false-positive or incorrect diagnoses calling the efficiency of respectively applied therapies into question. The masculine and fitness-focused military culture itself can inadvertently facilitate functional decline among military personnel. Service members may (un-) wittingly suppress their physiologically sourced symptoms in order to be perceived strong and fit. However, a failure to seek medical assistance in a timely manner can worsen the prognosis, increasing the cost and the length of treatment. A multidimensional approach to functional fitness is proposed to highlight the importance of understanding performance restrictions by considering both physical and psychological factors.

Fit for military

Practices to improve soldier's battle performance trace back to the times even before the Greek civilisation. Through centuries of training, techniques have been carefully advanced to meet the challenges of changed battlegrounds. Increasingly sophisticated training techniques have been developed with an intention to design physical training programs to be more combat-like (for an extensive overview see East, 2013). Despite this the aim of training remains unchanged and all efforts are directed to developing combat stamina and improve service member's military readiness. In the military, failure in functional performance is often attributed to physical weakness. Fitness for duty is usually evaluated by more or less standardised versions of physical fitness tests, and good performance is honourably rewarded (Hammermeister et al., 2010). However, whether or not physical fitness tests are able to capture the necessary performance components in combat environments is debatable. It has been recognised by field practitioners that being physically fit and equipped with all necessary skills does not necessarily mean that those virtues are actually applied in real-life situations. Recognising the role of service members' psychological resources, the Military Demand-Resource model has been proposed. The model takes into account situational demands (e.g. risks, routines, daily hassles), the performer's internal and external resource environment (e.g. engagement, coping, leadership), and outputs (e.g. functional health,

> *The physical readiness training is a joke that trains Soldiers for the lowest standards and fails to prepare Soldiers to move their wounded battle buddy from the X to safety. The push-ups will not prepare someone to carry a litter 100 yards or an even longer distance to a landing zone a helicopter can actually land in.*
>
> Spc. Joshua Woodward,
> Military medic at Fort Hood, Texas

performance, retention) (see Bates et al., 2010; Bates et al., 2013). From the perspective of functionality it is important to explore what happens inside this resource environment which mediates situational demands and desired outcome.

For each individual, there are environments and jobs which are a better match with their wants and wishes. It has been shown that interaction between job characteristics and personality predispositions predict work-related outcomes and also that job enrichment interventions intended to motivate employees may have the opposite effect if work design and individual characteristics are not calibrated to match (Chung-Yan & Butler, 2011). From that perspective, an interactional approach to personnel management could be classified as a first-level prevention strategy for various outcomes of poor fitness. Stress is created in the mind of stressed (Krueger, 2008), and external events by themselves do not automatically upset anybody. Whether the event is perceived as a stress or challenge is related to how threatening it is perceived by an individual (Rademaker, 2009) and how well they believe they are able to cope with it (Delahaij, 2009). Recognising challenge relates to personal growth and triggers active problem-solving. Feeling threatened relates to the potential to harm and triggers passive coping (Lepine, Podsakoff, & Lepine, 2005).

Within the comprehensive framework of the Total Force Fitness different domains of military fitness are defined in 10 categories: physical, psychological, behavioural, occupational, medical, environmental, nutritional, spiritual, social, and family fitness. However, the operational value of this framework can be a victim of its own success because of blending and occasional overlaps in proposed definitions. In occupational fitness, for example, overlap is recognised between behavioural and psychological aspects (see Bray et al., 2010), and the full scope of individual physiological and psychological capacities, including elements from psychological, behavioural, and family fitness, is effectively covered in the medical fitness category alone (see O'Connor et al., 2010). Considering the scope of the framework, some degree of overlap is conceptually understandable but may compromise its practical usability for understanding functional decline. However, when dealing effectively with functional decline, medicine should be able to differentiate cases where clinical attention is necessary for functional recovery from those where non-medical interventions should rather be considered. Last but not least, cases of functional decline without explicit somatic complaints should be identified in military organisations in order to avoid a worsened prognosis caused by delayed medical intervention.

Neglected side of military healthcare

Medicine tends to treat the body as a machine instead of a system. However, all complaints are not necessarily symptoms, and all perceptions of bodily irregularities are not necessarily complaints (Hiller, Rief, & Brähler, 2006). The observation that an increased quantity of provided health services in the military is not necessarily associated with improved health (Shelton, Ondra, & Levin, 2015) may refer to occasions of misdiagnoses and mistreatment in military healthcare. Wakefield (2010) discusses the problem of false positives (diagnose that mistakenly attributes a disorder when it does not exist) indicating that the symptom-based system fails to distinguish normal distress from disorder. On the other hand, the problem of false negatives must also be noted (not seeing the problem when it is actually there; Hiller et al., 2006). For effective intervention, cases without obvious underlying physiological pathology should be differentiated from cases where clinical attention is necessary for functional recovery. Identifying physically troubled individuals as medical cases and psychologically distressed people as non-medical ones may not be very straightforward though. The origins of manifested symptoms are not always clearly distinguishable. Potential overlaps between physical and motivational deficits give rise to further diagnostic complications and complex interactions between somatic processes. Regardless of the presence or absence of medical explanations, physical symptoms are an important component of depression and anxiety and predict health service use in community populations (Escobar et al., 2010). Identifying cases of somatic complaints with

> *Some, for example, consider that functional disorders are dependent on increased suggestibility arising from fear, horror, or other emotional or fatiguing conditions; while others maintain that, quite apart from suggestion, emotional conflict or excitement is capable of producing functional disorders.*
>
> Charles S. Myers
> The Lancet, 1919

other than physiological origins poses a challenge to medical services. Failure to filter out people whose bodily symptoms are actually stress-induced can overload military primary care units by a number of chronic service users and leave unattended those service members who tend to withhold or suppress their symptoms.

Functional fitness

The *Oxford Dictionary* defines functionality as 'The quality of being suited to serve a purpose well', relating it to the 'likelihood to be successful'. Drawing on that definition, a person can be considered functionally fit if they exhibit psychological willingness and the physical abilities to be successful in real-life situations. Functional fitness, thus, can be defined as the integration of individual physical and psychological resources that are required to succeed in serving a purpose in the particular task environment. A tentative model is proposed below which emphasises the role of both components of the functional fitness along axes of physiological and physiological functionality based on available resources (see Figure 1).

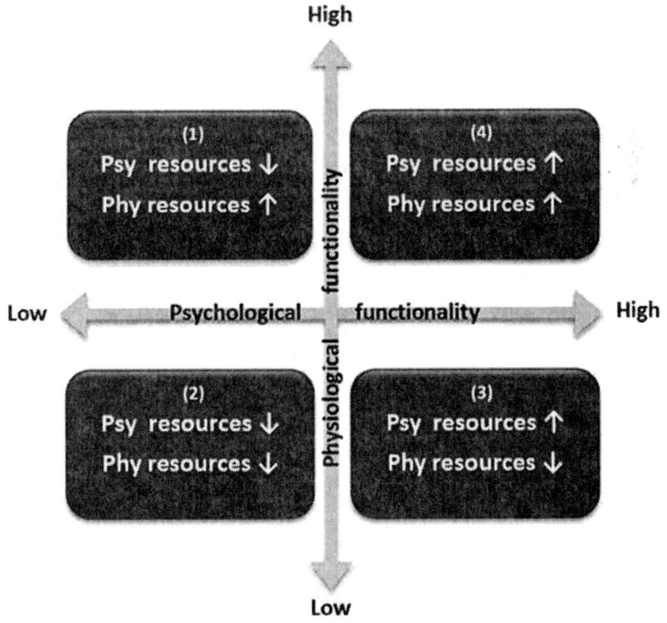

Figure 1. The multidimensional model of functional fitness.

The dimension of physiological functionality refers to physical well-being and capabilities, and the dimension of psychological functionality refers to psychological well-being and willingness to contribute in a particular task environment. The first dimension can be hampered by acute or chronic somatic symptoms with or without physiological origin and the latter by psychosocial, mental, or moral issues.

Descriptions of psycho-physiological combinations of functional fitness follow:

1. Physically unimpaired, but the actual performance may be impacted by depleted psychological resources.
2. Physically impaired, and the actual performance may further be impacted by depleted psychological resources.
3. Physically impaired, but the actual performance may not be impacted due to applied psychological resources.
4. Physically unimpaired, and the actual performance is further boosted due to applied psychological resources.

Some functional deficits could be expected in all but the fourth group and addressed according to the origin of the deficit. Moving individuals from the first, second, and third groups to the fourth can be considered as an organisational challenge calling for integrated efforts. Leadership should consider not only how to enhance psychological well-being among physically fit soldiers in the first group but also keep an eye on currently well-functioning soldiers in the fourth group. Remaining unnoticed, the migration of soldiers from the fourth group to the first group can take place with a risk of soldiers developing physical complaints and ending up in the third group thus becoming subjects of medical treatment.

To identify the most optimal form of care, sources of functional decline can be divided into three broad categories based on if and what type of symptoms are manifested. Figure 2 is provided to illustrate the perspectives of medical, non-medical, and integrated care.

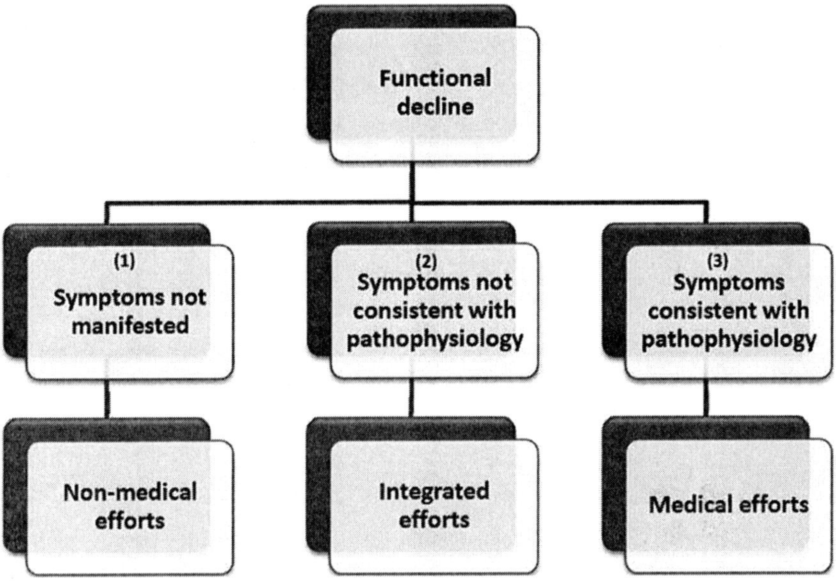

Figure 2. Integrated approach to functional decline interventions.

1. Non-medical interventions. It is known that the characteristics of the work environment can have positive and negative effects on performance and on the well-being of the performer (Gaillard, 2008). Service members whose individual characteristics are matched to their task-environments may be better motivated for their assignments, have a potential to grow thorough challenging situations, and recover faster from their professional exertions. The variable nature of military deployments requires soldiers not only to fight an enemy but also, for example, to provide humanitarian assistance, build schools, or hold warring tribes apart. These diverging tasks mean that soldiers have to be able to

Target group (1): Service members are physically well able to accomplish all aspects of assigned duties but their actual performance is hindered although no physical symptoms manifested.

switch between roles encompassing fighting and using force and roles that involve helping and protecting people (Broesder, 2011). Findings reveal that although troops are generally able to adapt to environmental demands, there are soldiers for whom the particular types of environments are psychologically more difficult to endure (Parmak, 2011). A strong correlation between psychosocial variables and symptom-reporting has been reported by Kinman and Griffi (2008), who explored a *sick building syndrome* and showed that employees report more somatic complaints in their work environment when their job-related mood is negative. Results are supported by findings that negative emotions can lead to or exacerbate pain (Wiech & Tracey, 2009). Effects of distress can be expressed in physical symptoms which in turn are related to withdrawal, intentions to quit, and job dissatisfaction (Shoss and Shoss, 2011).

2. Integrated interventions. Among police officers it has been found that higher levels of reported daily hassles are associated positively with reported physical symptoms but negatively with competence support from superiors (Otis & Pelletier, 2005). Presence of multiple physical symptoms among military personnel is found to be associated with functional deficits but not with a higher exposure to potentially traumatic events (de Silva, Jayasekera, & Hanwella, 2013). Somatisation can be defined as the expression of personal and social distress in bodily complaints which are usually attributed to physical disorder (Kleinman & Kleinman, 1985). Medically unexplained symptoms (MUS) are a heterogeneous group of conditions characterised by persistent physical symptoms that cannot be explained by medical illness or injury. The vague nature of MUS is recognised (Kapfhammer, 2011) and poses a challenge to military healthcare in several ways. On one hand, there is a risk that symptoms thought to be medically unexplained are

Target group (2): Service members are physically not able to accomplish all aspects of assigned duties but his symptoms are not consistent with pathophysiology.

masking some serious disorder causing a delayed diagnosis (Röhricht, Gudi, & Lewis-Fernandez, 2010). On the other, physical symptoms are experienced by an individual objectively as painful and restrictive calling for medical health check and interventions whatever the cause. An integrated approach to interventions makes it possible to see the relevance of combined responsibilities in cases of somatised symptoms.

Although medical diseases require medical treatment, developing chronic pain, for instance, may well be preventable using non-medical approaches (Jonas et al., 2010). A key role for military leaders in maintaining mental readiness in their unit has been recognised by researchers as well as field practitioners. A pyramid approach has been proposed for suggesting that different situations may need different kinds of support to be effective. The lowest and broadest level involves self-help and support provided via leadership action, the second level involves specialists' consultations, and the third level consists of specialised treatment. The model suggests that higher levels of interventions should be initiated according to the severity and persistence of symptoms. Although originally proposed for dealing with potentially traumatic events on deployments, the model can be well used to illustrate that the best results for dealing with MUS in military organisations could be achieved by combining medical care and leadership efforts.

Adapted from: NATO STO/HFM-181, 2008

3. Medical interventions. Suffering from MUS is almost identical to suffering from medically explained symptoms (MES), even though a serious organic condition cannot be detected. However, people differ in terms of whether symptoms lead them to seek healthcare (Klaus et al., 2013). The military is a highly performance- and functionality-orientated structure. Competitive behaviour among service members is encouraged and being the best is rewarded. This type of organisational culture may lead to an unusual workplace situation where, instead of the risk of malingering, real physical symptoms are hidden or even believed to be absent. People can tolerate bodily discomfort or even pain for a long time if they are motivated to do so. There is evidence that pain tolerance (Fernbach, Hagmayer, & Sloman, 2014) as well as pain perception can be altered and should be considered within a context of goal pursuit (Van Damme et al., 2010) as well as a person's mood (Villemure & Bushnell, 2002). While recognising accompanying risks, it has been suggested that sub-acute somatisation may not be a maladaptive but an adaptive response, as those unsympathetic to psychological illness do not adopt the sick role when psychologically distressed (Bridges et al., 1991). However, physical warning signs may actually indicate a serious physiological condition or malfunction. It is the responsibility of medical services to identify cases where clinical attention is necessary for functional recovery even if functional decline cannot be objectively observed.

Target group (3): Service members are not physically able to accomplish all aspects of assigned duties although his actual performance may not be considerably declined.

Value of integrated healthcare

Throughout history, the military has always been the world of arms and heroism – the brotherhood of strong, brave, and invulnerable man. In that environment it can be perceived as more acceptable to develop multiple physical symptoms than psychological issues. Complaints include various types of pain, musculoskeletal symptoms, and fatigue and also food intolerance and sexual dysfunctions (Hiller et al., 2006; Aamland,

Malterud, & Werner, 2014). Somatised symptoms are usually objectively distressing but not always consistent with identifiable pathophysiology which may call into question the effectiveness of medical treatments. But the medical component of fitness is determined by medical metrics (O'Connor et al., 2010) and identified based on the presence of physical symptoms. On the other hand, some increasingly serious conditions can remain out of sight as troubled mental health does not belong in the tough warrior model, preventing adequate treatment to be sought (Kulesza, Pedersen, & Corrigan, 2015; Wright et al., 2009).

Healthcare in military organisations starts with selection. If people are unsatisfied with their jobs, residual effects of this dissatisfaction will affect both the quality of life and health (Kanda, 2011). We do know that not all of us are equally enthusiastic and motivated facing certain types of tasks or environments. Discomfort may be most likely to occur when particular situations do not accord with personality-related needs and preferences. This mismatch may appear to be an impediment in demanding environments where prolonged persistence is necessary for a successful outcome. A person who perceives his environment as congenial is willing to endure and adapt. On the contrary, a person who does not perceive the environment as matching with his needs is not motivated to invest his energy into necessary adjustments. Even the most sophisticated medications cannot increase soldiers' engagement, nor is the most motivating military leadership able to cure their wounds. Functional decline may not stem from solely physical issues. Behind the failure, even if it is apparently physical, the presence of underlying psychological factors can usefully be considered. In this chapter, a multidimensional approach was proposed to address functional decline in military organisations by analysing medical and non-medical aspects simultaneously.

References

Aamland, A., Malterud, K., & Werner, E.L. (2014). Patients with persistent medically unexplained physical symptoms: A descriptive study from Norwegian general practice. *BMC Family Practice*, 15, 107.

Bates, M.J., Bowles, S.V., Hammermeister, J., Stokes, C., Pinder, E., Moore, M., … Burbelo, G. (2010). Psychological fitness: A military demand-resource model. *Military Medicine*, 175(8S), 21–38.

Bates, M.J., Fallesen, J.J., Huey, W.S., Packard, G.A., Ryan, D.M., Burke, C.S., ... Bowles, S.V. (2013). Total force fitness in units Part 1: Military Demand-Resource Model. *Military Medicine*, 175(8S), 1164–1175.

Bray, R.M., Spira, J.L., Rae Olmsted, K., & Hout, J.J. (2010). Behavioural and occupational fitness. *Military Medicine*, 157(8S), 39–56.

Bridges, K., Goldberg, D., Evans, B., & Sharp, T. (1991). Determinants of somatization in primary care. *Psychological Medicine*, 21, 473–483.

Broesder, W. (2011). *Soldiers wielding swords and ploughshares* (Doctoral thesis). Leuven: W. Broesder.

Chung-Yan, G.A., & Butler, A.M. (2011). Proactive personality in the context of job complexity. *Canadian Journal of Behavioural Science*, 43, 279–286.

de Silva, V.A., Jayasekera, N.E., & Hanwella, R. (2013). Multiple physical symptoms in a military population: A cross-sectional study. *Annals of General Psychiatry*, 12–24.

Delahaij, R. (2009). *Coping under acute stress: The role of person characteristics* (Doctoral thesis). Breda: Roos Delahaij.

East, W.B. (2013). *A historical review and analysis of Army physical readiness training and assessment*. Fort Leavenworth, KS: Combat Studies Institute Press.

Escobar, J.I., Cookc, B., Chenc, C., Garaa, M.A., Alegríac, M., Interiana, A., & Diaz, E. (2010). Whether medically unexplained or not, three or more concurrent somatic symptoms predict psychopathology and service use in community populations. *Journal of Psychosomatic Research*, 69, 1–8.

Fernbach, P.M., Hagmayer, Y., & Sloman, S.A. (2014). Effort denial in self-deception. *Organizational Behavior and Human Decision Processes*, 123, 1–8.

Gaillard, A.W.K. (2008). Concentration, stress and performance. In P.A. Hancock & J.L. Szalma (eds), *Performance under stress* (pp. 59–75). Aldershot, UK: Ashgate.

Hammermeister, J., Pickering, M.A., McGraw, L., & Ohlson, C. (2010). Relationship between psychological skill profiles and soldier physical fitness performance. *Military Psychology*, 22, 399–411.

Hiller, W., Rief, W., & Brähler, E. (2006). Somatization in the population: From mild bodily misperceptions to disabling symptoms. *Social Psychiatry Psychiatric Epidemiology*, 41, 704–712.

Jonas, W.B., O'Connor, F.G., Deuster, P., Peck, J., Shake, C., & Frost, S.S. (2010). Why total force fitness. *Military Medicine*, 175(8S), 6–13.

Kanda, J. (2011). The effects of work-related variables on mental health of employees in manufactory. *Journal of US-China Public Administration*, 8, 577–585.

Kapfhammer, H.-P. (2011). CS03–04 – Concept of somatoform disorder. *European Psychiatry, 26*, 1777–1777.

Kinman, G., & Griffi, M. (2008). Psychosocial factors and gender as predictors of symptoms associated with sick building syndrome. *Stress and Health*, 24, 165–171.

Klaus, K., Rief, W., Brähler, E., Martin, A., Glaesmer, H., & Mewes, R. (2013). The distinction between 'medically unexplained' and 'medically explained' in the context of somatoform disorders. *International Journal of Behavioural Medicine*, 20, 161–171.

Kleinman, A., & Kleinman, J. (1985). Somatization: The interconnections in Chinese society among culture, depressive experiences, and the meanings of pain. In A. Kleinman & B. Good (eds), *Culture and depression* (pp. 429–490). Berkeley, CA: University of California Press.

Krueger, G.P. (2008). Contemporary and future battlefields: Soldier stresses and performance. In P.A. Hancock & J.L. Szalma (eds), *Performance under stress* (pp. 19–44). Aldershot, UK: Ashgate.

Kulesza, M., Pedersen, E.R., & Corrigan, P.W. (2015). Help-seeking stigma and mental health treatment seeking among young adult veterans. *Military Behavioural Health*, 3, 230–239.

Lepine, J.A., Podsakoff, N.P., & Lepine, M.A. (2005). A meta-analytic test of the challenge stressor – Hindrance stressor framework: An explanation for inconsistent relationships among stressors and performance. *Academy of Management Journal*, 48, 764–775.

O'Connor, F.G., Deuster, P.A., DeGroot, D.W., & White, D.W. (2010). Medical and environmental fitness. *Military Medicine*, 175(8S), 57– 4.

Otis, N., & Pelletier, L.G. (2005). A motivational model of daily hassles, physical symptoms, and future work intentions among police officers. *Journal of Applied Social Psychology*, 35, 2193–2214.

Parmak, M. (2011). *Should all soldiers be sensation seekers? The role of personality* (Doctoral thesis). Leuven: Author.

Rademaker, A.R. (2009). *Personality and adaptation to military trauma* (Doctoral thesis). Utrecht: Author.

Röhricht, F., Gudi, A., & Lewis-Fernandez, R. (2010). Medically unexplained physical symptoms masking (cenesthopathic) schizophrenia: A case series. *Journal of Psychiatric Practice*, 16, 258–264.

Shelton, H.H., Ondra, S.L., & Levin, P.L. (2015, February). Reforming the military health system: The opportunity and dire need for change in how we care for military personnel and their families. *Future of the All-Volunteer Force series*. Retrieved from http://www.cnas.org/

Shoss, M.K., & Shoss, B.L. (2011). Check-up time: A closer look at physical symptoms in occupational health research. *Stress and Health*, 28, 193–201.

Van Damme, S., Legrain, V., Vogt, J., & Crombez, G. (2010). Keeping pain in mind: A motivational account of attention to pain. *Neuroscience and Biobehavioral Reviews*, 34, 204–213.

Villemure, C., & Bushnell, M.C. (2002). Cognitive modulation of pain: How do attention and emotion influence pain processing? *Pain*, 95, 195–199.

Wakefield, J.C. (2010). Misdiagnosing normality: Psychiatry's failure to address the problem of false positive diagnoses of mental disorder in a changing professional environment. *Journal of Mental Health*, 19, 337–351.

Wiech, K., & Tracey, I. (2009). The influence of negative emotions on pain: Behavioural effects and neural mechanisms. *NeuroImage*, 47, 987–994.

Wright, K.M., Cabrera, O.A., Bliese, P.D., Adler, A.B., Hoge, C.W., & Castro, C.A. (2009). Stigma and barriers to care in soldiers post-combat. *Psychological Services*, 6, 108–116.

10

Cultural competence and leadership in multinational military operations

Yvonne R. Masakowski

Introduction

The twenty-first-century military environment has been characterised by numerous cross-cultural battle spaces, such as those in Iraq and Afghanistan. This is in stark contrast to the operational environment of the twentieth century during which the military prepared to deal with traditional warfare. During the Cold War, the United States clearly understood who their adversaries were and developed a centralised approach and a specific set of strategies, tactics, and techniques for defending against them.

Today, military leaders are challenged by a decentralised adversary, one which is geographically distributed in power and organisation, culturally diverse, ideologically driven, and able to act as non-state actors who function within a coordinated social network. This distributed and networked capability affords the adversary an asymmetric advantage. Furthermore, these capabilities highlight the importance of understanding the cultural and sociopolitical underpinnings of such ideologies that challenge global security.

To this end, each nation must deem cross-cultural competence as a vital skill in conducting war in the twenty-first century and a prerequisite for all future military leaders. Cross-cultural competence (3C) refers to the knowledge, skills/abilities, and motivation that enable individuals to adapt to and communicate effectively in cross-cultural environments (Abbe et al., 2008). This ability affords the military leader the means to understand cultural perspectives and facilitate their ability to build relationships based on trust.

The future security environment is characterised by dynamic, complex situations that will require an ability to adapt to a wide range of cultural, social, and political challenges. Military leaders must be prepared to understand cross-cultural impacts, influences, and behaviours. Cultural intelligence, social intelligence, and emotional intelligence will play a pivotal role in optimising operational efficiency.

As Major General Robert Scales (US Army, Ret.) has stated, 'To win World War IV, the military must be culturally knowledgeable enough to thrive in an alien environment. Victory will be defined more in terms of capturing the psycho-cultural rather than the geographical high ground. Understanding and empathy will be important weapons of war.'

Nations must come together to address the emerging threats in the security environment. Today, in this new, complex dynamic operational environment, it is insufficient for our military leaders to be merely tactically and technically competent. This dynamic environment requires that military leaders are able to communicate their intent both within their teams and forces and with their allies and coalition partners. The transparency of today's social media environment mandates that leaders understand the cultural consequences of their decisions as they attempt to form unity of effort and unity of command during coalition operations. To do so, leaders must first understand the cultural diversity of those they command as well as their adversaries in order to make informed, effective decisions. Each step of the way, leaders must be cognizant of the potential cultural consequences of their decisions and actions. They must communicate their intentions and build trust and confidence among their teams. To this end, the twenty-first-century military leader must be adaptive and transformational in their leadership style.

Leadership styles

Leadership style describes the approach that leaders take in influencing and shaping their command climate. Media attention has largely focused on negative and toxic leadership (Doty & Fenlason, 2013). Traditionally, the military has fostered a transactional leadership style wherein subordinates perform tasks assigned by their leaders in a management/ subordinate relationship. Transformational leaders are those who have the ability to share their vision and inspire trust and confidence in their subordinates while supporting the needs of the individual and the team (Bass, 1985; Yammarino & Bass, 1990a).

Research on leadership during the past decades has provided further evidence that flexible, adaptive leadership is critical when there is significant change in the situation and in the requirements for leadership (Yukl, 2008). Flexible, adaptive leadership is important when dynamic and uncertain situations emerge in the environment, presenting new emergent threats. Research suggests that the leader must learn to analyse the situation quickly and achieve an understanding of those behaviours that will ensure a successful outcome (Yukl, 2006). Flexible leaders must identify potential problems and take steps to avoid them or to prepare for them. Leaders must also learn about the effects of their actions and decisions and use this information to make revisions while strategically ignoring or denying bad news. Leaders must use feedback to integrate new information into their cognitive mental model (Yukl, 2008). As leaders learn to adapt to changes in the complex, dynamic environment, they must also learn to evaluate multiple objectives simultaneously to understand how the changing environment can modify their priorities. The complexity of the environment, the risk assessment of potential options, and an understanding of potential consequences for their decisions provide significant learning challenges to the leader.

Avolio (2013) has conducted extensive research dedicated to leader development and leadership effectiveness. He has examined the role of self-awareness and moral perspectives in the development of 'authentic leadership' (Avolio, 2010). Among the constructs for the development of authentic leaders, he posits that self-awareness, balanced processing, moral perspectives, and transparency are positively related to effective leadership. Furthermore, he describes the impact of maintaining a positive and ethical environment that fosters growth and development. In his view, he portends a future in which we will develop 'exemplary followership' as an antecedent to develop effective leaders. In other words, we should teach leaders and followers to process and reflect versus developing a specific style of behaviours. Leader development would thereby be optimised by preparing followers to become leaders. However, followers are individuals who are attracted to leaders whom they trust and believe to be credible. Thus, shaping and influencing the follower's behaviour relies on the extent to which the follower trusts their leader.

Each of these leadership constructs provides a perspective on various styles of leadership. However, military leadership is really a combination of talent, skills, and abilities as well as character and an ability to communicate and share a vision that inspires subordinates. Successful military leaders are those who have a keen sense of self-awareness, character, and integrity as well as an understanding of the organisation and the people that they will lead.

However, for the multinational military leader, there is one additional requirement. These leaders must have the ability to understand cultural diversity in the environment in order to set the conditions for building relationships based on trust. Lacking that capability, leadership styles, by themselves, will fail to inspire trust and confidence among their teams and fail to build relationships required to achieve unity of effort and unity of command. To accomplish this end, military leaders must first acquire cultural competence.

Understanding cultural diversity and uncertainty in the operational environment

Today's multinational military operation demands the ability to successfully operate across cultures and cultural teams. There is a great deal of uncertainty in the operational environment in settings such as in Iraq and Afghanistan that has cost the lives of many military personnel. Misunderstandings of the cultural social network and the role of cultural values often create conflicts that the military must address. Understanding each culture's societal rules impacts a military operation on foreign soil. The importance of this must not be understated. Rather, military leaders, as well as subordinate military and civilian personnel working in these environments, must gain an understanding of the cultural nuances and perspectives of the people in the operational environment. The military has a set of specialists such as intelligence, Foreign Area Officers (FAOs), as well as civilian Human Terrain Teams (HTT) who provide support for leaders to achieve an understanding of the human terrain (McFate & Laurence, 2015). However, there is a need for civilians, such as social scientists, to provide to the military leaders the cultural perspectives of the local population. Social scientists are better prepared to understand the cultural lens of the local people and achieve an understanding of their cultural values and perspectives. These cultural insights are an asset to military leaders and inform their decision-making in relation to the potential cultural consequences of their operational decisions. As General Petraeus states in the Foreword of this text, 'the most important lesson of our post 9/11 campaigns has been that the key terrain is the human terrain' (McFate & Laurence, 2015).

Thus, understanding the complexities of local cultures in the operational environment, such as in Iraq and in Afghanistan, mandates the need to develop cultural competency and fluency. There have been many reports and texts written on this topic; however, few have taken the perspective of the locals themselves. Rather, we must reverse our cultural lens and view each culture from their perspective. How do they see us, the military team, as interlopers in their cultural environment? We must turn the cultural prism on ourselves, the multinational military force, in order to understand how our actions are perceived by them, the local population. For it is only through achieving an understanding of their cultural perspective on us, the military force, can we begin to break through the cultural barriers set before us. To do this, we must first understand the culture, beliefs, and cultural values of those in a culturally diverse region if we are to lead multinational military operations. We must achieve the ability for perspective taking through the lens of the local population.

Furthermore, we must also do this with our allies and coalition partners as well if we are to share leadership responsibilities. For many years, the United States has led multinational forces, in large part because they have had the technological advantage. More recently, NATO military operations have been sharing responsibilities among various nations. The complexities of achieving consensus among culturally diverse military forces are increased when one thinks of the diversity in organisational and national cultures which participate in the multinational force.

Organisations have a culture of their own wherein relationships, values, and behaviours are established (Schein, 2010). Indeed, the values of a leader may also become integrated in the tapestry of the organisational culture at all levels. (Schein, 2010). National cultures have also been examined from a cultural perspective extensively by Hofstede in terms of power distance (Hofstede, 2001). Taken in combination, the national and organisational cultures also present challenges for us to work together in a seamless manner.

Military leaders must be aware of the cultural perspectives of their adversaries as they form military strategic and tactical plans. As Sun Tzu stated, 'All men can see these tactics whereby I conquer, but what none can see is the strategy out of which victory is evolved.' For it is by achieving an understanding the culture of your adversaries that leaders can develop strategies for mission success.

The dynamic nature of the complex operational environment pose numerous challenges for multinational military operations as evidenced by an increase in humanitarian, peacekeeping, counterterrorism, and combat operations. These diverse challenges on a global scale highlight the need to develop military leaders capable of establishing coalition teams among multinational and culturally diverse teams. To this end, we must prepare our military leaders to be ready to address these challenges by developing leaders who will be effective across a range of military operations.

The twenty-first-century leader is required not only to be tactically proficient but must also be capable of building consensus among culturally diverse teams. Successful leaders are those who can instil trust and confidence with others as they build teams. Leaders must earn the respect and trust of their teams, colleagues, and coalition partners. Leaders of the twenty-first-century military must understand the culture of those working with them to achieve these objectives as well as that of their adversaries. To realise this objective, leaders must achieve a level of cultural competence which facilitates their interactions and communications with their coalition partners as well as within and among culturally diverse teams.

Leadership in multinational military operations

As the frequency and number of multinational military operations increase, there is a need to address leadership in terms of the leadership team. While there may be a lead nation for a military operation, all coalition partners play a role in making the mission a success. The integration of each nation's military structure, therefore, presents challenges in terms of their contribution to the effectiveness of the mission. For example, NATO hosts multinational exercises to evaluate how information is shared and disseminated. These military exercises afford NATO the ability to evaluate the effectiveness of each nation's contribution towards a particular mission paradigm. As each nation participates and serves a supporting role, leaders must understand and value each nation's contribution to the exercise. For English-speaking nations, such as Australia, Canada, New Zealand, the United Kingdom, and the United States, there is no language barrier to impede the exchange of information. In contrast, non-English-speaking nations may suffer the consequences of not being able to achieve coalition cohesiveness due to their inability to communicate effectively. This failure in communication will negatively impact the ability to build relationships based on trust.

Building effective relationships is a key characteristic of multinational military operations. The cultural diversity of many regions often presents significant challenges for achieving team cohesion. One means of addressing these differences is to bring coalition team members into the command structure itself. Such integrated commands have been shown to be effective in multinational military operations such as NATO. Indeed, NATO's (2011, 2016) command structure reform provides evidence of the reform of the command structure to address current and future challenges.

Leaders of multinational teams require a capacity for communicating a common objective and direction (i.e. commander's intent). Traditionally, the military has considered language proficiency and a geographic regional briefing sufficient preparation for deployment in a culturally diverse environment. Time has shown that this is an inadequate approach to achieving cultural understanding. If future leaders are to transcend cultural barriers, we must prepare them to understand the cultural challenges that they will face in an environment foreign to them. Specifically, we must help them see through the lens of their coalition and/or adversary's cultural lens in order to understand the influence and potential impact of their uninformed decisions.

This task is made more complex by the fact that leaders must also be effective at communicating their intentions in a clear manner. Leaders must be culturally competent, articulate, persuasive and must have developed an ability to resolve conflicts, mediate problems, and remain culturally sensitive as they move the team towards achieving mission success. The need to achieve consensus in an environment of trust presents critical challenges to military leaders when striving for unity of command and effort. According to Gurstein (1999), there is a need for multinational military leaders to achieve abilities in mediation, conflict resolution, and cultural sensitivity.

Although it is the war fighter who must conduct the operation, it is left to the military leader to develop the tactical plan, inspire trust and confidence, and build a cohesive team that will execute the plan. Thus, leaders must be adaptive and aware of the cultural and sociopolitical networks that exist within the operational environment in order to become effective leaders. This chapter will explore the requirements for effective leadership in multinational military operations as well as the required knowledge, skills, and abilities that must be developed to achieve this goal.

Historically, the United States has struggled with this issue throughout the years where nations joined forces to achieve a common goal. Both First and Second World Wars provide evidence of the complexities of sharing leadership and responsibilities according to capabilities, competencies, and cultural knowledge. Since the Cold War ended, the United States has reached out to its partners for numerous multinational military operations in support of military missions. Indeed, the operational tempo and diversity of missions has increased (e.g. Afghanistan, Iraq, Iran, Syria, etc.) and made us clearly aware of the need for cultural sensitivity and leader development. Active engagement with our coalition partners enables us to extend our capabilities and level of cooperation and support for those facing security and humanitarian challenges. The recent events in Syria serve as an example of the complexity of the multinational operational mission. Leaders must achieve an understanding of the operational environment, the culture of its people, the sociopolitical environment, and the potential consequences for the interactions and/ or interventions. The refugee crisis of Syria has raised challenges from both the humanitarian perspective and the security perspective. Leaders must weigh and balance the costs of intervention in a responsible way with a view towards both humanitarian and security implications for their interactions and decisions.

Conclusion

The twenty-first century is a time of complexity and profound change on a global security level where terrorist threats and attacks continue to emerge. There has also been an increase in humanitarian/refugee crises not seen since the Second World War. To address these challenges, the military must emphasise the education and training of its leaders and military personnel on the value of cultural perspective taking, cultural competency, and fluency in order to address these challenges. It is left to us to rebuild good will and improve relationships around the globe based on our willingness to reach out and understand the influence and impact of each other's cultural lens.

References

Abbe, A., & Halpin, S.M. (2009). The cultural imperative for professional military education and leader development. *Parameters*, 10, 20–31.

Abbe, A., Gulick, L.M.V., & Herman, J.L. (2008). *Cross-cultural competence in army leaders: A conceptual and empirical foundation* (Study Report 2008–01). Arlington, VA: US Army Research Institute for the Behavioral and Social Sciences (DTIC No. ADA 476072).

Avolio, B. (2010). Pursuing authentic leadership development. In *Handbook of Leadership Theory and Practice* (ed. N. Nohria & R. Khurana). Boston, MA: Harvard Business School Publishing.

Avolio, B.J., & Gardner, W.L. (2005). Authentic leadership development: Getting to the root of positive forms of leadership. *Leadership Quarterly*, 16, 315–338.

Avolio, B.J., Sosik, J.J., Kahai, S.S., & Baker, B. (2014). Introduction to 25th anniversary issue of the Leadership Quarterly. *Leadership Quarterly*, 25, 105–131.

Bass, B.M. (1985). *Leadership and performance beyond expectations*. New York: Free Press.

Bass, B.M. (1988b). The inspirational process of leadership. *Journal of Management Development*, 7, 21–31.

Bouchard, T.J., Jr. (2004). Genetic influence on human psychological traits: A survey. *Journal of American Psychological Society*, 13, 148–151.

Bouchard, T.J., Lykken, D.T., Mcgue, M., Segal, N.L., & Tellegen, A. (1990). Sources of human psychological differences: The Minnesota Study of Twins Reared Apart. *Science*, 250, 223–228.

Doty, J., & Fenlason, J. (2013). Narcissism and toxic leaders. *Military Review*, 55–60.

Earley, P.C., & Ang, S. (2003). *Cultural intelligence: Individual interactions across cultures*. Palo Alto, CA: Stanford University Press.

Eberly, M.B., Johnson, M.D., Hernandez, M., & Avolio, B.J. (2013). An integrative process model of leadership: Examining loci, mechanisms, and event cycles. *American Psychologist*, 68, 427–443.

Finkelstein, S., & Hambrick, D.C. (1996). *Strategic leadership: Top executives and their effects on organizations*. St. Paul, MN: West Publishing.

Finkelstein, S., Hambrick, D.C., & Cannella, A.A. (2009). *Strategic leadership: Theory and research on executives, top management teams, and boards*. Oxford, UK: Oxford University Press.

Grandstaff, M., & Sorenson, G. (2009). *Strategic leadership: The general's art*. Vienna, VA: Management Concepts.

Greenert, J.W. (2013). *The navy leader development strategy*. Newport, RI: US Naval War College.

Gurstein, M. (1999). *Leadership in the peacekeeping army of the future*. In J.G. Hunt, G.E. Dodge, & L. Wong (eds), *Out-of-the-box leadership: Transforming the twenty-first century army and other top-performing organizations* (pp. 195–218). Stamford, CT: JAI Press.

Hayes, C. (2008). Developing the navy's operational leaders. *Naval War College Review*, 61, 77–108.

Heifetz, R., & Linsky, M. (2002). *Leadership on the line*. Boston, MA: Harvard Business School Press.

Heifetz, R., Grashow, A., & Linsky, M. (2009, July-August). Leadership in a (permanent) crisis. *Harvard Business Review*. Available online from https://hbr.org/2009/07/leadership-in-a-permanent-crisis

Heifetz, R.A., Linsky, M., & Grashow, A. (2009). *The practice of adaptive leadership: Tools and tactics for changing your organization and the world*. Boston, MA: Harvard Business Press.

Hofstede, G. (1980). *Culture's consequences: International differences in work related values*. Newbury Park, CA: Sage.

Hoftsede, G. (2001). *Culture's consequences* (2nd ed.). Thousand Oaks, CA: Sage.

Lowe, K.B., Kroeck, K.G., & Sivasubramaniam, N. (1996). Effectiveness correlates of transformational and transactional leadership: A meta-analytic review of the MLQ literature. *Leadership Quarterly*, 7, 385–415.

McFate, M., & Laurence, J.H. (2015). *Social science goes to war*. Oxford, UK: Oxford University Press.

Northouse, P.G. (2007). *Leadership: Theory and practice*. Thousand Oaks, CA: Sage.

Schein, E.H. (2010). *Organizational culture and leadership* (4th ed.). New York: John Wiley.

Singleton, R., & Straits, B.C. (2009). *Approaches to social research.* Oxford, UK: Oxford University Press.

Stavridis, J., & Hagerott, M. (2009). The heart of an officer. *Naval War College Review,* 62, 26–41.

Ulmer, W.F., Shaler, M.D., Bullis, R.C., Snodgrass, W.M., Brockman, D., Jacobs, T.O., & Funk, P.E. (2011). *Leadership lessons at division command level – 2010.* Carlisle Barracks, PA: United States Army War College.

Van Velsor, E., Criswell, C., Puryear, K., & Hollenbeck, N. (2011). *Learning leadership in the military: Key developmental events and lessons from senior officers.* Greensboro, NC: Center for Creative Leadership.

Yammarino, F.J., & Bass, B.M. (1990b). Transformational leadership and multiple levels of analysis. *Human Relations,* 43, 975–995.

Yukl, G. (2010). *Leadership in organizations.* Englewood Cliffs, NJ: Prentice Hall.

Yukl, G.A. (1989). Managerial leadership: A review of theory and research. *Journal of Management,* 15, 251–289.

Contributors

Colonel Dr Hubert Annen (PhD, Swiss Armed Forces) is currently Department Head of Military Psychology and Military Pedagogy at the Swiss Military Academy at the Swiss Federal Institute of Technology in Zurich (in German, Eidgenössische Technische Hochschule or ETH Zürich). In 1996, he earned his master's degree in Psychology, Pedagogy, and Neuropsychology at the University of Zurich. In his master thesis he carried out a validation study of the Assessment Centre for Prospective Career Officers of the Swiss Armed Forces (ACABO). Subsequently, he was assigned as research assistant at the Swiss Military Academy where he took over responsibility for the ACABO, taught Military Psychology, and worked on his dissertation thesis. After earning his PhD in 1999 he was elected as Head of the newly created Department of Military Psychology and Military Pedagogy. In this function, Hubert Annen teaches prospective career officers as well as experienced military leaders in basic and advanced training; is responsible for several pivotal selection tools in the Armed Forces; and conducts research mainly in the areas of personnel selection, motivation in the military, leadership development, and stress in military training. He is a member of the board of the International Military Testing Association (IMTA), and in 2012 he received the Harry Greer Award for long-standing exceptional work contributing to the purpose and aims of the IMTA. After completion of his military basic training as a conscript, Hubert Annen decided to volunteer as military cadre. After the officer's school he served as a platoon leader in the cyclist troops, at that time a specific, not to say peculiar, branch that is now history. During his subsequent career as a reserve officer he has served as the press and information officer (PIO) at the battalion, regiment, and brigade levels and as the personnel advisor to the commander of an Infantry Brigade. Since 2009, he is the Head of Research of the Psycho-Pedagogical Service of the Swiss Armed Forces

Tintisha Basu is a Counselling Psychologist and a Researcher at the Military MIND Academy, Pune, in India. She completed her Masters in Counselling Psychology from the prestigious SNDT Women's University and is now practicing as a counselling psychologist in diverse spaces, including the military setting. Coming from a military family where she grew up travelling along with her father (who is a combat veteran from the Infantry and has served in various military operations, including operation PAWAN in Sri Lanka) to different cantonments all over the country, Tintisha has gathered cross-cultural competencies which allow her to use her experiential learning using an eclectic approach in providing her expertise to different target populations to include children and families of military personnel, soldiers with substance abuse issues referred at Military Command Hospitals and other institutions. She also provides counselling at the National AIDS Research Institute (NARI) for HIV/AIDS as well as psycho-education to clients recovering from tuberculosis and other comorbidities. Her interests lie in the field of research on military personnel and their families.

Captain Dr Ole Boe has previously served as an operational officer, with the rank of Captain (R), for many years in a Norwegian military special unit conducting VIP protection, hostage rescue, and close combat training. He has served on several international operations all over the world, from Congo to Cambodia. Dr Boe received his PhD in psychology in June 2000 from the University of Gothenburg in Sweden. He has served as an Associate Professor of leadership and leadership development at the Section of Leadership and Tactics at the Norwegian Military Academy since 2003. He has previously served as the Norwegian Armed Forces representative in NATO's RTO panel HFM-ET-104 on mental training. Dr Boe now leads the Norwegian Military Academy's largest research project: Character in military leaders. He is also responsible for the Norwegian Military Academy concept of stress management and for preparing officers both physically and mentally for combat. Dr Boe has been the author or co-author of over 250 different publications on topics such as judgment and decision-making, leadership, leadership development, education, mental and physical reactions to combat, stress and coping with stress, selection, personality traits, character strengths, and simulation-based training. He currently serves as a reviewer for journals such as *Military Medicine, Military Psychology, Small Group Research,* and *Journal of Defense Management.*

Col Dr Cristian Dobre is a career officer and psychologist with extensive international experience, both as a military diplomat and military psychologist. His passion for psychology sought him to work in diverse psychological topics: Diplomatic Psychology, War Psychology, Cyber-Psychology, Operational Psychology, Emergency Psychology, Military Family Psychology, and others. He has published the following books – *Diplomatic Psychology* (2013) and *Operational Psychology* (2016) – as author and has published four other books on *Military Psychology* as coordinator. As an avid fan of science fiction literature, he has published as co-author the novel titled *The Secret Zamolxe* too.

Lt. Col. Dr Jacques Gouws is a registered psychologist in independent clinical psychological practice in Ontario, Canada. He is also the President and CEO of Human and System Interface Consulting, Inc., providing multidisciplinary integrated mental and physical health status assessment services. Dr Gouws first registered as a psychologist in South Africa in 1985. He completed postgraduate training and internship programs in Industrial Psychology (1985), Counselling Psychology (1992), and Clinical Psychology (1996). He is registered with the College of Psychologists of Ontario, providing independent Clinical Psychology services since February 1997. Dr Gouws' military service commenced in 1973, when he was selected as trainee pilot in the then South African Air Force. After his withdrawal from pilot's training, he completed compulsory national military service at the then Rooikop Air Force Station, Walvis Bay, in what is today Namibia. After working with the then South African Railways and Harbours (SAR and H), during which time he completed the degree Baccalaureus Artium through extra-mural studies at the University of Pretoria, he was recruited back to the SA Air Force in 1979, continuing his military career in 1980. He completed the degrees Baccalaureus Artium Honores in Psychology (1983), Magister Artium in Psychology

(1984), and Doctor Philosophae (Psychology) (1986) at the University of Pretoria, all through extra-mural studies.

Colonel Dr Eri Radityawara Hidayat is currently the head of the Psychological Selection and Classification, the Psychological Service of the Indonesian Army; holds a BSc. from the University of Wisconsin, Madison; an MBA from the University of Pittsburgh; and a Master of Human Resource Management and Coaching (Psychology) from the University of Sydney; he also has a Doctorate in Psychology from the University of Indonesia. During his doctorate studies, he was awarded a Fulbright Doctoral Dissertation Research Scholarship at the PhD Program in Organizational Behavior with concentration in Cross-cultural Psychology, Columbia University, New York. A graduate of the Indonesian Defence Forces Officer's School in 1990, Colonel Hidayat attended the Indonesian Army Command and Staff School in 2006, and the Netherlands Defence Course in 2008. Colonel Hidayat is also a regular contributor for book chapters published by the International Military Leadership Association (IMLA), which is a working group of the International Military Testing Association (IMTA). During the 2015 IMTA Conference in Sweden, Colonel Hidayat received the Harry Greer Award for his contribution in military psychology.

Yvonne R. Masakowski is an Associate Professor at the US Naval War College (USNWC), in the College of Operational and Strategic Leadership. Dr Masakowski has a distinguished career in Human Factors and Human Systems Design spanning over 20 years. Prior to her appointment at USNWC, Dr Masakowski was the Lead for the Human Performance & Technology Group in the Advanced Concepts Division at The Naval Undersea Warfare Centre (NUWC) in Newport, RI. During her tenure at NUWC, Dr Masakowski served as the Lead, Human Systems Engineer for the Littoral Combat Ship ASW MP Program and for the OHIO Replacement Program. Her research interests include decision-making, stress, leader development, and intercultural impacts on multinational military operations. Dr Masakowski received her BA in Experimental Psychology from Rutgers University, a Master's Degree in Psychology from The University of Connecticut, a Master's Degree in Philosophy from The City University of New York, and a PhD in Psychology (Biopsychology) from The City University of New York.

Lt. Col. Dr Samir Rawat (Retd) is a tanktrooper with over 25 years of military service and has commanded tank squadrons deployed along the entire border states of Punjab, Jammu and Kashmir, and Rajasthan in the Thar deserts. He has served as a volunteer officer in OPERATION MEGHDOOT in the Siachen Glacier which, at 21,000 feet, is the highest battlefield in the world where he commanded an Infantry Rifle Company. Besides extensive combat experience in Counter Insurgency (CI) operations during peak of militancy in Punjab, and Jammu and Kashmir, during OPERATION PARAKRAM, he has also served with Ladakh Scouts during OPERATION VIJAY where he led an infantry assault and recaptured enemy-held positions in Batalik Sector of Kargil, for which he was conferred a President's Gallantry Award for Bravery. With a PhD in Psychology, Masters in Management, and an MPhil in Defence and Strategic Studies, Lt. Col. Dr Samir Rawat brings with him over three decades of experience in training and human resource optimisation in the Armed Forces. He has served as the first Psychologist in premier Category 'A' Training institutions like Junior Leaders Academy, Bareilly; and the prestigious National Defence Academy, Khadakwasla, in India. He has been a visiting faculty, among others, at the Army War College, Mhow, where he taught Commanding Officers on matters pertaining to stress optimisation, soldier and leader performance, and psychological fitness. His efforts revolve around improving psychological fitness and well-being of soldiers and their families. Based on principles of Positive Psychology, he provided extensive training and imparted knowledge in building and enriching of human strengths, assessment of soldiers' readiness in relation to such strengths, and evidence-based methods of enhancing emotional, social, family, and spiritual fitness of uniformed personnel. He plays a key role in crafting personal growth strategies as well as creating long-term benefits for organisational development in the Armed Forces. Lt. Col. Dr Samir Rawat has recently set up his own institution in Pune – Military MIND Academy – which is the cradle of Military Psychology and Counselling in India.

Capt Dr Merle Parmak is Lecturer in Organisational Psychology in the University of Huddersfield (United Kingdom) and Advisor in Security Psychology in the Centre for Defence and Security Studies in Tallinn University of Technology (Estonia). At Huddersfield University, she is a member of the Centre for Applied Psychological Research and the Institute for Research in Citizenship and Applied Human Sciences. Her research interests draw on an interactional approach examining human behaviour in context, with a particular interest in complex or harsh situational conditions. Her current research projects are related to national and international security concentrating on societal resilience in multinational societies. She is also involved in research into situational awareness, decision-making, and emergent behaviour in critical situations. Before shifting to the civil academic world, she was contributing to the field of military psychology as a uniformed research psychologist in Estonian Defence Forces. For the past 10 years she has been actively involved in international military psychology research, contributing actively to NATO and EDA collaboration projects. She also made efforts to introduce and develop military psychology in Estonia by producing educational materials and organising conferences. Her contribution to military psychology was recognised with the Harry Greer Award by the IMTA Steering Committee on 2013. After retiring from Estonian Defence Forces she continues to contribute to international security via her teaching and research in United Kingdom.

Vrashali Patil is a Learning-Development child psychologist and a Researcher at the Military MIND Academy, Pune, in India. She has a distinction in Psychology during her academic studies at the graduate level and an outstanding rank at the Masters in Psychology from Pune University. Her military family background helps her in instilling discipline among children including young children in infancy, early childhood, and teenagers transitioning through adolescence. Using a cognitive behavioural approach, she provides progressive training in helping parents optimise potential of children and develop an overall healthy personality in all domains. Her interests lie in the fields of counselling and research on children as well as parenting styles using the structured military model for creating future leaders in the country.